I CAN EXPLAIN

Lessons Learned on my Journey from
Chelsea to the Ballroom and Beyond

Jamie Laing

with Justin Myers

SEVEN DIALS

First published in Great Britain in 2021 by Seven Dials
This paperback edition published in 2022 by Seven Dials,
an imprint of The Orion Publishing Group Ltd
Carmelite House, 50 Victoria Embankment
London EC4Y 0DZ

An Hachette UK Company

1 3 5 7 9 10 8 6 4 2

A CIP catalogue record for this book is
available from the British Library.

ISBN (Mass Market Paperback) 978 1 8418 8549 0
ISBN (eBook) 978 1 8418 8550 6

Typeset by Born Group
Printed and bound in Great Britain by Clays Ltd, Elcograf S.p.A.

MIX
Paper from
responsible sources
FSC® C104740

www.orionbooks.co.uk

To my wonderful family, who have always put up with me and taught me what unconditional love is. Mentally and physically, you have helped me so much. I wouldn't be who I am without you.

Contents

Trailer

Who the hell does Jamie Laing think he is? Excellent question. If you'd asked me, a few years ago, I could have told you very easily. I'm that boy from *Made in Chelsea* who doesn't *do* dull moments. You want to carry on the party? I'm into it. More champagne? Let's do it. Have a race in our underwear down the middle of the street at three in the morning? No problemo, on your marks, get set go! Got something on your mind and need support? Share it with me, I'm here. Need a favour doing? I'm on it. This is who I am, I used to think, it's what I do, I bring the fun, I bring the creativity, I make it loud and as big and as brilliant as it can possibly be.

What do *you* think of me? Or better yet, what do you think you know about me? Go on, you can be honest, I can take it. Be as brutal as you like: I can't hear you anyway, because this is a book and we're not standing in the same room as each other. Do you think good things about me, or bad? Fine either way. Maybe you don't think about me at all! That's also fine, but you may find the book a bit of a struggle if you're not that interested in me.

I *think* I have a fairly good idea of what people think of me. It's a spectrum, I know that. If I asked you to chuck some adjectives at me, there are things I *know* you will say – and these might be true or they might be false, whether I want to hear them or not. And there are words I *hope* you might say, and these might be things I already know about myself or just lovely things that would be nice to hear. You see, I have to be realistic about this, I have to summon up a bit of self-awareness because the thing with being in the public eye for the best part of a decade is that it's like permanently walking into a room where people are talking about you, but stop as soon as you come in. Over and over. Nobody ever really tells you to your face. When I was a kid, I'd have to steal someone's secret diary or something to find out whether they loved or hated me but now it's all just a few clicks away – sometimes they even @ me in to make sure I see it. Absolute strangers making huge assumptions – some right, some wrong – and there's not a lot I can do about it other than try to be a good person. So, those adjectives, then:

Posh. That was your first one, right? Knew it! Look, don't feel bad for going for the obvious choice first – I totally get this. Posh, I'll accept. What next? Did you go for looks or personality?

For the sake of speed and efficiency, I'll assume you're going to say I'm **cute** and/or **good-looking** – not quite the same thing but very good to hear both – and maybe you've got **blond** and . . . **tall**? No, you weren't going to say tall?! Worth a try, I suppose. You still said I was cute, though, right? Oh, go on, just for me.

Personality then, go on, hit me with your best shot. **Funny**? I hope you said that. It's important to me that people think I'm funny – I don't know why. Funny people are the kind of people you want to keep around you, aren't they? That's a nice feeling.

Maybe some of the other adjectives you had up your sleeve are **silly** (so true), **loud** (100 per cent yes), **wild** (I have my moments), **scatty** (possibly) or **a bit all-over-the-place** (I can be), **flirty** (guilty as charged), **sweet** (aw, thanks), **loyal** (stop laughing! I am! Honestly!), and maybe we could finish off with . . . **generally a nice guy**? Yes? Ah, you spoil me!

But hang on: what about **wanker**? Was that in there? What about **dim**? Or **arrogant**, or **selfish**? Ah, come on, I've seen the tweets, I know people say these things, and I know what they think of reality TV in general. You don't have to be embarrassed. And you know what, it's all true, or has been at some point. Yes, I am all the things you think I am, and all the things I claim to be, good and bad.

So how do I see myself now? Well, I'm just me. I like pretty simple things. I'm at my most calm sitting on the floor, naked, playing backgammon. Seriously! I'm caring. I think I'm insecure, though. I love life. I'm sensitive. I have a strong mind. I know I'm confident and loud and I'm very aware of my need to be the centre of attention all the time. But, just to contradict myself, there's also a kind of shyness about me. Lots of us are like that, aren't we? Huge extroverts getting on everybody's nerves one minute, then sitting quiet as a mouse and tongue-tied in front of strangers the next. Some people accept their shyness or lack of confidence and just go with it, and some people just don't. I choose not to accept it, I fight against it, because there's one thing about me: I want to be loved. Honestly. I have proper imposter syndrome and if you've ever found yourself wondering why the hell is Jamie Laing famous, believe me, I've asked myself that question hundreds of times. People might say they don't care what others think but I'm calling bullshit on that. You don't have to like me, but, you know, I'm happier when you do.

Maybe I seem full of self-confidence, the kind of guy who's never met a mirror he didn't want to kiss. But here's another thing you might not know about me: I am pretty tough on myself. It's like I'm my own evil twin and I must be stopped. I hardly ever give myself a break. If I could kick myself, I probably would. A few years ago, I didn't actually like myself very much. But maybe back then I deserved a bit of a self-kicking, because, to be honest, I'd been a bit of a pain to be around. Okay, okay, a lot of a pain.

I've been struggling with something since I was 22, you see. Something very heavy, and unwieldy, something I couldn't manage. No, not a monogrammed Louis Vuitton trunk, more's the pity – although I would totally love one if you're offering, thanks. It's anxiety. What have I got to be anxious about, you might ask? Aren't I, like, the heir to a huge fortune, the owner of every biscuit ever baked? Actually, there's no time like the present to clear up this McVitie's business before I go on:

OFFICIAL STATEMENT BY JAMES ROBIN GRANT LAING
REGARDING RUMOURS HE IS AN HEIR TO
THE 'MCVITIE'S MILLIONS'

McVitie's, for anyone who has never known the joy of a Jaffa Cake, is one of the most famous biscuit companies in the country, maybe on earth, I'm not sure. If you google me, once you've read the long list of people I've dated, and seen *that* naked photo (we need to talk about that, too, later), you'll see that I am, apparently, the heir to the McVitie's fortune. All of it, every penny. I have numerous siblings, but do they get any? According to the press, no they don't. All these millions are heading my way. How exciting! Whatever shall I spend it all on? To be honest, I wish this were true, if only to see the look on my brothers' and sisters' faces. Yes, I come from a privileged background, and, yes, it is true that one of my great-great-great-great grandparents (there may be a few more greats in there, I haven't counted) invented the digestive biscuit, and my family did run McVitie's for many years, but our stake in the company was sold off years ago, when I was tiny, so sadly, I will never be the sole owner of every Hobnob ever baked. Basically, if I'm being honest – which I will be, on every page of this book – my connection to McVitie's was played up a little when I joined *Made in Chelsea*, because I suppose it makes a good story and does kind of explain why I am so posh. It's true that I've never gone hungry, and I've always had a roof over my head and the priceless love of my parents and family – whether I deserved it or not – but from the moment I left university I've had to earn my own money. So, I am not 'rich' in the proper sense, like the Queen, or Jeff Bezos, or the guy who plays Charlie on *Casualty*. I still have to go to work, because if I don't, my rent doesn't get paid and my lights and radiators go off. I don't eat caviar for breakfast, I don't have a special room for wrapping presents in my flat, and I have never owned a pet swan. Glad we could clear that up. And, no, I can't get you any free biscuits. Sorry. I don't even *eat* biscuits!

– – – STATEMENT ENDS – – –

Right, where were we? So, the old anxiety thing. Yeah, weird one. You might wonder what I've ever had to feel anxious about. I was travelling the world with loads of gorgeous people, we rode about in big cars, sat on yachts and in huge manor houses looking amazing and were never further than two metres from a freshly chilled bottle of champagne. All we had to do was get paid to have fun, party, snog, and fall out for a bit before going off and snogging someone else. We all had lovely skin and our clothes were always freshly laundered and the world was our oyster. Boo-fucking-hoo, am I right? All this is true: I was having the time of my life and was so grateful to be where I was, I can't tell you. Most mornings I got out of bed and wanted to kiss the floor in gratitude, like a pope kissing the tarmac when he got off a plane. There wasn't any other place I wanted to be, no other life I wanted to live. But all the time there was an undercurrent: what happens when it all ends? (By which I mean my career rather than the actual apocalypse.) All these little doubts were bubbling away in my head: what about this thing that might never happen, or this other thing that's probably quite ridiculous and will probably never happen, but just might? So I lived in the moment and tried to drown out the negative energy as much as possible. To nudge out the anxiety, I turned up all the biggest, the boldest and most boisterous parts of my personality even higher – imagine! – but I don't want you to think I was faking it, living it up just for the cameras. Oh no. I was being my true self, showing my favourite side of myself. Some people serve up beef wellington as a speciality; my speciality is fun! But I always know what's expected of me and I can control my emotions or let them loose a little. It's like a volume button: up and down, whenever I think I need it. But this time, someone else was pushing the button – not even someone else, but another side of me, that I'd never really confronted before.

Let me try to describe it. It's like being at the best party in the world, but knowing as soon as you leave the party, you have to pay a penalty for having so much fun. And that penalty is to be continuously stung by wasps, all over your most intimate areas, for a full hour. So, you know, you're having the time of your life but you know those wasps are coming to sting you in the balls. In fact, on bad days, you can see the swarm, waiting, out of the corner of your eye, as you lift the glass of champagne to your mouth. The wasps are coming. They're always coming. I dunno, maybe you're into wasps; I'm quite open minded, whatever gets you off, you know, but I'm definitely one to one to avoid wasps if I can.

Don't get me wrong, I was living the dream! Ever since I was little, I'd wanted to be famous – I like to be liked. I'd wanted to perform ever since I was tiny – let me tell you: no Hollywood actor has worked harder at an audition than I did for the role of Joseph at the school nativity, aged five. I even trained in acting at university in Leeds. The way I tend to work is: I don't worry about risk, or how things turn out, I just jump in and start doing something and worry about the consequences later. One of my mottos is: 'Ask for forgiveness, rather than permission'. This can be both a good and a bad thing, as many of my friends will tell you. So, when it came to getting cast in *Made in Chelsea*, I didn't really think about what that would mean. My face was everywhere, and it looked like my dreams were coming true. Brilliant! But I thought if I didn't grab every opportunity, like a game of Hungry Hippos, it would all come to an end, and I'd be forgotten. I thought I'd end up losing absolutely everything – my family, my friends, my home – which sounds so silly and deluded given all these nonexistent biscuit millions or whatever. But anxiety isn't rational, and that's the huge hold it had over me. Those bloody wasps, waiting to sting. And the most annoying thing? This anxious, nervous, miserable person wasn't the real me. I didn't want this to become the default. I wanted to stay the friendly, popular guy everyone loved to know. Sometimes, it felt like the real me was disappearing. Any second that I wasn't living in the moment, during downtime or time alone – whenever I had any time, any space, to think – it was as if the anxiety saw its opportunity and would start pounding me with mallets and I'd feel like I was crashing. I'd be sitting there, thinking, 'Why am I relaxing? I'm in my twenties, I should be having fun, right?' The world was a theme park, but any time I wasn't on a ride I felt like I was in the lost kids' area, listening to everyone else having the best time ever. Like I didn't even have a 50p coin for the vending machine.

So I just kept going, tasting the highs of being on *Made in Chelsea* and chasing excitement and fun. And then the contrast between the ups and down started to get wider. I'd look at social media and read comments by people saying I was funny, or whatever, and think, well, I have to be even *more* like that, to stop them getting bored. I was almost playing a role, that of a person who slept with loads of women and was a party boy, and I acted far more confident than I really was. It was me – yes – but on steroids. Thing is, you can't live on heightened alert for long. So, in short, most of the time I was very 'YAY!!' but sometimes I felt 'BOOOOOO' and the boos were threatening to outnumber the yays and, as you can imagine, this was a huge pain in the arse. I didn't have time for this.

I became selfish and a bit irritating to be around. When you're not looking after yourself, you drop the ball with being there for others too. I probably wasn't a great son around this time, either. I mean, I didn't do anything too bad like poison a great aunt and steal all my McVitie's inheritance (because that doesn't exist, remember), but I was just kind of . . . crap. I missed my mum's 60th birthday, didn't go home for Christmas a few times, and didn't really see either as a big deal. Yeah, I still feel bad about that sometimes, don't worry. I guess if you were a very clever therapist in chunky spectacles, you might say that I wasn't making myself available, emotionally, for my family – I would describe it as acting like a pain in the arse. My proper friends, I kind of pushed away, because I always wanted more of everything: cooler friends, better nights out. I was a bit like a kid, who didn't want to do anything 'boring' that would take me away from my amazing high-rolling party lifestyle for longer than five minutes.

Not a bad person, I promise, just a bit 'ugh'. Sometimes I'm amazed anyone still talks to me!

I had my very first panic attack at the age of 22. If you've ever had one, you'll understand exactly how terrifying they can be. It came from nowhere and I had no idea what it was. One minute I was watching TV – *The Voice*, if you're into details – and the next minute I had this overwhelming feeling that something was very wrong. My chest was tight, my muscles tense, and my throat felt like it was closing up. I didn't know what was happening, or why, but I was absolutely certain that I was about to die, right there, halfway through an episode of *The Voice*. What a way to go. At the hospital, still struggling for breath, entire body tingling in fear, I was shocked to hear there was 'nothing' wrong with me – I'd 'just' had a panic attack. That day, that awful day, where it felt like it was the end, was only the beginning – my friend Anxiety had come to visit and planned on hanging around for a while. I tried lots of different things to get over my anxiety attacks. I called my mum for reassurance all the time, I saw a therapist for a while too but I'd just nod and smile my way through my sessions and head out to another party, planning to worry about the big stuff later. I even tried doing colonic irrigation to try and – I don't know – flush the anxiety out of me? Why are you laughing? It's a thing! All I'll say is, if you're going to have your colon hosed out, do not eat a prawn laksa the night before and when they ask you if you want to watch what comes out, decline. Politely. Seriously, it's like Facebook comments – never look!

Things got so bad, I turned into a zombie. Well, no, not a proper one; I didn't eat anybody's brains or anything – and the more unkind among you might say I wouldn't have found much to munch on in the way of brains in the *Made in Chelsea* cast, anyway (which is very funny but terribly naughty of you. It would also be very much untrue, as lots of us had degrees, you know). Anyway, I got this thing called *depersonalisation*. I knew nothing about it except that it would get a great word score on Scrabble. One day I was sitting in a restaurant with my then-girlfriend Frankie bickering over our pasta − not an unusual occurrence − when this strange feeling came over me. It was like I was shrouded in fog, like I was staring out at the world through a crap Instagram filter. Everything was where it was supposed to be, but I felt like I was removed from my body, like . . . I don't know . . . I had farted out my own spirit and I was hovering above myself. And it didn't fade like a head-rush or a migraine − it lasted for six sodding months! Half a year suspended in a weird misty, slow-motion parallel universe. You know how in dreams when you're wandering about, and your body feels strangely heavy and floaty at the same time, but also like you're not controlling it, like you're on autopilot, or being moved like a puppet from scene to scene, and you're aware this isn't real and could never be real, because it's a dream? (I hope you answered yes to that question otherwise this will be even harder to explain.) Well, it was like that. I thought I was totally losing it, that I would be like this forever, my head absolute jelly. I made the zombies from *The Walking Dead* look like tap-dancing toddlers full of Red Bull and sweeties. A doctor explained to me it was depersonalisation: not just 10 Across on *The Times'* crossword but a culmination of my stress and anxiety, and that I needed to make changes if I wanted to get through it. The thing is, I'd been running all my life. Running away from security, messing things up, and running toward disaster. Something had to give; I had to rebuild. The fog did lift, randomly, one day on holiday, but I was terrified it would come back, and if I'm honest I still am, even now, when my life couldn't be better.

So why am I telling you this? Why am I even writing this book? This is a good question. Even my darling mum, when I told her about it, said, 'Who the fuck is going to want to read that?' – she can definitely pay for her own copy. But, like I said, I jump into things and worry about the consequences later. Life's like a series of auditions, and we're all trying to get that perfect role. I think a lot of us do what I've always done and play different roles, as we try to find our place in the world. That's what this book is about: me working out who I really wanted to be. I'm not ready for the end credits any time soon, but I do sometimes think: how do I want to be remembered? I want to be the kind of leading man you might admire. I know my life might not be the most relatable you'll ever read about; I can imagine what people might think. I'm not going to pretend I've had it hard, this isn't a zillion pages of 'Poor me!' or anything like that. But if you are interested, and open to taking a look, I guess I'm finally ready to lift the lid on what it's like to be Jamie Laing. There have been lots of highs, a few lows, but it's never been boring!

I might seem like an open book, if you like, but there are many more pages to turn; there are still things you don't know. I'm not here to change your mind, or make you love me, or even confirm everything you thought about me in the first place, I just wanted to explain, if you'll let me, that I'm both exactly who you think I am and . . . also not that guy at all.

And, please, let's not hear any more about the biscuits. Seriously.

Supporting Cast

You can't have a leading man without a supporting cast. I've been so lucky in my life to have a supportive (and patient) family, and friends who have stuck by me no matter what, even when I . . . well, as you'll see later on in the book, I can be quite challenging.

It might sound strange, but almost everyone I've ever met has had an impact on my life in some way. Sometimes all it takes is meeting someone once and I'll remember what they've told me forever. People talk about learning your lesson from things you've done or things that happen to you, but I don't think you ever stop learning. You're never done – everyone has something to teach you, no matter how insignificant it might seem at the time. The mother of the woman I hooked up with in South Africa, for example, taught me to always make sure your underwear is a) the right way round and b) clean before talking to someone while wearing just your boxers. A very kind agent, from the James Grant Agency, who said a polite 'thank you but no thank you' when it came to representing me, told me 'Jamie, when you're driving to Leeds, don't turn off for Manchester', which sounds like the most ridiculous and obvious advice ever but what he was actually saying was 'stay focused on where you're going, stay on the right path'. In hindsight, maybe it would've been easier for him to say 'stay focused on where you're going, stay on the right path' rather than what he actually said, but at least he made it memorable.

But it's the close relationships that really form you, isn't it? Without these guys, I wouldn't be where I am today. I mean, there's every chance that without some of them I'd actually be *more* successful, but for the purposes of this exercise let's pretend otherwise. And if I haven't mentioned you here, please don't be upset and think that I don't love you or appreciate you, because obviously I do – it's just that I love you *so* much, I'd need a whole other book to tell the world why. Either that, or think yourself lucky that your scandalous connection to me will remain undiscovered – for now.

Mum

My mum is always there for me no matter what. No matter how much I annoy her or try her patience – which I know I have done, often, in the past – she has stuck by me through thick and thin. My mum is dedicated, and nothing will stand in the way of her coming through for her children. I remember when I was away at my first boarding school, Summer Fields, there was going to be a mother and son tennis tournament and we were set to compete together. My mum and I are super-close anyway, but there's also a competitive streak that we both share, and, more importantly, we like spending time together, and are both very good at tennis. You could see why Mum was keen – my poor brother was useless at it; I used to get so annoyed with him when we played. This was bound to be an epic match; we were both so looking forward to it. So my mum was all set to drive out to my school and, together, we would thrash the opposition. I'm not ashamed to say I've always been a bit of a mummy's boy, especially when I was younger, so I waited keenly for her to come that day, looking out for her car and badgering adults to ask if they'd seen her arrive. But she didn't show. Now this was very out of character for my mum; no way would she miss this; there had to be a very good reason. I started to panic and wondered what the hell had happened to her. Eventually, I saw my friend's mum, whose face changed when she saw me. Uh-oh. She told me Mum had been in a car accident on the motorway and naturally I thought the worst, and tried to keep all my emotions in. I think this was the first time it occurred to me that people could actually die. So, in my head, Mum is gone and I'm all alone in the world and we never even got to play our tennis match and romp home to victory. I remember being so frightened and sad but trying to be stoic about it. As it turns out, I needn't have worried quite as much – story of my life. There was no motorway crash; what actually happened was Mum was packing the boot of the car with all her tennis gear when a van reversed into her car and knocked her out. She was heavily concussed, so was taken to hospital, and was barely making sense. Such was her dedication though, that when the nursing staff were trying to treat her, all she could say was 'I have to get to Summer Fields', to play tennis with me. All the nurses heard was Somerfield, a long-defunct supermarket, and they said to her, 'Don't worry, love, you'll have to do your shopping another day.' Mum, you're a legend.

Dad

My dad is amazing and I couldn't love my step-mum Katya more, but I was definitely a mummy's boy growing up. All I've ever wanted to do is make my dad proud. I think that's a pretty normal thing for kids to want, but I knew with my brother, I had some pretty impressive footsteps to follow. My brother did everything right: he worked hard at school, went to university and got a brilliant degree, got a good job, and basically never gave my dad a moment's trouble. And then there was me. Well, I didn't quite do any of that. I didn't get the amazing grades, I went to university, but I didn't do something that he might have seen as 'useful'. And, as for jobs . . . I ended up on a reality TV show. Not exactly a career trajectory my dad could identify with, you see, and I used to worry that I'd disappointed him. I used to imagine that my dad was probably wondering if I would ever get a real job. I don't know what it was about me and my need for approval – my dad had always been very supportive of everything I'd done and had forgiven a lot of my (many) misdemeanours, but I still didn't feel like I'd done enough to make him proud. Looking back, this was just me being hard on myself as usual and looking for issues that weren't there. But when I did *Strictly*, something clicked and I thought, 'Ha! Maybe this time I've actually done it!'. I'd got to the final, and my partner Karen Hauer and I were doing the *It Takes Two* show talking about it, and suddenly Claudia Winkleman said she had a message from my dad. He popped up on the screen, looking a little bit awkward, but adorably so, and he said, 'I'm so proud of you', and I thought, 'Wow'. As men, we don't really talk about things or say stuff like that. That's not who we are, so the fact that he said that on camera was pretty amazing. I think as a child you want to do all you can to make your parents able to say, 'That's my son', or 'That's my daughter' and feel proud of your contribution to the world, no matter how big or small. And that day, I got that feeling.

Xander

Xander is my big brother. Well, he's actually called Alexander, but when I was little I had no time for syllables and couldn't say his name properly, so I've always called him Xander. As you will read later on, I adore my brother. I have also made his life hell, totally accidentally, just by being me. And he's such a gentleman, he's never got cross. Well, not often. We lived together for a bit when I started on *Made in Chelsea* and although my brother loves me, I probably tested this love – and certainly his patience – many times during that period. He was always saying to me that our flat was like a madhouse, and couldn't I just be normal for once – but . . . my normal and his normal are very different. He's super academic and erudite and I'm . . . well, I'm smart and I'm hardworking, but in different ways. On one occasion my poor brother came home to find me out but could sense there was someone else in the house. He crept upstairs, prepared for a confrontation with an intruder, only to find a very beautiful woman in his bed. Now, she had definitely not been there when he left, so he was quite puzzled. The lady had, of course, been with me, and we'd been . . . erm . . . using my brother's room to get to know one another better. The woman smiled and said, 'Oh hi, I'm with Jamie, but he's not here; you don't mind if I stay a bit, do you?' And Xander, being Xander, said, 'Oh no, of course not. Would you like some tea?' He was always trying to get me to calm down a little and used to beg me to have a night in with him for a change. No dramas, no late-night cab rides to parties – just the two of us and a movie. And we did it, and it was great. Then we played a shooting game and it was pretty intense, but loads of fun. Just us. When it came time for bed, we said our good nights, congratulated ourselves on our clean-living evening, and hit the hay. Once in bed, I could hear a scratching noise at my skylight. Someone was trying to get in. I called, Hello – no answer. It happened again. No response. Remember, I'm kind of wired from the shooting game at this point, so I burrowed down into my bed, feeling super alert, when the skylight flew open and what I *thought* was an intruder on a zip wire slid down into the room. I was screaming like I never have in my life, like you can't imagine, and then I saw something leave the room. A panther! An actual panther! I'd heard these stories that panthers had, like, escaped zoos and they lived in London, but you never saw them. (I can't remember where I heard this bullshit, but it felt real at the time.) I screamed for Xander and he came running. I told him there was a panther in the house and he took it pretty well.

'God, Jamie,' he said. 'You're lying, or imagining things. You can't just have one night in and be a normal person; there has to be a panther.' But then he saw the skylight was open. We searched every room in the house until we came to the windowless box room that we never went in. We could sense it was in there, so I got a broom and banged on the door and WHOOSH, out rushes an extremely frightened and agitated cat and ZOOM, there it went running up and down our freshly painted walls and SPLAT there it was, cat pee and cat poo shat and sprayed over every surface. Everywhere, covered in paw tracks, and faeces, and urine. I was no use whatsoever; I jumped on a table and screamed. That was it, my brother had had enough. 'One night in and this happens,' he yelled as he somehow managed to usher the cat out of the flat, 'I can't live with you anymore.' It wasn't my fault the cat had broken in, of course but . . . I don't know, this kind of stuff has a habit of happening to me.

Emily

My baby sister. I was always leaving her out as a child so it will be no surprise to her that I'm leaving her out here too. (I love you, Emily; there's a whole part about you later on, so please don't worry.)

Sophie

My girlfriend Sophie is better than me in every single way. I've never met anyone like her before. When we first met, I used to be so nervous around her, like I wanted to impress her – in fact, even now, when we've been together all these years, I still sometimes feel my stomach do a little cartwheel when I'm with her, but in a good way. I like it; she keeps me on my toes. But back when we first started dating . . . well, you know what it's like: you're on your best behaviour. You want to show them they've made the right decision, that you're worth sticking with, and that you were well brought up. So, there's this period of being very polite, and sneaking off to brush your teeth before they wake up so you're minty-fresh for any early morning kisses – you know the drill.

But there's also the farting. Well, you can't, can you? Not in front of them, not in the same room; not even in the same house, maybe. The idea of actually admitting you have normal bodily functions when you're still trying to be sexy and mysterious and hot . . . so you just don't. One night, early on, Sophie is staying over, and we're both in that stage where we're a bit nervous around each other, it's all pretty new. The flat I'm living in at the time isn't that big, just one bedroom and one bathroom, so there isn't much personal space. And . . . I just happened to have tummy problems that night. Can you see where this is going? Whoa! No, not that far, don't worry, you can carry on reading. Anyway, we get into bed, it's late, and we're about to go to sleep and I'm lying there thinking, 'Oh God I really need to fart.' I don't really know what to do; I have the most beautiful woman in the world next to me, I can't *fart*. Disgusting. Anyway, I hold fire – literally – and wait until she's asleep. Great. I shuffle over a little to the edge of the bed and do that thing we all do when the time comes, and lift my bum cheek a little and . . . release. But it makes such a weird noise, like a hiss and a whoosh in one, like a snake trying to suck helium out of a balloon. Sophie sits bolt upright in bed. Not asleep at all. Very much awake.

'What was that noise?'

'I don't know.'

'You don't know?'

'No.'

'It's midnight, for God's sake.'

Sophie rolls her eyes. 'I mean, seriously, why is someone sweeping leaves outside at this time of night?'

Sweeping leaves? What the . . .? Obviously I collapse into laughter because she thinks that weird helium fart I've just done is a street-sweeper doing some serious overtime. I had to confess, and luckily she sees the funny side, while I'm wondering if I should maybe see a doctor about my farts. Are they supposed to sound like that? What does a healthy fart sound like? God, I'm overthinking this, aren't I?

Jonathan

My stepdad is possibly the most patient man I know. I mean, he's had to be – imagine taking me on as a teenager. We haven't always seen eye to eye, mainly because I used to come home with eyebrow piercings and wild ideas or . . . well, you'll be treated to a non-exhaustive list of my crimes against poor Jonathan later on. But now, we get on terrifically well, he's like a mentor to me and I admire him so much. He's been an absolute rock and has helped me build up Candy Kittens into what it is today.

Georgie

Ah, Georgie. The absolute best. I've known her since I was about 14; she went to a girls' school near my school. She lived with my ex-girlfriend for a while at university so, and probably after hearing a few stories about what a nightmare I was as a boyfriend, decided she didn't like me that much. But I eventually won her over and we soon became best friends. Her family would invite me on holidays with them every single year and we even lived together for a year which was . . . well, it was interesting. Georgie used to say our flat was like the wild west, with my friends always coming and going.

It did get quite crazy at times. I suppose we started as we meant to go on, when we turned up to sign the contract for the flat dressed as a cat and a bat. Just to say: this wasn't our normal clothing. It was Hallowe'en, and we were going to a big party. Oh well, you might think, if they were on their way to a party and had to pop in and sign the lease, maybe it's no big deal, probably a funny story the landlord might tell someone one day. Thing is, we weren't going to a party – we'd just left it. It was the next day. The sensible thing to do the night before you sign a very important contract, is to get plenty of sleep and arrive well rested and groomed so that the landlord doesn't think he's made a terrible mistake. I didn't really do sensible back then, though. Instead, we decided to stay up all night at the party and rock up to sign our lives away for the next year dressed as animals. I must say, we'd looked great the night before as we headed out, we were pretty pleased with ourselves. We were in a sorrier state the following day but, still reeking of booze and a little tipsy, we signed on the dotted line. Once it was done and the flat was ours, I thought it would be a great idea to make an even better impression than we already had (absolutely mangled from a night's partying), and I laughed maniacally and shouted 'You fools!' as we handed the contract over. I still wonder what they must have thought of us. No, I can probably guess. It took us a while to settle in. When we first started living together, I used to come back to the flat and the kitchen would be a complete mess. Now, I'm quite a tidy person, so I'd be really annoyed but because these were the early days, we were kind of tiptoeing around each other, not wanting to rock the boat. So I'd tidy up and think no more about it. This went on for a while. Then one day Georgie came home with a very formal look on her face and said, 'Hey, so . . . um, by the way, I'll just say this and then say no more about it, but there was a bit of a mess in the kitchen earlier and I cleared it up.' I was, like, what?! She was the messy one! But, not wanting to argue, I just said okay and we carried on for a while, each clearing up the other's mess and feeling a little resentful but biting our tongues because we loved each other. And then, one day, we came home together to find a CAT marauding through the kitchen, eating stuff and knocking things over and generally destroying the place. And it was doing this every single day! Whether it was the same cat that dropped through my skylight and shat all over my flat, I have no idea, but at least Georgie's and my friendship remained intact. Feline home invasion aside – and a few other stories we'll be coming to later – I can truly say that Georgie is the absolute greatest and one of my best friends. She knows my mind better than I do. She's always been there, through everything. One day, if I get married, Georgie will 100 per cent be my best man. Or woman. Whatever you want to call it, she's the best.

Spencer

If you know anything about my time on *Made in Chelsea*, you'll know all about me and Spencer – maybe 'partners-in-crime' isn't the right phrase, but we're certainly close. One of the funny things about being on TV a lot – and especially on a show that is, on the surface, about very rich people – is that people think you have loads of money just lying around. If only! But sometimes living up to this image and keeping up appearances only make things worse. Once, Spencer and

I were invited to a charity auction (where various prizes and experiences are auctioned off for pretty large sums and the proceeds go to good causes). We were there to drum up a bit of publicity, attract photographers to the event, that kind of thing. One of the goodies up for grabs was a skiing holiday. Nobody wanted it – and we certainly didn't – but being among the 'famous' people in the room, people started looking to us to step in and get the bids going. They kept shouting, 'Go on Jamie! Go on Spencer! Bid on it! Go on!' Now, this started getting intense. The bids were creeping up: a grand, £1,500; £1,600. And still the crowd is shouting at us, 'It's for a good cause, Spencer, come on!', I said to Spencer. The pressure was on; it was mortifying. They kept heckling, and shouting, and goading, and as the bids managed to creep to around £2,800, Spencer just snapped and shouted, 'FOUR!' And the auctioneer banged his gavel and said 'Sold!'. Four. Thousand. Pounds. My jaw was on the floor. The place erupted in cheers and congratulations. The pressure to live up to our Chelsea image was insane and, on this occasion, we'd gone too far.

I looked at Spencer. 'What the hell have you done?'

Now, Spencer was usually unflappable, but I could see panic on his face. 'I wasn't intending to win this. I don't even want the holiday,' he said. 'What are we going to do?'

We? It wasn't me shouting out 'four' like I was lost on a golf course, buddy. But I couldn't abandon him now. 'We'll just have to tell them you didn't mean to do it.'

'I can't!'

But what else could we do? We slinked backstage to speak to the organisers and explained, very sheepishly, that

Spencer hadn't been intending to win the auction. It still cost him money, though: to avoid having to pay for a holiday he didn't want, he ended up giving them a cash donation of about £1,500. I laughed about it all the way home. Spencer did too, later. Much, much later.

Ed Williams

Going into business with someone is a bit like getting married. You have to totally trust one another and ride out any storms together, no matter what. I lucked out when I met my business partner Ed, who has been there since the beginning and helped make my dream a reality, to get our confectionery business Candy Kittens off the ground. We work very well together, he's an absolute rock, but it hasn't always been plain sailing, for many reasons – for most of which, I have to admit, I am to blame. Once, we'd just had a huge success with our first pop-up shop in London and were all set to open another one in Bath. We'd planned a huge press launch for the opening and almost all the media in the south-west of England was going to be there. The BBC, ITV, newspapers, the lot. I was so excited. Actually, I was too excited. I got a little ahead of myself and went out to celebrate our new shop the night before the opening and . . . slept through my alarm. So while I should have been on a train to Bath, facing the press and showing the world our amazing new shop, I was . . . running around my flat, cursing my alarm, cursing myself, and cursing the fact that while I wasn't in Bath, Ed certainly was. Now, Ed is a terrific guy, and the business would not exist without him, but . . . he's never been on TV. He's handsome enough, but his face is not widely known so all these journalists and reporters were there, cameras trained on the shop, and Ed stood there facing them all alone, with nobody having a clue who he was, while I raced to get there as fast as I could . . . which turned out to be not that fast at all. I was two hours late! I've said it before and, no doubt, I'll say it again: sorry, Ed.

Francis Boulle and Oliver Proudlock

Francis, Ollie and I have been through a lot. In fact, we are still going through it – Francis is my podcast partner on *Private Parts* and there's not much he doesn't know about me. This isn't always a good thing. I still consider Ollie one of my best friends. All three of us even lived together for a while. We were like a team, and called ourselves 'the lost boys', like the characters in *Peter Pan*, because we were young and out in the world on our own and didn't really have a clue what we were doing. We even got matching 'Lost Bois' tattoos – well, we nearly did. Francis flatly refused, claiming in his usual modest manner, 'Why put a bumper sticker on a Ferrari?' So it was just me and Ollie. The idea was that my tattoo would say 'Lost Bois' in Ollie's handwriting, and Ollie's tattoo would say the same, but would be in my handwriting. After I had mine done, however, Ollie decided my handwriting was too terrible and that there was no way he was having my scrawl permanently etched upon his skin, so he went with his own design. In my defence, Ollie's handwriting isn't that great either and everyone who's seen it thinks my tattoo says 'Less Boi'.

Mal, my therapist

I know what you're thinking. Typical, privileged celebrity, droning on to a therapist about their feelings. I know I'm super lucky to have access to a therapist, but I think everybody should; every single person on the planet would benefit from being open about their problems and talking things through. It's so important that men speak openly about their challenges with mental health. There's so much pressure on guys to stay strong, and keep a stiff upper lip, and it's hugely harmful – not just to men, but to everyone who has to be around us. I don't know where I'd be if I hadn't found someone I can trust like Maleha Khan – or Mal, as I like to call her. She has really helped me. The thing about anxiety is it always makes you overthink things like your relationships, or your work or where you live – it's so hard to just let things 'be' and go with the flow. Mal was the first person I opened up to properly about my struggles. When I'd been going to see her about six months, she said to me, 'You know, Jamie, I'm kind of surprised you stuck with me.'

Oh. I was quite shocked to hear this. Was I even a little offended? Not sure. But Mal explained: 'I know in your head everything would've been telling you to change, to go to someone else, to try a different therapist, because I wasn't giving you the answers you wanted to hear.'

See, she knows me so well! To be honest, I'm surprised she stuck with *me*!

Tinnitus

Nope, not another posh friend with a weird made-up name, but actual tinnitus. Where would I be without my ringing, pinging, buzzing constant companion? Well, I'd probably be a lot less tetchy when trying to concentrate in a quiet room. Like all the best love stories, Tinnitus turned up one day and changed my life forever. When I was 27 and living with Georgie, I woke up one morning and could hear this ringing noise. It sounded like an alarm going off somewhere, faintly, in the distance. I tore the place apart looking for this insistent beeping – I truly knew the meaning of madness that day. And when I realised, through a process of elimination, that the noise was actually inside my own head, I was thrilled! Tinnitus became my new best friend who refused to leave. When I confided in Alex Mytton about my tinnitus, he suggested trying to burn the thing out using one of those ear candles that claim to burn all the wax out of your ear. I wasn't sure you could actually burn a sound to death, but I was willing to give it a try, and lay on my side while Alex, with the solemnity and reverence of someone performing open-heart surgery, jabbed a flaming cylinder in my ear. Did it cure my tinnitus? It did not, but it certainly took my mind off it for around 15 minutes. Tinnitus, my faithful, noisy pal – thanks for always being there. But please, for my sake, sod off.

Now we've met the players, it's time for the main event, our feature presentation. We're going right back to the very beginning, and the very first role I took on. Get ready.

Chapter One
Child Star

I'm not exaggerating when I say I've been causing mayhem since the moment I was born. Well, before that actually. According to my mum, I was playing rugby in her tummy constantly, and she had to stay in hospital for weeks while she waited for me to make an appearance. She was given permission by the matron to have one evening out of bed so she could go to a local restaurant for her anniversary dinner but – guess what? Starting as I meant to go on and wanting to be part of the fun, I decided to gatecrash and arrived at 5 o'clock that morning, by emergency caesarean. No dinner for mum and dad, sadly, but the biggest adventure of their lives was about to start: being parents to me. Imagine! My mum tells a brilliant story of how, coming round from her anaesthetic, she watched me next to her – with an angelic look on my face, I'm guessing – and picked up a horoscope book she had by her bedside. 'Let's see what this little boy is going to be like,' she said to herself, flicking through to find the right date and time. Oh dear. Her eyes fell on this: *'Beware the Scorpio child born at dawn'*. Well, you can't say she wasn't warned.

My early childhood was pretty idyllic, I have to admit. We weren't billionaires, but we were more fortunate than most – we lived in a big house in the Oxfordshire countryside and it had everything a boisterous little firecracker like me could want: a tennis court, a swimming pool, loads of fun places to hide, or pretend to get lost in. I was always climbing trees or running around naked. I haven't changed much! You know when you cast your mind back to the best moments of your childhood and it feels like it was permanently summer, just day after day of blue skies and sepia smiles and ice cream all over your face? That's what it was like for me; every day was an adventure and I loved it.

Obviously, there was mum and there was dad. My long-suffering brother Alexander, who's two years older than me, and my two half-sisters, Tash and Jems, who were a bit older than both of us and were from my dad's first marriage, were there too. Then came my little sister Emily. You might think I felt pushed out when she arrived, but, to be honest, I didn't. I know it's an unspoken rule among parents not to choose favourites and to say that you love all your children equally (and I'm sure that's true of my parents too) but . . . look, I have to be real here. There's no question that I was, and remain to this day, my mum's favourite child. She'll tell you that herself! She once said to me, 'When I had you children, I never loved anything more. But you in particular, I loved you more than anyone else.' I even said to her, 'You can't say that!', and she just said, 'But it's true!' Btw, my siblings are fully aware of this; they will not be surprised to read this and, believe it or not, they do still talk to me. Jumping ahead a bit here, but I have another sibling too, who comes along later. George is my half-brother from my dad's next marriage to my stepmum Katya – apologies for the spoiler there – and he's fifteen years younger than me. When he was a baby, he looked like Matt Lucas, and the first time I ever babysat him, when he was about three, he had a wild coughing fit and I was convinced that he was going to die right there and then and that everyone would think I'd done the little mite in because I was jealous. He lived to tell the tale, though, and he's a terrific boy and he's even been doing some interning for me at Candy Kittens, so we could have another entrepreneur on our hands.

But let's get back to when I was little. It may not shock you to learn that I liked being the centre of attention when I was a kid. Anything happening, I wanted to be there, right in the middle of it. I have a few special images in my memory from earlier in my life and, even as they were taking place, I remember thinking 'I never want to let this moment go, it's so wonderful'. That's why, in later years, I'd always have a video camera with me, just in case a 'forever moment' happens; I hate the idea of forgetting something magical. I want to remember it all. This may be the reason why I am the main star in all of my family's extensive library of home videos. At the first sign of a video camera, I used to home in like a shark, throwing myself in front of the lens. 'Watch me, Mummy! Watch!' You might call it middle child syndrome; I just saw it as me being me. And so did my family. At least I was entertaining!

The minute the focus was off me, I had a knack for bringing it right back. To me. Being naughty tended to do the trick. I was very light-fingered as a child. I was fascinated by things I didn't own myself; I didn't like to be left out or feel hard done by. I wanted everything that anyone else had. When I was very small, I would steal things – the stupidest of things like a jar of mayonnaise or a fizzy drink – and spirit them away. I wouldn't even drink the drinks: I just liked to have them, and hide them somewhere. The mayonnaise . . . well, this sounds very weird, but I used to bury it, a bit like a dog, then dig it up later and sniff it, a bit like . . . I don't know, a serial killer? I was obsessed by shiny things too, a proper little jackdaw. I didn't really understand what money was, but I knew it was good to have some. My dad had a pot of loose change on his dressing table, and I used to raid it, and take the coins to my secret hiding place. You know how at the end of banisters on a staircase, there's a post at the end? Ours had acorns on top of them – these are called caps, by the way, I had to google that – and I used to take these acorns off and slip the coins into the gap inside. So here I was, squirrelling money away and creating my first savings account; I was both a hoarder and kleptomaniac rolled into one. The house keys were another favourite obsession. If left unattended, there was a very good chance I would nick my mum's keys and chuck them down the drain outside the house. Why? Who knows? A little bit of excitement, or mystery, maybe? Or the guarantee that my mum would spend the next god-knows-how-many hours trying to get me to confess what I'd done with them. She would ask me their whereabouts over and over, and I would always shake my head and say I didn't know. She would take me round the whole house in the hope of exposing my hiding place, but I took forever to break. Eventually – and this could go on a while – I'd take her outside and point down the drain.

This behaviour soon earned me a bit of a reputation. My grandma lived nearby, and used to call me up and ask if I'd like to come over for a biscuit. Obviously, all children will say yes to a biscuit, and I'd go there and have a wonderful time. I remember my grandma saying she was going to spend a penny and, fascinated by money at that age, would go with her to the bathroom and wait patiently for her to give me this penny. I couldn't understand. I was like, 'Where the fuck is my money?' (Well, I didn't swear when I was tiny, but the depth of feeling was definitely there.) Once, when my grandma lost a peanut bowl, I found myself under suspicion. What do you mean, 'What's a peanut bowl?' It's a bowl, for putting peanuts in. Anyway, I hadn't taken it, but was made to search for it all weekend. I remember looking all over the house thinking, 'If I were Jamie' – kind of not realising that, obviously, I *was* Jamie – 'where would I hide this bowl?' I can't remember where it turned up, eventually. Maybe they should have looked down the drain.

If I wasn't helping myself to other people's possessions, I was screaming. Like, actual screaming. Constant tantrums. I was always being told off, always felt I was doing something wrong. My mum remembers carrying me out of shops under her arm, my body stiff as a board, face red and veins throbbing, as I screamed the place down, while other shoppers looked on and tutted and, probably, thanked whichever God they believed in that I wasn't *their* child. I was strong-headed and would often refuse to get in the car. Sometimes my mum would do that thing parents do and threaten to leave without me – except I was such a nightmare that she would actually get in the car and start driving. Savage!

'And then I'd hear your little legs running on the gravel,' she told me once, 'and my heart would break, so I'd stop and come back and get out.' And I, of course, would then start running in the opposite direction, screaming.

I would scream so hard and loud that I made myself sick. And others – my brother once had to ask to stop the car so he could get out and throw up, I was stressing him out so much. My mum would get so cross with me, she used to lift me up and put me behind a child safety gate because she was so afraid that my hollering and bawling would trigger some kind of detonator inside her and end with her smacking me. I don't blame her at all, looking back. Obviously then, realising I had annoyed her, I would try to be nice and call out to her. I didn't like anyone being upset with me; I still don't. Luckily, I reckon I could probably climb over a safety gate quite easily now, just in case Mum is thinking of trying that one again.

It wasn't that my parents weren't strict, I just didn't take punishment seriously at all, because I knew that eventually someone would give in. I remember during my naughtiest period, my mum produced a chart for the wall, and told me if I got five gold stars for being good that week, we could watch the movie *Free Willy*. I'm sure you can guess how many stars I got – yes, that's right, a big fat zero. But, because Mum didn't want my brother and sister to miss out, we watched *Free Willy* anyway. So, you know, literally no consequences for me there at all. My brother, who was an absolute angel his entire childhood, always says that he never got rewarded for being constantly good, yet if I behaved well, it was such a rare occurrence that I'd be showered with praise and treats. I suppose he has a point – and I wonder if he wishes he'd been a bit naughtier. But I always knew, as long as I said sorry, everything would be okay. Yes, people would get angry with me for not being good or doing my homework or breaking a window or whatever, but I would always get away with it because I would say sorry and actually mean it. This did mean the real world came as a bit of a shock when I slowly realised that not everybody would be charmed by my apologies, but back then, little terror that I was, I knew it would all work out absolutely fine.

One person whose punishment always hit the spot was my nanny, Julie. Now, she was no Mary Poppins, let me tell you. She was a young, yet formidable, Northern woman and although I loved her dearly, she absolutely terrified me at the same time. She did not mince her words – her favourite threat was to say 'I'll come down on you like a ton of bricks', and I actually believed she would. During my screaming matches, she would grab me tightly and shout right back at me, 'Scream louder, Jamie, Swindon can't hear you.' Honestly, nothing fazed her. For a time, I was borderline feral. I never sat still and would refuse to use my potty, preferring to slink off to pee in the corner of the room. Told you, feral. Julie's solution? Tie me to the potty until I did what I had to do! As for having elbows on the table during meals, Julie wasn't having any of it, and because I never sat up straight at the table, Julie constructed what I can only describe as an instrument of torture: she'd tie a fork behind my body and if I slouched, I'd be jabbed by the fork and sit bolt upright again. I know it sounds like Julie might have been better suited to working in a dictatorial regime instead of looking after a small boy, but even she struggled to control me sometimes. Once she threatened to have me arrested and even drove me to the police station and sat outside. I was terrified . . . but then we drove home again, and I remember thinking, 'Well, she didn't actually take me in, so I'll probably be okay.' I was always pushing buttons and boundaries just to see how much I could get away with.

I know what you're thinking: this child was a monster, those poor parents! And I agree, but the thing is, the reason I often got away with all these little crimes is that I was also genuinely the most loving little boy. I was so warm, just the sweetest. You know how some children hide away when people come over to visit, and are shy in front of adults? Not me. Oh no. I just wanted affection all the time, and I didn't care who from. I was always sitting on people's knees, always kissing people, always hugging them. Even Julie thought I was sweet, and I must have made her life hell – she entered me in a bonny baby contest once. I didn't win, though. Shocking.

But because I could be so sweet and friendly and affectionate, I would win people over, and everyone kind of forgave me being hard work for some of the time, because I was just this cute blond kid who would always say sorry and always promise to try harder to be good. I wish I could say that this didn't follow me through life and I learned some hard lessons, but people have always found it hard to be mad at me for long. One of my school reports once said, 'Getting mad at Jamie is like drowning puppies.' Insufferable! I know!

My biggest cheerleader was, perhaps surprisingly, my brother Xander. He was my saviour. He would often take the rap for things I'd done or defend me to stop anyone getting mad at me. 'Jamie didn't mean it,' he would always say. He was so protective of me and so patient. My brother is so sensitive and gentle, and making him mad is the hardest thing in the world, but I have certainly pushed him as far as I could over the years, especially when we were little. I knew if he was ever angry with me, I was absolutely for the high-jump. He would get me back in other ways, though. For example, we once peered over the edge of an old well, and Xander told me if I dropped my prized silly-putty down the well, it would bounce back up. Now, I believed Xander's word over everybody else's, so gamely chucked the sticky stuff down the well and . . . waited. It did not bounce. But we were so close, as thick as thieves. If any of our cousins or other kids came over, we would still just play between ourselves and leave them out. We were a little gang – all we had was each other and we loved it. (My sister was too little and we weren't that interested in her back then, sorry Emily. We do love you, though!)

Xander really looked after me, especially at bedtime. He used to play the violin in the evening, and when I was sent to bed, I would sit at the top of the stairs and wait for him to finish playing, because I couldn't go to bed without him. It would be the scariest thing in the world hearing this violin because he was absolutely terrible at it, it sounded like ten cats in a tombola, so I'd sit with my little hands over my ears, hoping it wouldn't last much longer. I was scared of the dark and hated sleeping alone, so I was always crawling into bed with him. Many big brothers might have told little ones to buzz off back to their own bed, but Xander let me in and would quietly tell me stories. I was obsessed with sweets when I was little and, perhaps understandably, rarely allowed to eat them because I was so hyper all the time, which only made me more obsessed. So Xander would invent amazing stories featuring me as a main character – Jamie in Sweet World – living in this incredible place where every single thing was made of sweets. Houses, gardens, everything. And the best thing of all was that because the sweets in Sweet World were magic, they wouldn't rot your teeth. He would lie there and tell me these brilliant tales and I would imagine this fantasy world, fully visualising it as if I were right there. It became the inspiration for my sweet business Candy Kittens. And yes, I really do love sweets that much.

Although I loved listening to my brother's sugary sagas, night times weren't great for me. I was a very deep thinker as a kid, and quite obsessive. I'd worry about all sorts of things late at night. Did dinosaurs go to heaven? And if they did, did that mean when I died and went to heaven, I would spend all eternity trying not to get eaten by a T-Rex? I was always too scared to say 'night-night' to my brother when we were going to bed, too, because it sounded very final, like we would never see each other again. So instead, I used to say, 'Talk to you a lot in the morning', and he would say it back.

I also had an obsession with going to the bathroom. I was always too scared to get up and go, which meant I peed my bed all the time. Off I would trudge to my parents' room, to clamber into their bed, every night without fail. Yes, you could say I was bed-hopping from a very early age, well done. Of course, being me, I wouldn't just slip quietly in between my parents or whatever; I used to sleep across their pillows, right at the top of the heads. On unlucky occasions when my bladder wasn't quite empty, I would pee again – and thanks to my weird sleeping position, I would end up peeing into the back of my dad's head. Dad, I'm not sure if there's any scientific evidence to support this, but if I am responsible for your hair loss, I'm deeply sorry.

My poor brother, who always stayed in his own bed and never complained, had a nightmare once and came crying into my parents' room for a scrap of attention, only to find I had already taken up residence. No way was Mum having two children wrecking her night's sleep, so Xander was sent back to his room to deal with the monsters under his bed, while I stayed exactly where I was. I adored it. I always wanted to be in among the family and feel loved.

My sister Tash was probably the coolest person I knew when I was little. I can't describe how cool I thought she was. She was ten years older than me, and all the boys fancied her; her friends were amazing and I found them fascinating, because they could do whatever they wanted – or, at least it seemed like that to me, the little boy who was always being told off. I remember I caught them smoking once and I just thought, wow, they are so grown up. I'd always felt so frustrated as a child because I couldn't understand why there were rules, or why I couldn't do what I liked – nobody really explained and it took me a long time to figure it out. Decades, even! All I knew is that it seemed that children couldn't do anything, but as soon as you were older, the world belonged to you. And that was it, my obsession with being older was born. I wanted to be fifteen, not five. Tash and her friends seemed so free, they could say no if they didn't want to do something, which I thought was amazing, and I would try to copy them. For instance, if Tash said she wasn't going to go swimming – because she was so cool – then I used to say I wasn't going swimming either. I was a tiny six-year-old boy who was pouting like a surly teenager. I was desperate to be part of their gang and, for some reason, they indulged me. Like I said, people really loved me, in spite of everything! They let me watch movies with them, and Tash used to have posters of movie idols like Tom Cruise and Brad Pitt on her wall, and she'd say, 'One day, Jamie, you're going to be just like these guys.' I couldn't wait.

I remember Tash and her friends would speak very frankly to one another in front of me. They would talk about sex, and although I didn't have a clue what any of it meant, it sounded exciting.

So . . . this is the part where I tell you about the first sexual experience I ever had. Yes, already and quite young. I'm not sure you could call it sexual, really; it was more of an experiment. It all starts with overhearing Tash and her friends talking about sex, and my silkies. What are my silkies, you may wonder? You may regret asking.

I don't know if you had, like, a favourite security blanket or a special pillowcase when you were younger, just something like a comforter that you would cling to and it would make you feel safe? Well, I had my silkies. When I was a baby, I had a little rug that had silken edges, like a border of soft, silky material, and as time went on, the edges became detached, and I named them my silkies. There was Big Silky – the longer edge of the rug – and Little Silky – I'm sure it doesn't need a diagram to explain. They were about the width of a decent tie, and to say I loved these things would be an understatement. I would have died for them. As a comfort thing, where some kids would suck their thumb or play with their hair, I used to do something called 'lipping', which was basically rubbing the silkies between my fingers. It felt so nice, and if the silk was cold, or slightly dirty, the change in texture made it more exciting. You think this is weird? Look, I used to bury mayonnaise and drop keys down the drains – this is nothing, this is on an almost Disney level of cute in comparison to my other antics. And anyway, the silkies were the loves of my life, and picking up on what Tash and her pals were saying, it seemed if you really liked someone, you should have some kind of sexual experience with them. So, I got resourceful. Selecting Big Silky as the lucky recipient, I tied one end of it to a doorhandle, and wrapped the other end round my . . . well, round me. Do you see? And then? I slammed the door shut. I wasn't sure what sex was and I didn't really know what was happening, but I'm telling you, it blew my mind.

So far, my early years are sounding pretty lovely, I imagine – well, apart from the screaming and fixation on the silky remnants of a rug. But my childhood of eternal summer was about to change. I started school, and cried buckets on the first day. One highlight was sitting in a circle with the other children for a story and a kid called Joshua threw up right into the centre of it. I did love my teacher, and I made friends, but I started to notice I was different. My first school was just a local one near my house, and I remember my friends making fun of me for the way I said 'Yeah'. Well, if you are reading this you might not know what I mean, but if you have heard me speak on the TV or my podcast, and you don't talk like me, you might understand it as 'Yah'. You know, yah, what posh people say. But back then, as a little boy, I had no concept of poshness, or even being lucky. I'd grown up in a big house with a pool, and tennis courts, and I just thought . . . that everyone's house was like that. Why wouldn't it be? And as for accents, well, I had noticed nanny Julie's was different, I suppose, but it never occurred to me why, so when I went to school and was just myself, other kids noticed. I was never bullied, or anything like that, but it did make me feel strange that there was something they'd spotted about me and kept mentioning. But you know what kids are like – even ones who like you still latch onto any differences and can't resist having a dig. My first sign that not every child lived like me was when I went over to my friend Tom's house and was puzzled by how small it was. Like, just two bedrooms. Where did they put all their stuff? Where did everyone sleep? And when I went to the back of the house, I was even more shocked to find just a back garden. No swimming pool. No tennis courts. But where did he go swimming? What about tennis? Why no big lawn to play football on? Now, as a 32-year-old man, I know how ridiculous this sounds, and I imagine some of you are looking to send me to the guillotine, but I just had no idea. Quite an eye-opener: there will not always be tennis courts wherever you go, Jamie. Crushing!

I wasn't that keen on school, generally – so many rules! – so sometimes I used to pretend to be ill so I could stay home with Julie. Earaches were my speciality as they were harder to disprove. Nobody cared about headaches, and high temperatures were hard to fake, but earache – the worst pain of all – was easily faked, so Julie and I would sit watching *Home and Away* and other programmes all day eating her favourite meal of jacket potato, baked beans, tuna and grated cheese on top. She literally ate it every day. So we would sit and watch mindless daytime TV – the poor woman must've been bored out of her mind. At least when I was being naughty, she'd had something to do.

Being so small, it feels like your life is packed with life-changing events and, of course, firsts. I think that's what keeps me so enthusiastic about stuff, makes me want to try things, because I love the idea of experiencing something for the first time. Although you now know about how intimate I was with my beloved silkies, you might be wondering when I first gave romance a go – after all, it would eventually be something I'd become quite well-known for. I loved the idea of being in love. I think it was part of why I used to be able to charm ladies so much when I was a little boy. I wanted to make them feel special, and adore me – that's never left me, really, I still love to make someone feel like they're my number one priority. My early forays into love came from adoring teachers and sticking to my mum like glue, but I really liked the idea of being properly in love. I assumed being older meant having romances and I was desperate to grow up and be in love. It sounded like the coolest thing ever, so I started early, at the age of six, with my very first girlfriends – yes, plural. At the same time, in fact. Aged six, I dated two girls – Hannah was my proper girlfriend and Eliza was my . . . what would you call her? My mistress? At six? Is that a thing? Seems a little bit over-the-top. Anyway, Hannah would write love letters to me and it was all very sweet and lovely, while Eliza and I would enjoy very chaste, but adorable, kisses in secret. Even then I knew it was wrong, and that if Hannah saw me together with Eliza, she would be upset. But there was something so grown up about it, of being somehow aware of the morality of it, that made me feel like I wanted to do it.

Disaster struck for me around that time, however – my beloved older brother, my teammate, my hero, went off to boarding school. I was probably told about it before he left but to me it seemed like he'd just disappeared. He went off to Summer Fields – spoiler: I end up there in the next chapter – and I was left behind, my world in pieces. No more bedtime stories about Sweet World, no more Xander getting me out of scrapes, or fighting my corner. When you first go away to Summer Fields, you're not allowed to talk to your parents for the first two weeks, to help you settle in. Imagine! I can see why they do it, but it does feel barbaric. After that fortnight, they have something called the Teddy Bears' Picnic which the parents are invited to attend to see how their little darlings are getting on.

When I was small I always tried to hide emotion. If I was upset or annoyed about something, then I would cry, I would scream, and I would shout. But if something upset me that I was embarrassed about, I wouldn't, and I was acutely embarrassed that I missed Xander, my brother, so much.

Crying and screaming seemed like such babyish things to do and, remember, I just really wanted to be a grown-up. After the picnic, I remember how I watched him walking away and I started to cry. But because I didn't want my mum to know how much I was missing him, I told her I was crying because I'd seen his face as he walked away and he'd looked unhappy. This wasn't true at all.

I love my sister but it wasn't the same when it was just the two of us. I was quite mean to her. We would argue all the time. She had a little pony called Teazal and every time she annoyed me, I would pick up a stone, throw it and say that it had hit Teazal – even though he wasn't anywhere near us at the time or even in our line of vision. Sometimes I'd say that he was 'dead', and she'd start crying. I feel really terrible about it now.

It's funny, but after Xander left and even though I'd found the sound of his violin terrifying, I used to sit at the top of the stairs and wish I could hear it again. I knew that if I did hear that screeching of the strings again, I wouldn't mind a bit for it would mean Xander was at home with me and that was all I wanted.

I didn't know it then, but even as I pined for my hero, I was about to grow up very fast indeed. Soon, this part of my adventure was over. Everything changed.

Chapter Two
Boy Wonder

When I was eight years old, my biggest worry was getting eaten by dinosaurs. That, and my parents getting divorced. I was kind of obsessed with it happening – I was aware that my elder sisters had come from my dad's first marriage, so there'd definitely been a divorce there. I used to ask my parents all the time, whether there was a cross word between them or not, 'You're not going to get divorced, are you?' Over and over again. My little mind was busy with catastrophe. The answer was always 'No, of course not', until one day and it wasn't. I'd never really seen my mum cry, but I remember seeing her upset once when I caught the tail-end of an argument between them. I remember badgering them, asking them what was happening. And then I asked, 'You're not getting a divorce, are you?' and, horrifyingly, my dad replied, 'Yes, we are.' He obviously didn't mean to blurt it out like that, but I was stunned. My mum and I got in the car and she took me water-skiing, like nothing had happened. But she looked different and she was pretending she wasn't crying. I pretended not to notice that she was pretending she wasn't crying. I knew something big was happening, but I didn't say anything to my siblings at all. Then one day, my mum and dad took all of us – except for my little sister – aside and told us they were getting a divorce. I remember trying not to laugh, not because it was funny, but because it was an awkward reaction to a tense situation. It was the same when our dog died: I was so shocked by the reality of it that I started laughing. I suppose my body didn't know what else to do. It's stayed with me too. Any time I'm feeling awkward or want to defuse a situation, I'll reach for humour, make 'em' laugh, I'm always like that.

Obviously, I knew what divorce was, but I didn't understand what it would mean for me. As a child – in fact, if you're an adult too – you don't know how it's going to affect you. It's like wandering into the unknown. I have never been a huge fan of change and I think it all started here. This was the first time I understood that people can leave you, and from then on I was on high alert for that.

Bombshell number two: we left the countryside and moved to London. I understand why my mum wanted to come back to the big city. She must've felt like there was nothing left in Oxfordshire for her. Although at the time I was desperately sad to leave the home I'd always known, I look back and feel glad we came to London; it's a wonderful place and I've had so much fun there.

The only problem – well, not the only problem, I had loads, but the most immediate at that time – was the house we came to live in. I remember pulling up outside the house in Kensington, a beautiful part of London, and standing in front of the house and thinking, 'Where's the rest of it?' Now, before you declare I'm a spoilt brat, please remember that my parents are splitting up, I am tiny, and I have only ever known one house. I now see it was a very beautiful townhouse, and I was lucky to have a roof over my head, but back then all I could think was, 'This is not home'. Mum has a further shock for me: our house was only *half* the building I was looking at. My house in the country stood on its own, in fantastic grounds, but this new one . . . well, it was attached to other people's houses and that didn't seem normal at all. I wouldn't be able to do a full lap of the outside without hopping into someone else's garden. Where were the nooks and crannies for me and my brother to play hide-and-seek? Where was the tennis court or the pool or the gardens where I could play when I was bored? I could see trees, but they looked lovingly pruned and I didn't think I'd be allowed to climb them. Worst of all: Dad wasn't there.

But the bombshells didn't stop coming. The house may have been a let-down, but it was worse: I wouldn't even be living in it all the time. I was going away to boarding school. I still don't really know why people send their children to boarding school. For my family, it was just something that had always been done. My father went, his father before him had gone and my brother was already there. It was just what our family did, so at eight years old and barely settled into the house I was expected to call home, I was off again, to a strange place where there were even less people I knew. And just to stick the boot in, my nanny Julie was leaving too, because there weren't enough children for her to look after. Everything I knew was being obliterated. This is a lot for an eight-year-old to deal with. I thought it then and I'm thinking it now: 'what the hell was happening?'

When we first arrived at my boarding school, Summer Fields, I didn't really understand I was supposed to stay there overnight. I'm sure it had been explained to me, but, well, you know, I probably wasn't paying attention or was burying cans of Fanta in the garden or something – priorities, right? It was a warm day, and I had a huge multi-coloured suitcase, and I remember looking up at the building and everything seeming so huge and new and strange. I was looking around at the other boys thinking 'Are any of these people going to be my friends?' I'm sure we must have said goodbye, but I didn't really notice I was there, all by myself, until my mother had left. And there I was. Like I live here now? What?! I was assigned a number – 237 – and also a 'shadow'. Now, just to be clear, I hadn't joined a wizards' school; a shadow is a boy from an older year who shows you the ropes and makes sure you don't end up late or getting lost during your first few days. I remember being incredibly overwhelmed as he showed me the various landmarks. And the smell. There's something so unsettling about unfamiliar smells when you're small. And they were everywhere – carpet and chlorine, rubber flooring. There was the distant sound of doors banging. My shadow showed me the wash area – known as the 'vins' – and I saw the showers for the first time. I was used to having baths at home; there were none in sight, just showers with buttons you pressed that would automatically turn the water off after a short amount of time. My routine was explained to me: everything had my number on it, toothbrush, pyjamas, hair brush. I was shown my dorm and I remember feeling my guts churn as I saw it. The dorms were named after cartoon characters and mine was Snoopy. There were 14 beds including mine. Lights went out at seven, and I remember trying to fall asleep, my mind in overdrive, wondering what on earth was going to happen to me and these 13 other very scared little boys. Just when I was dropping off, one boy in the next bed sat bolt upright and shouted for his mum, wondering where the hell she was. Relatable!

The next day, my shadow picked me up and took me down for breakfast. Those smells again, of cooking this time, but not a homely, hearty smell. It was more of an industrial smell, how I imagine lunch in the cafeteria of a factory might smell. Functional, not welcoming or comforting. I remember that feeling of being intimidated by the newness, hating not knowing where I was going, or what was going on. It was so unsettling. In that first week, when I peed my bed, I didn't know what to do, so I didn't tell anyone. I just slept in it. Miserable, right?

When I used to see my mum, or go home for a while, I used to cling to her neck begging her not to send me back. Once I got back, and was distracted, I was fine, but those last few moments together and the first few moments apart were really crushing. I look back now and realise how hard it must have been for my mum. She was coping with the end of her marriage, trying to settle into a new home with her two boys away at school and one of them used to nearly strangle her because he didn't want to be away from her. She never showed us what she was going through and her loyalty to us never wavered, not once. I can say this now, all these years later, and it has always been true: my mum has never let me down. She has always been there for me. Every Sunday, we attended Chapel in our school, and parents could come along to the service. But we could never see them as we had to sit high up on a balcony and all the rest of the congregation sat below us. I remember being up there with my friends, listening very carefully for a telltale sign that Mum was there – a little cough or a sneeze, or the jangle of her bracelets. And I would, every week, without fail, hear that little sign. She would drive up to Oxfordshire from London for Chapel, every single Sunday, just to let us know she was still there for us. I've never forgotten it.

But Mum couldn't be there all the time, and I was really worried about not making any friends. I remember asking my teacher, 'Does anyone make friends here? I haven't got any.' But little rascals always find their kind in the end and one day a boy called Edmund Miller came up to me and said, 'Mrs Logan keeps Mega Refreshers in her desk'. Now I don't know if you remember Mega Refreshers but they were huge, fizzy, chewy bars of sugary badness and I loved them – remember my obsession with sweets? Edmund and I worked out a way to steal these holy bars at break so we could run off and eat them, and a friendship was born. We bonded over being a little naughty. I liked him because he was dangerous, and anybody who can help get your hands on not only free sweets, but free sweets stolen from a teacher – the ultimate dangerous quest – has to be cherished. I was going through my stuntman phase, always flipping myself upside down and narrowly avoiding serious injury, and Edmund was such a daredevil that we clicked straight away. Also, my silkies had come to boarding school with me and I was embarrassed by them, but Ed Miller had a tiny cow called

Moo, and I thought, 'Well, if he has a security blanket, it must be okay for me to have one too.' Side note: my silkies were eventually stolen from me by a mystery assailant. I was devastated. If I ever find out who it was, they'll be sorry. My precious silkies will be avenged!

I began to settle in, but I never really liked it. All the rules. So many. 24/7. I know everyone has strict rules at school but when lessons were over, we were still there, in what was supposed to be our home, but with loads of regulations and routines. I can't help wondering if this is why I so loathe being restricted now. At the time, I could never understand why you had to do everything you were told to do and why nothing was ever explained. My friend Rupert always used to say, 'Why are teachers allowed to get cross with you? And scream and shout at you? You can't shout back or you'll get into trouble.' I remember thinking he had a point. I get it now, that it's about learning how to behave and be respectful and being prepared for the real world but as a little boy all I could think was, 'This is like prison.'

Even though there were so many rules and regulations, my naughtiness could not be curbed. I didn't do anything truly terrible or criminal, I was just always pushing the boundaries to see what I could get away with. I have always, always, craved excitement – I still do! – and that's what it was all about for me. Why stick to the rules? That's what everybody else did! Let's see what happens when you bend them a little. I think a lot of it came from wanting people to think I was cool. People like you if you're cool, right? Especially as a kid. They might not want to break the rules and get into trouble, but they can live vicariously through you. I was very conscious of being cool, of being the naughty one. Even though I was a very sweet kid, I used to amplify my mischievous side for attention. In a way I think it helped me to stop feeling sad about being away from home. I remember being in bed one night and my friend Marcus asking: 'What part of school do you like best, the night-time or the day-time?' He liked night-time best, but frankly, neither appealed very much to me. At least in the day-time I wasn't left with my own thoughts, overthinking all the time.

The weird thing about being naughty is that although I liked the attention, I hated getting into trouble. Couldn't think of anything worse, didn't want anyone to turn against me. I didn't even think of the consequences of anything I did, I just . . . decided I'd worry about it later. (And that's another thing that's stayed with me far longer than it should have!) It did help that one of my talents was being a good liar. I would lie and lie and lie way beyond the abilities of any other child. My thinking was that even if the teacher knew I was lying about being bad, they couldn't prove it, so we'd have to get past it eventually. They knew I was lying, and I knew I was lying but I would never break. I could hold out, I always had that strength. And even then, I was fully aware of the safety net under me. No matter what my parents or teachers threatened, no matter how many detentions hung over my head like daggers, I knew I would be okay. I was never going to be thrown out on the street, or not have people who cared for me. Experience had shown me that no matter what I did – climbing out of windows, stealing the house keys, upsetting my sister – I'd be forgiven in the end. So, my reasoning was, do the bad thing, ride out the storm, and everything will come good in the end. If you think about it, this is a pretty electrifying realisation for a child to have; it's almost like discovering you have a superpower. Chasing the excitement, getting my hands on the sweets, or doing things I shouldn't, made the awkwardness of getting caught worth it, because I knew it would soon be over. I was also aware it wasn't like that for everyone, but really – what was the worst that could happen?

Early on I found an army of supporters, in the under matrons, and that probably helped. The under matrons were a group of young women who worked at our school looking after us. They would probably have been women doing their gap year, were 18–19 years old, and many of us attached ourselves to them straight away. My favourite was Faith – who we knew as Miss Faith, because we were taught to be respectful. Remember, rules are rules. I used to go to her every single day and the under matrons were all like surrogate mums to us. I find it interesting that I always sought comfort from women; I think men intimidated me when I was a child. Needless to say, I was their favourite. I genuinely don't know how or why this happens and I promise I'm not being big-headed. But Miss Faith and the other under matrons were like my best friends. Again, they were older, and so much cooler in my mind than anybody else.

Just as I was climbing the ranks, making the right connections, and getting used to being a big fish in a little pond at Summer Fields, I found myself right at the bottom again when, at the age of 13, I moved on to Radley College. The experience of moving from junior school to senior school is like stepping out into a gladiatorial arena. You assess everyone who's there and see what role they're all playing. You have your top dogs, and the jokers, and the sporting heroes, and the popular kids, and the quiet kids. Loads of hierarchies sprout out in all directions, and you don't really know where you fit in; it's not normally your decision anyway. Some boys might hang back, suss everything out and wait – but not me! I gained instant notoriety. But it was a total accident, honestly. On the very first day, a group of us were playing a game called Bums – yes, good old private school and its clichés. It's basically a silly game where you have to keep a football in the air and if you drop it, you have to go on all fours and someone kicks the football right at your bum as a forfeit. A boy in the year above cheated and, rather than remember I was an absolute nobody at this place and keep my mouth shut, I spoke up. We argued. And that was that: I was labelled as cocky and my name spread round the school like wildfire; the other boys were determined to take this mouthy little upstart down a peg or two. The place was run by the boys, and if you stepped out of line, they were onto you. I would never say that I was bullied there, it was more like . . . how can I put this? Light, enjoyable torture. It was tough. They once sprayed Lynx deodorant all over me and tried to set fire to me. One night I had to sleep in a metal trunk as a test of endurance. And another time they peed on me as I slept. I'd be held up and punched in the ribs and constantly roughed up or given sharp kicks and digs. But I didn't mind. That they found me worth bothering with was almost like a mark of respect, like I had rattled them, so they were keeping me in line. I obviously had their atten- tion. I didn't see them as bullies – if you were quiet and sensitive, they wouldn't come near you, but if you were seen as a challenge, or a smug little shit as I was, you got their attention. My favourite!

I remember trying to tell my mum what was going on and blowing her mind. In our dorms at Radley, we each had our own cubicle to sleep in – and just like the ones in public loos, you could look over the top. When Mum brought me back after my first trip home, there was a big mass of melted cheese on my bedside table. And in it was written, 'You will die!' Mum was horrified, but I was elated. Actual death threats? From the older boys? Yes! I had made it! I was someone to be reckoned with, I'd been seen. It was better than being ignored. I've always liked to make waves.

I got into so many scrapes it could almost be a separate book. I was not to be deterred. I remember roof-running was a favourite, hopping and skipping over the rooftops at night. Me and a pal once even broke into the school kitchen through a skylight and shared a tub of Häagen-Dazs ice cream. Trouble was, he was larger than me and after all our scoffing, he couldn't get back through the skylight to escape – I could barely clear it myself with all that delicious ice cream churning about in my guts – so what else could I do? I sat and waited with him so we could get into trouble together. Roof-runner code: never leave them on their own. The ice cream made it worth it. No regrets.

Now I'd been noticed, my main goal was to be popular. It was my ultimate plan. I was pretty calculating about it, selecting potential buddies and then I persisted and persisted until they became my friends. I knew I could win people over. It wasn't an arrogant thing; it wasn't even a conscious thing. It was the same with girlfriends. I know I'm never going to walk down a Dolce & Gabbana catwalk; I'm five-foot nine on a good day. But I knew I was kind of cute and fun. And I never gave up.

Obviously, it helped that I liked these people in the first place. Being good at sport was a big plus too. To be quite honest, I was no academic, but I was excellent at almost every sport – especially rugby – and this helped me move up the food chain a few rungs. The weird thing about popularity is that it usually comes to people who don't even try to be cool, they just *are*. You can't just buy it off the rack – coolness just kind of happens to you. I wasn't willing to wait; I wanted it. Even though I did eventually find myself in the cool gang, I wasn't horrible to others. Maybe there was the odd bit of sniffy teenage attitude, (you know how nightmarish teens can be) but I could never be truly awful to someone. I was always nice. I could never be a bully. I would worry if I hurt someone's feelings for I cared about them too much.

I focused instead on battling teachers. I was still always getting into trouble. We had a system where you could be rewarded with a good mark, called an SUG, or 'show up for good' or punished with a bad mark, known as a SUB, or 'show up for bad'. I suppose you can easily guess that my SUBs outweighed my SUGs by a pretty wide margin. The simple truth was, apart from hating rules and being told what to do, I wasn't much good at studying. I didn't have the patience, or the attention span. I remember in Latin, my most hated lesson, my teacher threatened to give me yet another SUB if my test result was bad. This was bad enough news, but it was my birthday! Obviously, I knew the test result would be an absolute shocker but when I complained, the teacher said it didn't matter whether it was my birthday or not – bad work would be punished. Awful! I knew I had to do something to correct this injustice. It was too late to study, so, after handing in my exam paper, I snuck back into the classroom at break-time, jimmied open his cabinet, stole my exam paper, and ripped it up, before burying it in different parts of the school field. What, you think maybe this was over the top a little? Yes, looking back, I guess it has a touch of the twisted criminal about it, but I really didn't want that SUB. The next lesson, when the teacher inevitably asked where my test was, I said I had no idea – kind of true, as it was already rapidly decomposing in a number of locations under the field. He'd seen me hand it in after all, so it wasn't my fault. And remember, I could lie and lie and lie just as easily as breathing. Long story short: no SUB for me on my birthday. Win, win.

But this attitude was not impressing my parents. My school reports always made episodes of *EastEnders* look light and breezy. My dad was furious. 'Why on earth am I paying for this schooling if he's not going to learn anything?' he would shout. The thing was, I was learning plenty – just maybe not the kind of things you'd want to read about in a school report. Okay, so here's a plot twist: this is the part where I tell you when I had my first orgasm.

What, you can't remember yours? Really? That momentous occasion? Well, maybe there's a reason I remember mine. Being in a school full of teenage boys, we were all running on pure sugar and hormones. We were fascinated by sex, even if we weren't quite sure how it all worked. Anything we could find out about it was treated like it was magic and we were enchanted by it.

Let's go back to that very first money shot. We used to go to Normandy on school trips and learn very important stuff about how to be French, like dipping your baguette into hot chocolate (weird, yes, but delicious). On the ferry, Edmund Miller and I went to the toilet and happened upon a condom machine. How grown up! *So* adult! Obviously, we bought one condom each. Why? I had no idea and we were about as close to having sex as a death row inmate would be but when I got back to my dorm, I decided I would see what it felt like. Why? Well, you could say that about a lot of things. Why stick your finger in an electric socket? Or put your hands through a flame? Sometimes, you just follow your instinct. Anyway, on went the condom and immediately, within microseconds, off went my fireworks. I came straight away. The earth may not have moved for the condom, but I was happy enough. I remember the first time I saw a pornographic film too. Because I was always friends with the older kids, I managed to secure the hallowed disc from a boy in the year above. This disc was momentous, more precious than gold. We gathered, about 50 of us boys, around a laptop, brimming with excitement. You could have cut the hormonal energy with a knife; I can't remember ever going to a movie premiere as hotly anticipated as this one. This was like every *Star Wars* film being shown at once. So, I'm there, front and centre as ever, enjoying my moment, and I hit play. We watch it for 30 seconds when . . . boom! Off I went again. I didn't even touch myself, or anything; the power of the visual was enough. I didn't want anyone to know I'd jumped off the rocket too early, so I had to sit there in . . . shall we say, mild, squidgy discomfort for the rest of the show.

I prided myself on my ability to be a leader and trendsetter and once, when we were on holiday in France, a 17-year-old told me and Edmund Miller how to masturbate. Our minds were blown, along with everything else and I couldn't wait to get back to school and pass on this knowledge. In my dorm that night, I gathered everyone together, like a sensei, or like I was telling a story around a campfire. I explained, in great detail, what you had to do. My dorm-mates looked at me in horror. They just didn't believe me.

'That isn't how you do it!' they cried. 'You're lying!'

I was hurt but I knew they would come round to my way of thinking, eventually. All it would take was a few hours of alone-time. Sure enough, a couple of days later, one boy took me aside.

'Yeah, I tried it,' he said. 'You're definitely right.'

I felt thrilled I could pass on this gift to others, like it was an important secret I'd been trusted with. I can't remember if me and this guy high-fived, but we totally should've done.

As for the real thing, actual contact with girls . . . well, that's coming up later, but even though we were at an all-boys school, we did have some contact with girls. We had weekly 'socials' where we would be taken in a bus to meet girls from a nearby girls' school to check each other out. Mobile numbers would be exchanged – along with a few snogs if we were lucky – and then our little Nokia 8310s would be very busy.

But what I lacked in sexual prowess – or at least the

opportunity to do it properly – and academic success I made up for on the stage and the rugby pitch. My early desire to be a stuntman had given way to a love of acting and, of course, I had sport, my ticket to popularity. I loved both because it meant everyone could see me, I could perform. Acting and sport both gave me that validation. I was a decent enough actor and always got cast in school productions, and I could be loud and confident and in-your-face (and not get into trouble for it) but I wasn't great at learning lines. I was kind of just playing myself. But rugby was in my heart. I wanted to be a professional rugby player more than anything. I wasn't too sure how to achieve this goal; I just hoped that I would be discovered somehow, that I'd be scouted on the pitch and spirited away to World Cup superstardom. If you've followed my career at all, you will know that this never happened. On tour in Italy and going into my last year at Radley, another disaster struck: I was badly injured. I tore my ACL ligament that connects your shinbone to thighbone – and basically, my knee was fucked. I was told by a doctor that my rugby playing days were over. Just like that. I'll never forget his deadpan voice, the way he told me as if it were nothing, when for me it felt as though the floor beneath me had disappeared. Of course, like all teenagers, I assumed I was the centre of the universe, and I remember thinking, 'How can you just say that so matter-of-factly? How can you not be upset for me?' I was crushed at the time, but I know now that it was a blessing in disguise. I would never have made it. I used to get injured all the time; I would just throw myself into it and worry about the consequences later (spot the recurring theme). My career would only have ended in disappointment, and I wouldn't have the amazing life I have now.

Even though I loathed most of my school days – well, the learning part, anyway – I don't regret going to boarding school. I missed my family a lot, obviously, but I did have some amazingly fun times, and in a way it was these experiences at school that gave me many of the skills I still use today. I didn't perform that well, academically, but I knew I was smart, and from those lonely first few days, in a huge scary dorm full of strangers, I learned how to make friends quickly.

I can talk to anyone, and not feel shy or embarrassed – even though I do suffer bouts of shyness myself. I can stand up in front of any group of people and talk and be absolutely fine. In fact, I once went back to Radley to give a speech – my old teachers delighted in reminding me I still owed them plenty of homework. I genuinely think these are really important skills to have in life; I'm a firm believer that you will always get much further if you have the right group of people by your side.

Going away to school also made me more resilient. It taught me a lot about my strengths, and it gave me the competitive urge I still have, to do things as big and as brilliantly as possible and to take chances. I mean, I still go online sometimes and check whether my old school sport records have been broken. What's wrong with that? I'm happy to report that the under-10s javelin record at Summer Fields still belongs to me.

Chapter Three
Rebel

I have never liked being restricted. I remember, when I was younger, feeling so frustrated all the time, trapped almost. Sometimes I wasn't even sure what it was I actually wanted to do, or what exactly I thought was holding me back – all I knew was that whatever I did, I wanted it to be my own decision. Now I am a grown man, I'm not too proud or vain to say that, and yes, that frustration led to me behaving like a spoilt brat at times. But even when I was doing these things, it wasn't to be mean or spiteful, or to upset anyone, it was because of my addiction to fun. My ultimate downfall. As I say, I never met a boundary I wasn't willing to push just a little, just to see what would happen. If it ended in excitement, and everyone was happy, then great, and this was usually the case – or at least it was when I didn't get caught. But sometimes I would push things too far. Teenagers can't help themselves, can they? What didn't help was that by the time I was five I was already obsessed with being older, so when I hit my teens, with actual, proper, real adulthood just around the corner, I couldn't wait. I was obsessed with this freedom that I assumed magically came with turning 18.

Later I would discover that becoming a man was a little bit more than some random landmark birthday, and, boy, was that a rude awakening, but until then, my plan was just to get there as quickly as possible, having as much fun as the boring old rules that tried to contain me would allow . . . and then breaking one or two of them. Maybe a few. Okay, well, quite a lot actually. It wasn't just the teachers I was constantly up against. I was very close to my mum and loved her dearly – and still do, hello Mama if you are still reading this (you'd better be) – but I seriously put her through it during my teenage years (and a bit beyond). The parent-teen relationship is so bizarre: you love each other, you're blood, but, at times, you're sworn enemies. I must point out, before I continue and make you gasp in horror at some of my slightly more rebellious moments, that I have been more or less fully forgiven for my adolescent misdemeanours and I have done everything I can to make it up to everyone. Phew. Now we can start.

Where shall we go first? Okay, how about the time I broke into my stepfather's flat and had a massive party? Yes, that sounds pretty bad, I know. Mum's new husband, Jonathan, is a great man, and we get on very well. He's also a pretty patient man, as we will see. Anyway, so, yes, the break-in. It wasn't really my fault. Honestly. When I was at Radley, if you wanted to, you could get a weekend pass (called a chit), so you could go home and spend time with your parents. As you can imagine, by the time I got to my teens, I wasn't clawing at my mum's neck begging not to be sent back to school, and while I definitely did want to get out of school for the weekend, I had plans other than family time. My mum and Jonathan used to rent a little cottage in the country where they would spend the odd weekend to get out of London, and when they invited me to come along, I saw an opportunity.

'Oh no, I can't,' I would say, keeping my voice as level as possible to hide my excitement. 'There's a really important thing I have to do for school.' Conscientious, studious Jamie – how could she not smell a rat? Anyway, she didn't, and so I spread the word around. 'Party at my parents' place this weekend.'

It was the perfect cover – school thought I was at home, under my mum's watchful eye, and my mum thought I was at school, beneath the teachers' glare.

I hopped onto the coach at Oxford, acting the innocent, and prepared to open up the family homestead and play host to hordes of fun-seeking teens. Well, hordes may be an exaggeration – I'd say there were around twenty-five of us. But you know what even a small number of teenagers sound like when they're together, even having a normal conversation, let alone hyped up to the max on excitement, and illicit cigarettes, and booze pilfered from drinks cabinets. It could get super loud in there. As you can tell, this is yet another of those occasions where I didn't really think about how this was going to go. It's ironic really that some days I would be so anxious about what might happen in the future because, at this point, I was living fiercely in the moment. We were out of control – but, in a way, under my control – and I loved it. I had a habit of letting things go too far. I remember once, because we were too young to go to the shop to buy booze, we raided a vintage crate of wine that I'd been given for my christening in 1988. Just casually crowbarred open this case of priceless booze, with huge sentimental value – although not to me at that moment – and drank it. It wasn't even that nice! It was port! To a teenage tongue, it tasted terrible, and most of us probably threw it all up that same night.

Anyway, we're halfway through our teenage rampage, smoking cigarettes and knocking back booze like we're at an Oscars after-party and not just a bunch of adolescents home alone, when the doorbell goes. I check my watch. 11 p.m. Hmm, not a good sign, but at least it isn't a battering ram and armed police. I meekly open the door to find, sure enough, members of our local constabulary on the doorstep, looking reasonably pissed off.

'Your neighbours have made a complaint,' they said. 'There's too much noise. If you're throwing a party in here, you have to keep it down.'

I flashed my best Charming Smile 101 and looked suitably sorry and said it was no problem, promised to be good, bid them goodbye, and closed the door.

And then I made a very bad decision. I should've sent everyone home. Called it a night. Why didn't I? Why? Well, you've made it this far in the book, you should have a pretty good idea that at this point I simply will not be told what to do. But I didn't want to piss off the neighbours any further, so I made a grand announcement to my roomful of revellers, feeling like the Emperor of More Fun.

'We have to leave this house,' I said. 'But don't worry, the party can go on! My stepfather has a flat we can use.'

Bad decision. The worst. But it was true, he did have a flat, although it clearly wasn't meant to be used for my parties. He never stayed there, and there was nobody else living there; I knew the keys would be in the house somewhere. This is where my murky past as a childhood thief and hoarder came into play – there's not many a hidey-hole I can't sniff out. Sure enough, I was soon swinging the keyring round my fingers like I was Billy the Kid twirling a pistol, and we all trooped off to our party's second and more intimate venue.

What can I tell you? By now it's midnight. We are all at top-volume, reaching levels of 'Let's worry about this later' that you can hardly imagine. We were young, having fun, living in the moment and . . . making an absolute fucking mess.

I woke up in the morning feeling like I had spent all night being used as a ball for two lions playing catch with their teeth. Gross. I looked round me. This wasn't good. Oh no. The crumpled bodies of my friends lay on sofas, floors, slumped over chairs. And I had to be on that coach back to Radley sooner than I liked. Reality, finally, kicked in. We cleaned the place up and, thankfully, did an excellent job. You'd never know. Back to Radley I went, reputation as unrivalled party host and, of course, perfect son totally unspoiled. I had got away with it! For a few hours, anyway.

Phone goes. It's home. But it's Sunday evening; Mum never phones on Sunday evening. I pick it up.

'Hey, Mum, how are you doing?'

No hellos from Mum, nothing; she's straight into it. 'We've had a complaint about noise from the police. The neighbours said there was a party going on in this house. But of course, it wasn't you, because you weren't here. Right?'

Now, I think you know enough about my younger days

already to know how I was going to respond to this. 'Nope, wasn't me. Definitely not. I don't even know what you're talking about.'

She sighs. 'Was it you?'

I stay strong. 'No, wasn't me.'

She plays her next card. 'Okay, well, we've also been round to the flat, because we saw the keys had been moved.'

Still no idea how she spotted that, to be honest.

She went on: 'We went up there, and someone has had a party there as well. Was it you?'

Again: 'No, wasn't me.' I could keep this up all day, and she knows it. I was keen to know what had given me away though; we cleaned that place from top to bottom. 'What makes you think there was a party, Mama?'

Another card: 'The mattress was upside down.'

How the hell did she notice that? Also, how on earth had we turned a mattress upside down? Bizarre. No matter, I carried on lying through my teeth. On and on and on.

Then she played her ace: 'I see. In that case, we'll have to call the police, because the flat must've been broken into.'

Now, even I have limits. I'll push and push, but I don't like getting into proper trouble, especially with the police. I remember when nanny Julie took me down to the police station and threatened to take me in. That had been a proper deterrent for a good few minutes until I realised she wasn't going to go through with it. But this time, I couldn't take the chance. 'Okay, maybe it *was* me.'

Even then, at the age of 16, this felt like a watershed moment. I knew I had done some rebellious things, been a bit of a pain in the arse. You know what headstrong teenagers are like, everything they do kind of chips away at the parents but usually nothing's too bad to tip them over the edge and be hugely angry. But this was it. Jonathan and my mum came down to Radley to speak to me and I got an absolute rocketing by my housemaster. It all came out now: I wasn't working hard at school, not concentrating, I was disrespectful, all I wanted to do was be with my friends and have fun, and waste away my days. It was a shocking moment, and some of it was tough to hear, but I still had that teenage brain, and I just thought nobody understood me, that they didn't get me at all. Worst of all, I knew my mum had always loved me, and always would, but I could see something in her eyes. I had disappointed her one time too many – she loved me, but she didn't like me anymore, certainly not at that moment. She had always protected me from everything, but she wasn't stepping in this time. It was all on me. I tried my charm, apologised profusely, and, if I'm honest, kind of manipulated them into forgiving me, but that was the beginning of the end of the beginning, if you know what I mean.

I didn't do as well as I should have done at Radley and massively underperformed in my exams. As usual, I realised too late how important it was to get decent grades, so begged to do retakes, which I did at an exclusive sixth form college in London. This was a different world, let me tell you; I had never seen anything like it. You think I'm posh? I had nothing on some of these guys – students were turning up to school in Lamborghinis and Ferraris. On my first day, I walked into the bathroom to find someone doing actual cocaine in there. It was wild. I can't even imagine how much money it cost my parents to send me there, but back then and because I was a teenager wrapped up in my own world of instant gratification – no consequences, and no responsibilities – it never even occurred to me. It wasn't something I had to think about. I now know how lucky I was but, well, ungrateful teens are what they are. I have to say I didn't exactly excel at college either. Going to school in London, with all those opportunities to have fun? How do you think it went? That's right. I had somehow persuaded my mum to let me live in a little flat she owned across the road from where we lived, at the age of 16. She says now it was possibly the worst decision she's ever made. But, for me, it was a dream.

The pursuit of fun was more important to me than any grade. If I could go back in time and shake myself, I would. I remember before I was due to retake my English exam, there was a huge party in Fabric, an amazing nightclub in London. My mum caught me printing out tickets for it and forbade me to go. She reminded me of my responsibilities, told me how upset and angry she would be, and made me promise I wouldn't go.

'Of course, I won't,' I said, with a straight face. 'I would never do that.'

She believed me. Hell, maybe even I believed me at that point. Later that evening, while I was very much not studying for my exam and instead choosing my outfit for the party at Fabric, Mum sent me a message, just to make sure I wasn't going.

'You promised, remember? Just warning you again. Do not go!'

'I know, I won't,' I typed back, breezily, styling my hair, before turning my phone off, leaving it in the bedroom and

. . . going to the party. I know, I know. I'm a changed man, I promise.

I got back with my friend at two in the morning, thinking, 'Great, I've got away with it, I can still go to sleep and get up and do the exam.' On the stairs I found the printed receipt from the ticket and, scrawled over it in black marker, the unmistakable, severely annoyed script of my mum: 'Where the hell are you?'

Okay, so I thought, 'Shit', but knew I could smooth things over when I saw her the next day or something. I walked into the living room and got one of the biggest shocks of my life. Sitting there, like a ghostly apparition, with a face like thunder, and dressed in her nightie, was my mum. She rose up from the sofa like an angry spirit; she was so furious. Like, her blood must have been lava; she was so cross with me. And I remember her grabbing my face and looking into my eyes and saying, with anger and sadness, 'Where is my Jamie? Where have you gone?'

I didn't say anything, mainly because I didn't know where he'd gone; this was who I was now. She walked out and it was such a terrible moment. I am still living that one down.

But I really didn't like letting anyone down, or making people mad at me. I would always try to please everybody, which usually ended up with me making more people mad. I remember promising at least 15 people one of the five tickets I had to the Feathers Ball – some massive party that posh kids all go to, where tickets are like gold dust – because I wanted to look cool and make people feel included. I wanted them to feel good, get the buzz of knowing they were coming to the party – except ten of them . . . weren't. This is something that's really fed my anxiety over the years:

trying to do a good thing for as many people as possible and ending up with even more people pissed off with me because I wasn't honest in the first place. Or not being able to admit to my own limitations. I know now that in these circumstances it's best to bite the bullet and, if you have to let people down, let them down quickly. But back then I decided the best way not to let anyone down was to go on a solo mission – with nobody else to look after and nobody else to disappoint. Which is why, at seventeen, I found myself blagging my way into a casino.

I'd never gambled before, but my head was turned by a movie about high-stakes poker games called *Rounders*. It was like a light went on suddenly. 'Hang on,' I remember thinking, 'you can go into these places with, say, ten pounds, and maybe leave with a thousand pounds?' I didn't get this at all, but I loved the concept. Only problem: I was underage. But I had a plan. I walked into the casino which was just round the corner from my mum's house, with confidence. I acted like I belonged there. I remember there was a list of names on the wall of everybody who worked there, like a company hierarchy, and at the very top was the CEO. Let's call him John Smith, because I can't remember his name, and, more importantly, I don't want him coming after me. The guys on the door obviously took one look at me and thought, 'Child!' and asked for my ID.

I thought fast. 'Oh, I haven't got my wallet with me, or anything,' I said, 'but I'm John Smith's son. Him, there' – I pointed up at the photo on the wall – 'That's my dad.'

'Okay,' said one, cool as a cucumber. 'What's your name, then?'

'Well, it was nice while it lasted.' I thought, 'but I might as well try.' I don't know why this name came to me, but I just plucked it from nowhere: 'Robbie Smith'.

They checked their list, scrolled down slowly. It seemed to take forever. And there he was: Robbie Smith. I had somehow guessed correctly, totally by chance! I felt like a king as they held open the doors for me and I strolled in, victorious. Oh. My. God. This was it! It was so bright, and shiny. Lights everywhere, the gentle rattle and clink of gambling chips and the hum of machines and chatter, ice splashing into glasses. Tacky, maybe, but incredible all the same. I sat at the blackjack table; I had no clue what I was doing, I was so nervous. I had twenty pounds, which isn't very much to go into a casino with, but is a lot of money for a teenager to lose. I got some chips with it and watched the only other person at the table – a little old lady – to see what she did.

I'd played cards at school and knew you had to get close to 21, but that was it. At school we played a rule where, if you drew five cards and still didn't hit 21, you automatically won, but funnily enough the rules of Radley dorms didn't apply in this huge big-boy casino.

Regardless, I won! Two hundred pounds! I was amazed. I thought I'd cracked the system. I saw a new bright future opening up before me. I went home with my winnings and read all the books for tips and tricks, learning about mysterious systems and card counting, like I was going to spend my life as a professional poker player. I went back, with a tenner, and it happened again. £100 this time. I had no idea what to do with the money once I had it, at this point I was just wrapped up in the idea of winning, so I hid it in my bedside table. I think in a way I wanted my mum to find it. Maybe I wanted to brag about how grown up I was, or how clever I was for gaming the system.

Unfortunately, my mum took one look at this pile of fresh notes and jumped to what I guess was a more likely conclusion: that I was a drug dealer. I tried to explain, but the closer to the truth I stuck, the more bizarre and fantastical my tale sounded.

'So you're telling me that they let a 17-year-old into a casino because you pretended to be the boss's son? And you won every time, amassing £300?'

Hmmm, now I read it back, it does sound like I've made it up, and I did have quite a reputation for lying. My mum's first instinct was to part me from my money and put it into savings – she is all about saving for rainy days – but I refused. I knew I could do it again, I knew casinos inside out, this was my moment. So, ignoring my mum's objections, and denying yet again that I was dealing class A drugs to my classmates, I returned to the casino for my masterpiece win. I imagined myself giving a wry smile as I collected my winning chips, cashing them in and coming home to show Mum how clever I'd been. Except my luck ran out, my expertise turned out to be common old beginner's luck, and I lost the lot.

But I did gain some insight into the power of persuasion, that you can talk your way into most situations if you're confident enough – and this has been both a good and a bad thing over the years! Take the time when we first pitched Candy Kittens to Harvey Nichols. We had no sweets and no production line set up, but with a bit of charm and a lot of persistence we walked away with an order for £150,000 worth of sweets.

I'm jumping ahead of myself, though. Let's get back to when I was a teenager. There have been a few occasions where Mum has given me a short, sharp shock trying to keep me on the right path and make me be a responsible person. She once went to great lengths to get me an internship with an insurance company for two months over the summer. Maybe she thought as long as she could get me to sit at a desk for eight hours a day it might keep me out of trouble. This might not seem like the obvious career path for me, but I was fully committed. The stuntman thing clearly wasn't happening, rugby was off the table, I had no plans. 'I can do this,' I remember thinking, 'this is gonna be fun, the beginning of my life.' Grown-up stuff. I could make some friends, maybe even get offered a job at the end of it. Everything was going to work out okay. I got a suit, and a shirt and tie from Marks & Spencer. I was ready. I got up on the first morning, in time to get the Tube at 6:30 a.m. God, I was so tired, beyond exhausted. Everyone on the Tube looked like they would rather be anywhere else; they were all so grumpy and dour. But I dismissed it: maybe they had really boring jobs, or whatever – mine was going to be fun. I arrived at the office. It was quite exciting for the first 30 seconds or so. Everything was so shiny and professional. I was introduced to my mentor who worked in commerce, and I remember he was head to toe in beige – beige suit, beige shirt, beige tie, like a giant, talking sausage roll. He sat down at his desk, had me pull over a chair next to him and began explaining his job to me, and all about the insurance biz. Now, no disrespect to anyone who works in this industry, I know it is very important and fulfilling and all those kind of things, but . . . I couldn't keep my eyes open. Every time he turned away from me to look back at his screen to show me something, I would have to smack myself in the face to wake up. What time was it? Most people were probably still in bed. And beige dude was perfectly nice to me, but every word he said was like ten Nytols crushed up in an Old Fashioned. I remember trying to take notes, and my pen just kind of veering across the page like a speedometer because it was so dull. This couldn't be it, not for the next two months. I asked one guy why he did this job. I wasn't trying to be a smart arse, I thought maybe he had some wisdom to impart or some advice on how I could make it more appealing. His answer? 'It pays the bills.'

'Cool, cool, of course, very important, but do you love it?' Man, I needed *something*.

He looked me right in the eye and said, 'No, I don't love it. If you want to love your job, don't do this one.' I swear, if you looked deep enough into the pupils of his eyes, you'd have seen the word HELP.

I went to lunch, mind ticking over. I couldn't do it. It wasn't me. Not my kind of thing. But, my mum . . . she'd gone to great lengths to organise this for me and I had let her down so many times before. I couldn't have her angry at me again. I walked slowly back to the office and went to my mentor and said the first thing that came into my head.

'Sorry, I can't carry on with the internship; I've got a part in a film!'

They said it was fine, congratulated me even, and let me go. I went home and didn't say a word to my mum, just saying my first day had gone okay. And the next day, I got up at 6 a.m., got dressed in my suit, and left the house, just as if I was going to work, except I went round the corner to my friend's house to play PlayStation all day, before returning in the evening and pretending I'd been at work for nine hours. The next day, I did it again, and again, and . . . until the two months was up. Best of all: I've never even owned up to this before. The first my mum will hear about this is . . . right now.

Guess my rebellious phase is still not totally over. Sorry Mum.

Chapter Four
Adventurer

I talk myself into situations. Sometimes it works out, other times I have to talk my way back out of them as soon as I can. When my final A-level results came back and weren't what I'd hoped, I refused to take it lying down. Since I couldn't become a famous rugby player anymore, I turned my attention to wanting to be an actor, or, at the very least, performing to the crowd. I'd been limbering up for this ever since I was a toddler, presenting chat shows to a line of my favourite teddy bears. While I quite fancied the idea of fame, for me it was more about being seen, and being valued by as many people as possible, and making them happy. It was that need for approval, I guess, and the drive to entertain. The end goal was vague at this point, but being an actor seemed like a good distraction until I worked out what the hell I *was* going to do with my life. I was determined to go to Leeds to study theatre and performance and would do whatever it took to get there – well, except get the recommended grades, of course, but it was too late for that now and I had learned my lesson. I decided the only option was to get a train up to Leeds and knock on the drama department door, and ask them to take me in. I had a lot riding on it – the girl I was in love with, Lucy, was going to Leeds too. So, at 18, I got the train up there, banged on the door, and tried my best to convince them why they should take me. I begged, I pleaded, I gave it my all – the performance of a lifetime. And then I got the train home again. I learnt another valuable lesson that day: the importance of turning up, taking your destiny into your own hands. If you really want something, you need to go for it, full force and refuse to take no for an answer. You can never get those moments back. And, for once, my risk taking, just rushing in and worrying about the consequences later, paid off. Sure enough, a letter came through: unconditional offer. Brilliant! But first: gap year.

I know not everyone is in a position to take a year off between studies, but I would recommend it to anyone – it can be a life-changing experience, and I think you need that time to take stock, and kind of settle into yourself a little, you know? Exams are hard, school is tough, breathe a little before you carry on. Just . . . maybe don't do it like I did it, okay?

My friends and I all wanted a bit of freedom before we put our noses to the grindstone, or toes onto the stage in my case, so we settled on a few months in South America. The only problem was that I was in love. Deeply. Madly. Ridiculously. Lucy, my girlfriend was, like, the coolest, most fun person ever, and saying goodbye to her at the airport was a wrench. Looking back, we were idiots; it was like a movie, so many tears and hugs and promises of undying love. I remember thinking, 'Oh my God, I am going to marry this girl, so why am I leaving her?' This was the real thing; we made

Romeo and Juliet look like two strangers in a supermarket queue. But I had to seek adventure. We said goodbye with salty kisses, and off I went. Things started well when I was offered an upgrade to business class by a friendly lady on check-in who took pity on me. Looking back, I was this tiny, blond schoolboy; I must've looked so lost and pathetic and I'd never really travelled alone before. Most of my friends were already out there, and even though they'd given me directions to get to the flat they were renting, they actually all turned up at arrivals with a big banner saying JAMPOT, my nickname back then. Why was that my nickname? It's not too juicy a story, don't worry – but when I was little my mum used to say I was as sweet as a little pot of jam. Jamie Jampot, see?

Anyway, this trip, it felt like the start of something big. The apartment was nothing much, eight of us packed into two bedrooms, one lacking air-con, but we didn't care. There was such a sense of excitement. We were free, had no worries, and Buenos Aires was ours for the taking, a huge thrilling city throbbing with opportunity and adventure. One night we all organised a huge surprise birthday party for one of the guys, Jim, and were hysterical with excitement as we went up in the lift to the party, jumping up and down and shouting 'Happy birthday' at the top of our lungs. Thing is, the lift was more used to carrying sedate Argentinian grannies than boisterous British teenagers and so it promptly broke, leaving us trapped between floors, with no phone signal. Five of us were crammed into a tiny space getting hot, sweaty and grumpy and we completely missed the party. But at that age, nothing much could dampen our spirits, even if we couldn't go quite as wild as we'd imagined we would. The trouble was none of us could really speak Spanish and we didn't know anyone. The original plan was to bus it around South America, but we just hung around Buenos Aires for a month wasting time, so we missed our connections. Luckily, we met up with another group of friends, some amazing girls who were off to Brazil. I saw my chance. The boys had already done Brazil while I was still doing my retakes, and were going to Chile. They couldn't understand why I wanted to go off with the girls, but I was desperate to see Brazil and . . . uh oh, I had accidentally fallen in love with one of the girls. Amy. I was half-sure she felt the same way but wanted to see how things developed. My airport tears with Lucy were barely a memory. Oops.

Before we split into two groups, we all had an amazing last trip altogether to Iguazu Falls. It was so beautiful, one of the happiest experiences of my life. I'm not overly religious, but I did think as I looked at this gorgeous wonder, that there was a pretty good chance God did exist if he could make something so incredible. Then it was time to go. I remember an amazing moment as we waited at the bus stop: our coach was going in one direction and the boys' coach went in the other. And that's how we parted – just like that. Kind of cinematic.

In Rio, things didn't get off to a great start. We were staying in this amazing apartment, loaned to us by some friends of one of the girls' parents. It was so plush, it even had a sauna. Unfortunately, my gung-ho attitude would nearly burn it down. It was no big deal: I'd just heard from someone that if you put vodka in the bath, the fumes made you drunk, so figured it might work on the hot rocks heating up the sauna too, right? Wrong – it set them on fire, and I ended up in hospital with burned hands from trying to put them out, and a very red face from causing so much damage. But I wasn't put off – that's the thing about me, as long as there's fun to be had, I can just push through and I always get back up after every knock. A couple of days later, we went for drinks at a little bar at Copacabana beach and it was just the best time. It was so warm and the night was electric with excitement. Things certainly got more exciting when I decided to slip off for a pee on the beach. Copacabana beach has a kind of dip in it, that you can drop down and not be seen from the bar where everybody else is, so I thought it would be fine. Now, my mum has always told me to never go to the beach at night, because it's extremely dangerous. When we went on holiday to Portugal when I was small, she would discover I'd broken her rule by checking inside my shoes and emptying sand out of them. Before I left, she said to me, 'Promise me Jamie, you won't go on the beach at Rio after dark,' and I said, 'Of course I won't' – that's what I've always said. But I'm just off for a quick pee here; I'm super clear where the rest of my friends are, they just can't see me for a few seconds at most, what's the worst that could happen? I soon found out.

I was taking a pee and I remember looking around thinking, 'Oh, this is so fun', totally lost in the moment. Then I looked to my right. I wasn't alone. A group of guys were encircling me. I suddenly felt this cloud come over me, a sense of, 'Oh God, I really shouldn't be here.' Maybe you can guess the rest. I'll tell you anyway. Before I knew it, I was surrounded and there was a machete at my throat. They didn't stop to chat, they were just all over me, like bees taking pollen. They took everything they could. My trousers, my T-shirt, my lovely new shoes Mum had bought me, my necklace, they were rummaging around in my pants – which they let me keep on, thankfully – everything. And I was standing there, powerless, terrified. I remember thinking, 'I'm going to die here, my mum has always told me to not go on the beach, and I've done it. I've *done* it.' She was always right. I'd made another mistake. The man with the knife was smiling and tapping the machete either side of my mouth; it was like a Guy Ritchie movie. When I was stripped bare, they gave me a thumbs up, stopping only when I begged them to give me back my inhaler, which they did, which was pretty decent of them. Well, I say decent – they had just stripped me of all my possessions and made me think I was going to die. So I had to trudge back up the beach in my boxers and say what had happened. I'd never really understood before when people said they were really affected by things that had happened to them; I just thought you were glad to survive and moved on, but after that, I looked at life anew. I had total PTSD from it, and freaked out if anyone I didn't know came too near me. That was the first time I understood how powerful the mind is, and how it can play tricks on you. I think that was the scariest day of my life.

But I lived, and we moved on to La Paz, in Bolivia, the highest city in the world, which means you can't quite catch your breath the entire time you're there. And there I had another rocky start. After having to push our broken-down taxi up a hill to the hotel – my lungs have never forgiven me – we went to this dodgy speakeasy where everyone was smacking a huge piñata. Everyone was taking turns and they were pretty determined to get into it. I soon found out why – one big thwack revealed the whole thing was full of bags of cocaine. I'd eaten something dodgy, and started to feel ill so went to the loo to try and . . . you know, evacuate whatever was in me that was causing the problem, and it was so awful. The toilet made the gross one in *Trainspotting* look cleaner than an operating theatre. I had to hover above it, do what I had to do, and then I went home. I was so ill, and when you're feeling that unwell, you just want to be at home and safe. The girls decided to take me to hospital and, seriously, I remember being in the cab with my head out the window thinking, 'I would rather die right now than go on feeling this way.' Luckily, once I'd peed into a cup, pooed into a flask, and had a shot of steroids, I felt amazing again, so it was back to the adventure.

As we were leaving the hospital, overjoyed that I didn't have to die after all, we were approached in the street by a man who said his name was Johnny Cash. He didn't look much like the actual Johnny Cash – who had been dead a good five years or so by this point – but he had a proposition for us. Had we ever tried ayahuasca, he asked.

'What's that?' we cried in unison, already tasting our next escapade.

'Oh, you will love it,' he said, 'It's a cactus drink, and when you drink it, you have fantastic hallucinations, it's so much fun.'

'Okay, where do we do it?'

'You come to the middle of the beautiful Amazonian

jungle,' he said. 'I can have you flown there and back for $50, no other costs to you.'

Now, you might be thinking we should run for the hills – although we were as high as we could go in La Paz – but he was pretty convincing. He showed us these photos of where the ayahuasca drink would be taken – it was like a beautiful resort, packed with beautiful people laughing around campfires, or fishing, or having the loveliest time. And we all looked at each other – 18, and naive, and trusting and . . . just up for anything – and were fully on board. What serendipity to meet this man! He's giving us this freedom to go to this beautiful place and experience this amazing thing. All hail, Johnny Cash! So, obviously, we went. And let me tell you, I don't know where those photos came from, but our experience was . . . somewhat different.

I don't know where to start. Just disaster after disaster. It was exciting at first, I had my video camera – never far from a lens or a spotlight, you see – and we were all hyped up as we set off first thing the next morning. So we get on this plane, and it's rickety to say the least, like a self-assembly dining chair with a screw missing. It's tiny, and because of bad weather, the thing nearly crashes, and has to land somewhere else. One of the girls is crying and even though I can normally face anything with positivity, even I am thinking maybe this isn't such a good idea. We land and are shown to a truck that will take us to the deepest jungle for our once-in-a-lifetime experience. We're not the only passengers – indeed, half of Bolivia appears to be hitching a ride on it, along with quite a few chickens. This was obviously the supplies run for anyone living the remote jungle life. But we were young and optimistic, and the girls had calmed down a bit now, so on we leapt. And we drove. Ten minutes. Twenty. Thirty. An hour. Two hours. How deep was this jungle exactly? We drove and drove and drove and I started to get a feeling. We had no phone signal, no way out of here; it was just us and the chickens and Johnny Cash. Three hours later, we arrive at a clearing. No campfires, no fishing, nobody having a lovely time. We are shown to a small hut and Johnny Cash tells us he's off to bring the shaman, who will present us with the ayahuasca to drink. And off he goes. One hour. Two. Three. By now, the girls are hysterical, and I am down to my last shred of optimism, thinking, 'Okay, this is it, we've been kidnapped and taken to the middle of the jungle. We are going to be on the *News*. Not only that, but we have paid $50 for the pleasure.' But there is nothing we can do but wait. We sit there, trying not to lose our minds. Nobody else there speaks English. Five hours. Six. Seven. Eight! Eight fucking hours later, Johnny returns. I have never been so glad to see a practical stranger in my life. He says the shaman is ready to see us. We file into this hut, all in a line, like schoolchildren, and there is this guy sitting there with beads on his head. Next to him there was a machete and the girls, by now, porcelain white and hysterical with terror, motion for me to grab the machete and . . . murder everyone so we can escape? I was, like, I'm not going to do that! Then the shaman gives us some cocoa leaves, which we start eating, and some filterless cigarettes, which we smoke, and some ethanol to drink. And we're thinking, 'What the hell happened to our cactus drink,' but we thought maybe this was part of the ritual, and

87

our Spanish is terrible, so we just go along with it. Soon, it turns out this is not the ayahuasca at all – this is just an apology from the shaman because the ayahuasca won't be here until the next day. Yes, we have to stay over. But, on the bright side, they were being very nice to us and at least we weren't being kidnapped. Well, not yet anyway.

So, we sleep in this rather charmless brick hut with only one mattress, and I haven't eaten since my illness back in La Paz, which seems like a hundred years ago. The next day, we finally get to try the ayahuasca. I don't know what I was expecting – maybe some magical sparkling potion, or a glimmering elixir. Hmm, not so much. It looked like pond water and didn't taste much better. We sipped it demurely, asked each other if it was doing anything. We all shook our heads. So we drank more, and a bit more and . . . what can I say? Very soon, I felt like I was staring right into hell. I started throwing up and . . . it got quite busy at the other end too. I felt monumentally shocking, and began hallucinating, but rather than dancing with enchanted brooms in *Fantasia*, I thought I was a truffle pig. And what do truffle pigs do? They hunt for truffles incessantly, jamming their snout into the ground until they find one. And that's what I did. For eight hours. It was the most hideous experience. I remember thinking, in rare snatches of clarity between truffle hunts, that I was going to be like that forever, burying my snout into the undergrowth, life ruined. Thankfully, it did end; it was like a switch in me just turned off and I was back to normal. Amazing! Now all we had to do was ride three hours in a truck full of chickens, and get on a plane that was basically held together with Post-it notes and get the hell out of here. And I still hadn't eaten. 'Never, ever again,' I said to myself.

After all these scrapes, miles from home, it felt like the universe was definitely trying to tell me something. So I did what any other excitable young man thirsty for fun would do – I ignored it.

After university, I was preparing to get real. I was going to have to get a job. I'd had an interview with a wealth management company and even though I didn't know that much about what I'd have to do, I managed to wing it. What clinched it, I think, was that in desperation I told them a bad joke – 'What's Postman Pat's name after he retires? Pat, of course!' – and it somehow endeared me to them. Also looming in the background was the chance to be on *Made in Chelsea*. I'd seen my friends have a ball on the first series and yes, I wanted a piece of the action. The producers had been trawling the friends' lists of the cast members' social media accounts and I'd been picked out as someone who might be good fun. Well, they weren't wrong there, but it was a definite crossroads. A life of respectability and an eventually decent salary, versus a first step into the world of entertainment with no certainties, no promises, but probably loads of fun. I didn't know if I was going to take it, and the security of the office job lingered in the background. So what else to do but hold off reality (and reality TV) as long as possible, and go on a last hurrah? My friend Ed needed a little persuading – this is a different Ed from the Edmund at boarding school, btw; I have a lot of friends called Ed. But I made my case.

'We need to go clear our heads, and have fun,' I said.

'Because the rest of our lives is about to begin now.' He was going to become this broker; I was maybe off to work in wealth management. Ridiculous. You might think we'd decide to live it up on a luxury holiday or chill out at some idyllic resort. No, what we actually decided to do was travel round the south of Spain and end up in Pamplona, the town where they have the annual running of the bulls which, if you are unfamiliar, means they basically let a lot of angry bulls loose into the streets and you try to outrun them. What could possibly go wrong, apart from everything? Ed had been before on his gap year, and while he didn't actually fraternise up close and personal with the horned beasts, he did get a bull tattoo on his leg. This time, he wanted to do it for real. Why not, eh?

'You're on.'

That was almost *too* easy.

We flew to Barcelona with two of his other friends and, remember, we have just finished university, so we are as broke as broke can be. After a brief wander round Barcelona – and accidentally straying into a dodgy part of town that led to us being ordered to leave at knifepoint by a less than friendly local – we hired the one car we could afford, a shitty little Citroen. Road trip! In road trips in movies, there are mysterious strangers, which we were, beautiful vistas, which we had, and an iconic soundtrack which . . . well, the car was such a banger that the radio didn't work and the CD player had one disc stuck inside it. Ah well, maybe we could make the best of it, we thought, except this solitary disc played only one song all the way through – Nelly Furtado's 'I'm Like a Bird'. So from Barcelona, to Zaragoza, to San

Sebastian, to Pamplona, it was 'I'm like a bird, I'll only fly away . . .' the entire way. That song still haunts my dreams.

We had this vision that we were these four young British bucks, that the Spanish girls were going to love us and that we'd have a huge adventure. It was massive fun, obviously: we ate some incredible food, drank, and partied every night. What was great about back then was that there was no social media, really, so there were no distractions, or trying to get the right photo, or wasting time just broadcasting our opinions or reading every reaction to stuff – we were just living it. I had that real sense, for the first time, that I was going to have to be an adult as soon as this was over: back in London, on the Tube every day, off to work, that would be me done. Fun times over. So I was determined to enjoy this trip. Unfortunately, we didn't realise how expensive it would be to go on a road trip, stopping for meals and staying places, so by the time we got to Pamplona, we were skint. Pamplona is absolutely buzzing as we arrive – everyone's in red and white and throwing sangria down their necks and in a party spirit getting ready for the big event the next day, but we realise anywhere half-decent is already booked, we haven't made any reservations, we have no money, so we end up in a truly terrible apartment. You have to walk through someone else's kitchen, and past their bedroom, to get to it. It's utterly miserable, and so am I: my sensitive stomach is about to let me down yet again. Whatever I've been eating on my carefree days in the sun is severely disagreeing with my insides. We go out, but after a few drinks, I start to feel really unwell and begin puking everywhere, so badly that I have to leave the guys to it and go back to the hell-pit we're staying in. Once my stomach is utterly voided, and I am feeling about as sorry for myself as it's possible to feel, I crash out. At around six in the morning, I'm woken by a bashing at the door. I stumble out of bed, still feeling pretty grim, and it's Ed and the other guys, only just getting in! They are looking pretty hammered and, worst of all, Ed's leg is bleeding. What on earth have these boys been up to, I wonder, and is whoever's made Ed bleed still going to be looking for them? On closer inspection, this isn't a battle scar; he now has a bull tattoo on this other leg to match the first, except it's not such a professional job – it looks like it was carved into his leg with a staple gun. He reeks of sangria, and rather than do the decent thing and collapse into bed, he reminds me we have to go to the bull run, like *now*, and tosses me an outfit he's got for me to wear. There's a beret, and a red and white top. Red. Bulls don't respond that well to red, do they? But I think nothing of it, even at this stage. Determined to get into the spirit, I start to downplay the danger ahead – maybe the bull run will be a chilled affair. We set off, although the three other guys still have not slept, and arrive on the streets of Pamplona at about 6.45 a.m. The place is bouncing. It's like Glastonbury main-stage, totally packed so nobody can move. The streets are pretty narrow, and surrounded by walls and windows that people are looking over and out of, and everyone is wearing red and white and holding rolled-up newspapers and the atmosphere is electric – everyone's having the time of their lives and passing round the sangria. Then I see these people walking about with little pieces of paper, asking you to sign them. I ask what's going on, and they tell me it's a disclaimer, that you must sign to accept that you might actually, erm, die during this. It occurs to me that I probably haven't thought this through, that I'm wearing an outfit that may as well be a painted target, and there's a good chance I'll be spending a good few hours getting flung into the air by a pack of angry bulls like a crisp packet in a hurricane. But there's nothing a bit of adrenaline can't fix, and when it comes to the key moment, the life-or-death situation, I definitely always go for it. I'm so pumped up: let's do it, let's do it, let's do it. But also: shit, shit, shit, shit. I can see down the hill below me to the starting line and there's a sea of people all jumping and shouting and waiting. And the bell strikes for seven o'clock and everyone starts whistling 'Woooooooooooo'. There are thousands and thousands of people in the street and leaning out of windows, banging and making a racket. Then a firework is let off into the sky and explodes and . . . wow, it's like a tsunami. I see this wave of people start to move, and I realise everyone is running and what can I do but run along too? So we start to run, and I remember running alongside Ed and looking at him and seeing the fear in his eyes. The scythe of the reaper is reflected in those baby blues, I tell you. Fuck, fuck, fuck! We don't know what's going on, but we keep running and then we hear this screaming behind us, and Ed manages to jump up and grab a wall and hoist himself up off the street. I go to do the same and grab hold of Ed but he kicks me off in case I pull him back onto the street and into the path of the raging bulls. By the way: THANKS, ED. So I plunge back down into the street like a sack of potatoes and as I do, a bull runs right past me and kicks me in the shoulder

93

with its back leg. Ouch, yes, but I'm alive! A miracle! And I look behind me and see more bulls coming – there are, like, five of them – so I run and run and manage to jump up onto a different wall as they speed past to cause more chaos down the hill. I've never felt anything like it in my life, like an exhilarating, terrifying cocktail of excitement, joy, and fear – this hideous yet ecstatic adrenaline rush. It was just unbelievable. And though I loved it, I was definite this time: never again. Nope. No more danger, no more risks. It was time to grow up a bit.

Chapter Five
Buddy Movie

I know I'm really lucky to have so many friends. And my friends are everything to me. It's really important to have good people around you and although sometimes I have tested friendships to the limit – especially when I started on *Made in Chelsea* – most of them have stuck by me. Most people only get one or two best friends in their lives, but I've had many over the years. I form close attachments to people. I think it comes from always wanting to be liked, and doing everything in my power to make people like me – which, of course, sometimes has the opposite effect entirely! There are super-close friends I've had who go back years, who are nothing to do with *Made in Chelsea*. There's Olly and Toby. Toby was one of the first people I confided in about my panic attacks. And there's Georgie, of course – you'll be hearing more about her later! I remember how once, when I'd woken up hungover and naked in my bed, for some reason I thought I'd gone and ruined our amazing friendship by taking it to the next level. By which I mean sex. With my best friend. Not good. I couldn't remember anything about it – hence the hangover – but I somehow managed to convince myself that we'd done it. There was no sign of Georgie anywhere. I immediately began to catastrophise. Obviously, she too had been so mortified by what we'd done that she'd scurried off, too ashamed to face me. How could we have done this? After all these years?! I went to phone her, but then realised I couldn't. What would I say? So I avoided her for days, until one day she came home and I couldn't keep it in anymore. As soon as I saw her, I didn't notice that she seemed to be totally fine and wasn't hiding her face behind her hands in horror or anything, and apologies started falling out of my mouth. She looked at me like you might look at an excited child who's telling you they're in the same class as a stegosaurus, honest.

'What are you talking about, Jamie?'

'I'm so sorry!' I burbled. 'We've obviously had sex! I woke up naked. And you weren't there. I was so drunk I don't even remember it.'

I remember her sighing and then laughing. 'What the hell, Jamie? I stayed at my dad's house, God.'

Only I could make something as simple as waking up with no pants on into a friendship-destroying catastrophe. Despite the fact I'm clearly an idiot at times, Georgie has always had my back.

When it comes to close bonds, they don't get much closer than me and Spencer Matthews, who was my wingman, bestie, champion, and nemesis all in one when we were in *Made in Chelsea* together, and beyond. In fact, all this is his fault – me being famous, I mean. He was the one who convinced me to do *Made in Chelsea*. Literally everyone else I knew told me I shouldn't go on the show. My parents pleaded. My siblings told me I'd be crazy to do it. My close friends said I'd be making a big mistake. This obviously wasn't what I wanted to hear. Until I spoke to Spencer. Mind you, what you need to know about Spencer is that he's a sociopath – I am deadly serious. I mean, I love the guy, but honestly.

Spencer's always been very honest about his ups and downs. I've tried to help him through them as much as I can, while dealing with my own problems. I'm proud of him and I know he is of me. He is a bit of an enigma to a lot of people and in many ways he's the total opposite to me: I'm one of those people who wants everyone to love me, but he doesn't care. In a way that makes him more lovable to me.

Actually, I should go back to how we met. I remember our first encounter like it was yesterday. We were both teenagers – he went to Eton, and I went to Radley. I was 16, he was in the year above. I was with my girlfriend Lucy, walking to a nightclub in Ladbroke Grove called Neighbourhood. We walked past Spencer and his friend, who called something out to us. It turned out Lucy was this guy's ex-girlfriend and he was warning me to look after her. Looking back, this all seems very serious and intense when we're talking about teenage relationships, but you know what it's like at that age – you take things deadly seriously. Everything is the biggest drama; it's like it's the end of the world if you have a break-up or you can't be together. Good practice for *Made in Chelsea*, I guess. Anyway, boys being boys, we start having this very public-school argument, sneering at each other in the street. I must confess, I thought Spencer was the biggest douchebag in the world when I first met him; he was just a complete idiot. I'm sure he'd say the same about me, and I think we would both be right. You know what it's like sometimes, you actively hate someone for reasons you can't understand, until gradually, by sheer exposure, you start to tolerate them – in fact, again, that's a bit like how *Made in Chelsea* worked. You couldn't stay enemies long, because nobody was going anywhere, and you spent so much time together that you started to get crushes on people whether you initially fancied them or not. Anyway, in my late teens and early twenties I'd see Spencer out at places, or at parties, and we began to thaw. Scowls across a room became smiles, polite nods became warm hellos, handshakes became hugs. Not super intimate, or anything like that, where you'd call someone up if you need anything, but a friendly face when you go out, someone you might be glad to see. Little did I know just how much of Spencer I'd be seeing eventually.

Made in Chelsea came along and quite a few of my friends were doing it – Spencer, Caggie, Hugo, Millie. I remember hearing they were doing it and thinking it was so strange – *The Only Way is Essex* had only started the year before, so reality shows of this type weren't as huge here then. I remember sitting and watching the first episode and thinking, 'Wow, you have all made the biggest mistake of your lives.' I couldn't believe anyone would voluntarily do this to themselves – what idiots! You might think it was jealousy. After all, I wanted to be an actor, and definitely wanted to be on TV – but not like this, I told myself. Looking back now, I would say, yes I was definitely jealous; I wanted to be on this thing. But then, I pretended I was horrified on my friends' behalf. This TV show was probably going to wreck their lives. But what did I know? Clearly nothing, because when I was asked to do series 2, and everybody told me I'd be wrecking my life if I did it, I didn't listen and asked Spencer instead. Spencer, who probably doesn't really care about anyone. Spencer, who in all the time I'd known him had shown the empathy of an Ikea sofa.

'Do it,' he said. 'It's gonna be great. We'll have such a fun time together.'

That was all it took. I just wanted that one person to push me over the edge. And what a drop it was. Sometimes I think Spencer knew exactly what he was doing.

My very first scene was with Spencer, meeting me at the airport after Pamplona, and we soon became inseparable. We were thick as thieves, proper best friends, and we experienced most of our twenties together. It was a blast at first. Spencer and I had some nights together to remember – and quite a few that we can't. To say we enjoyed all the excesses of what it meant to be young and famous would be an understatement. Non-stop partying. And, yes, dating. All that stuff. The thing was, even though we were on TV all the time and people were starting to know who we were, the riches we assumed would come along from starring on TV didn't materialise at all but I thought I could top this up with . . . well, I don't know what I thought. Brand endorsements, maybe? Perhaps I could be the face of something? Why not? But even though we were famous, nobody wanted to give us any other work or anything like that – everyone just thought we were posh wankers. Which was kind of our own fault, really, for going on TV and . . . acting like posh wankers. What did we expect?

One thing Spencer started doing as a side hustle was personal appearances. They are exactly as they sound – someone phones your agency, and books you to appear in person somewhere, tells you how much they're going to pay you, and off you go. Usually it's a nightclub, one of those great big ones that crop up on the edges of towns, sometimes in a big retail park. You know the ones, they always have names like Icon or Envy or Adonis and can fit in thousands of people. According to Spencer, you didn't even have to do that much other than go up on the stage, say hello to everyone, and then maybe speak to a few of the clubbers – you might even meet some nice girls. I wasn't sure at first, but Spencer said they were amazing fun, and I was definitely intrigued – anything for a little bit of excitement and a new experience. So he invited me on one to see for myself.

The deal was that Spencer had to go to a club in Reading to make this appearance, and I was going along as an added bonus. The club owners said they'd be sending transport. I don't know what I'd imagined – maybe a limo, or at least a big car we could stretch out in and relax on our way to Reading. Instead, a black people-carrier turns up – and do you know what, it didn't matter. It was still a thrill – it could've been that shitty Citroen I hired in Spain. Someone had sent a car, just for us. We were loving it.

Then we open the back door and . . . it's like they're expecting the Gallagher brothers. There are bottles of champagne, and vodka, everywhere. Whatever we want to drink, it's there. We get in, and start on the booze. I remember thinking how weird it was, we were just two ordinary guys on a reality TV show, being given this VIP experience. Okay, so it wasn't that luxurious and glamorous, we were basically sitting in the world's booziest Uber to Reading, but this was just for us. I mean, they'd sent a driver just to pick us up, there was free alcohol all over the back of this car, and they were paying a decent amount of money just to have us there in physical form, and I admit I was starting to think, 'Okay, well maybe we *are* someone. Let's enjoy it! Who knows when this will be over?' I was just an excited guy in my early twenties, who couldn't believe his luck.

I must confess, Spencer and I weren't exactly looking our best at this point. We were out far too much and weren't looking after ourselves at all. When we arrive, I realise I'm quite drunk. Not ideal, but I can hold myself together, I think. I look at Spencer. Oh no. He's gone. Gone. We get out of the car and there's a huge queue snaking behind us; we ask one of the guys looking after us what's going on.

'This is for you,' he says. 'They're here to see you.'

Now, there were hundreds of people trying to get in, and in that moment I thought 'Wow, this must be what it's like to feel like one of the coolest people on the planet.' We go inside, and Spencer is still pretty drunk so I decide the best thing to do is get him something to eat, help him soak up the alcohol before he meets his adoring fans. We manage to get him a burrito, of all things, and we're taken to wait by the side of the stage. It sounds loud out there, the music is blasting and we hear people screaming and having fun, and there are lights and lasers and all kinds of things. Best of all, or so we think, their night is about to be made by having Spencer and me troop onto the stage to say hello. Watching Spencer gnaw through the burrito, however, brought it home to me – quite fast – that maybe we weren't actually the coolest people on the planet. It was fun, all right, but nothing about this was cool, we were just two guys in front of a huge crowd of strangers. Plus, that burrito smelt awful, but it was too late now. We were here. Yet again, I hadn't thought this through. Suddenly, the music stops and we hear the crowd murmuring, wondering what's going on. A guy gets on the mic and starts speaking to the crowd, really geeing them up like they're about to see something amazing.

'Guys, get ready for this! Are you ready? If you like *Made in Chelsea*, you're going to LOVE who we've got for you tonight.'

On and on, he goes, bigging us up like Barack Obama and David Beckham are about to walk out and start bopping with the crowd. And then:

'Please welcome to the stage . . . SPENCER MATTHEWS!'

Drunk as I was, it's a moment from my life I will never, ever forget. With the lights blazing, Spencer ambles onto the stage, blinking and peering out into the crowd. I notice now he's still clutching his burrito. The wretched thing is looking pretty shabby. The burrito, I mean, not Spencer. Although . . . Anyway, the crowd are cheering and whooping, while Spencer is waving at the crowd like Prince William cutting the ribbon at a local community centre. Right on cue, the burrito kind of collapses at the bottom and spills its guts over Spencer's front, and the crowd's excited cheers quickly turn into a huge, thundering 'Whooooooooa' like they're watching a train crash in slow motion – which they kind of were. Maybe to distract the crowd from the fact half a burrito had taken up residence all down his shirt, Spencer keeps gesturing at me to come out on stage. I think about this. Isn't this what I wanted, to get lots of attention, to have people come watch me perform? Well, there's plenty out there watching now, and I do like a buzz, so I saunter onstage – remember, the place is deathly quiet, as the music is off – and I start waving, meekly saying hi. There was a second or two of crystal-clear, unnerving silence before we heard it – not the joyous cheers for Spencer or even the loud 'OOF' for the dropped burrito but . . . boos. Actual booing! They were all heckling me. It felt shocking! So awful. In that moment it hit me; if I wanted anyone to respect me or to be interested in me and listen to what I have to say, I was probably going to have to do a little more than just be famous for being famous. The burrito got a better reception than me from the crowd; I definitely had some work to do. And to think that for a few brief moments I thought I'd made it.

The thing about Spencer and me is, on *Made in Chelsea*, we were always there for each other, but we were competitive too. We were, sort of, the two leading men on the show, and we would always try to date the most popular girls, or the newest girls coming into the show. We were definitely attracted to them, but we also knew it would make great entertainment too. You're in this intense environment and hanging out with the same people all the time – it's like a dating hothouse and we're a bunch of amorous tomatoes.

The relationships are real, but maybe sometimes the feelings are more heightened than they would be if you were left to it. The girls all knew this and had a similar goal – we all knew popular couples would get more screen time and would make the show more fun. Who wants to stand in the background? Certainly not us. So this meant there was some overlap between who Spencer and I dated, like characters in a soap. Mostly, Spencer and I were cool with it, but once we did veer into 'below the belt' territory when I dated Lucy Watson, who Spencer really liked. He dated her first, then I did, and I think he was hurt by that. Maybe in the real world, Lucy and I would never have got together, but there was something about being around each other all the time that drew us together.

Telling Spencer that Lucy and I had slept together was the only time I've sat in front of a friend and been scared about what I was about to say. This wouldn't be the first time I had overstepped the mark with a friend's girl, nor would it be the last – more about that later, I did promise to be honest, after all – but I was determined it wouldn't come between us. We knew if we messed up, or cheated, or something happened, we'd have to pull each other up on it. It could've been tough, and awkward, but Spencer always took it on the chin. I would give Spen a knowing look, and he'd always look back and say, 'Okay, bring it on.'

The thing about Spencer is he lives in a pretty small world, by which I mean he only has a small, trusted circle of people he's close to. I count myself lucky that I'm among them – most days, anyway – but seriously, in the nicest possible way, Spencer has no friends. None. His best friends are his wonderful wife Vogue, his amazing children, and his dog. Oh, and me. That's it. I think that's a bit . . . well, it's weird, but it's also a shame, isn't it? Spencer is a great guy, why shouldn't he have more friends? You know that old theory, about six degrees of separation, that says you can be linked to anyone in the world, even people you've never met, through people you already know? Well, I reckoned the exception to that rule was Spencer, who doesn't know anybody. It inspired me to talk to the BBC about an idea I'd had of starting a podcast where, basically, we would try to get Spencer some new friends and see how we were connected to all kinds of different people. I love an experiment, and I thought it would be fascinating to see how easy (or difficult) it would be to use our connections to get in touch with properly famous people. Well, I say 'our' connections – remember, Spencer doesn't have many.

I knew pitching to Spencer would be tricky. First of all, he had absolutely no idea what a podcast was. I remember his face as I was explaining it to him; it was like I was standing there speaking Japanese. Secondly, I had to make it sound like it was going to be worth his time doing. He gets bored pretty easily – I once had the idea of starting a YouTube channel with him, and booked for us to stay in a haunted house to film our reactions to the creepy goings-on. After an hour in the car on the journey to get there, he turned to me and said, 'You know what? I don't think I can be bothered with this. Can we go home?' The last thing I needed was Spencer wandering off halfway through a podcast because the special guest wasn't interesting enough; this had to be good. So I gave it my best shot, explained how it would work, that we'd be recording a podcast every week, shooting the breeze in front of microphones, getting some special guests on, trying to make contact with famous people, and it was with the BBC so, you know, this was serious stuff – but it was going to be huge fun too.

'The BBC, eh?' he said, mulling it over. 'I've always wanted to be a dragon on *Dragons' Den*. Do you think this could be my way in?'

Jokingly I said, 'Yes' – but actually, maybe he will get on *Dragons' Den* one day – he does do a great stern face.

'So I just get to chat to you, every week, for an hour?' he said.

'Yes!'

'Then that's all I want,' he said. 'If I get an extra hour of chat with you every week, I'm in.'

I was pretty touched. This was totally out of Spencer's comfort zone, but he knew that if I said it was going to be all right, it probably would be. It was very sweet, especially considering how, in most scenarios, Spencer has zero emotions. Honestly, open him up, and he's machinery, I'm convinced.

If you've listened to the *Six Degrees* podcast, you'll know Spencer is a natural. He has absolutely no filter, no pretensions at all – he can only ever be himself. He doesn't care what people think of him, mainly because only his family and his tight social circle are important to him. And yet, somehow, he manages to make it seem charming and endearing! He has this unbelievable magic that makes him so compelling. It doesn't matter who we have on the show – and we've had some huge names working our way through these six degrees – he is always 100 per cent himself.

Spencer's sense of humour is, to put it mildly, on the dry side, and he gives me an absolute roasting every week too. I wouldn't have it any other way, to be honest, but the podcast has definitely shown Spencer's tender side too. I remember we had Bear Grylls on once. Bear had known Spencer's brother Mike, who sadly died as he was returning from the summit of Mount Everest in 1999. Watching Bear and Spencer talk about Mike was really moving and even though Spencer never gives much away, I know he was really touched by it. Maybe that's the greatest thing about the podcast – even though it might not seem the most obvious place to share stories and be really intimate, there's something special about that space; it's just the two of us and we know we can talk about anything. And I mean anything – you should hear some of the stuff Spen says we should edit out. Regardless, I know he's got some softness in that old stone heart of his; I'll crack it one day.

Even though we love each other, we drive each other insane, and get each other into huge trouble. We lived together in New York for a while, filming *Made in Chelsea*, and had a blast, but we fell out constantly too. I can't believe we didn't kill each other – sometimes I think if I'd had a knife, I would've done it. We were pretty wild. We lived in a one-bedroom apartment in the Meatpacking District across the road from Soho House, and you can imagine what it was like for two young guys in their twenties living it up in New York. We were out partying most nights, having so much fun. On our very first night, we met these two older Swedish women in a bar, and went back to theirs. Cut to the next morning and I'm looking at my watch thinking,

'Hell, we only have an hour until filming.' Trouble was, we were not only still over at the Swedish ladies' place, they'd tied us to chairs, wearing only our pants. I'm never quite sure how I get myself into these situations, they just kind of . . . happen. I was usually never late for filming, but I certainly didn't make it on time that day.

Living with him in New York wasn't always easy – mainly because he took the bedroom and I slept on a camp bed on the floor – but then there were times when he was a true friend. One day there were a load of cleaners in the apartment and I had to go to the bathroom. I did what I had to do – quite a lot of it, as you will see – and came out shame-faced. My anxiety levels were all over the place and I was mortified, because I'd blocked the loo. I went and confided in Spencer.

'What do you mean you've blocked the loo?' he asked, glacially.

'Well, what do you think I mean?' I said, in a blind panic.

'Try to flush it.'

By now I was redder than a chilli. 'I can't! I've tried, it won't go. I don't want the cleaners to find it and get me into trouble.' The thing with anxiety is you get stressed about the small things. The cleaners probably wouldn't have been bothered, I'm sure they saw this all the time, but I didn't want to be 'that guy'.

Spencer could see how worried I was. He told me it would be okay. 'I've got this,' he said.

'What are you going to do?'

He silently got up and went to the kitchen drawer, and pulled out a knife. 'I'm going to take care of it.' He was like a mafia assassin. He slipped into the bathroom. Silence. Then, a flush, and Spencer emerged triumphant.

'What did you do?' I asked, strangely elated.

He waved the knife, vaguely. 'I chopped it up. All gone now.' He looked at the knife. 'Best put this in the dishwasher straightaway.'

That's when I realised it was true friendship, if he was willing to go to such lengths. Spencer, thank you, always, for slicing up my poo.

Perhaps the biggest test of our relationship was when we took part in a celebrity version of *Hunted*. If you're unfamiliar with the concept, contestants must stay on the run for two weeks, and not be caught by trained hunters, who are experts in finding people. All you have to help you is £100, and the kindness of strangers – plus a cameraman who doesn't assist, but documents your disasters. The most important thing is to evade capture. It was possibly the best TV show I've ever done, even though Spen was infuriating at times. Our strategy was an interesting one . . . in that we didn't have one. Our reasoning was, if we don't know where we're going every day, how the hell will the hunters work it out? At the beginning it was quite cool, we flew in a helicopter to a speedboat and zoomed off, it was exciting. Usually, though, we hitchhiked everywhere. As soon as we got into the car, Spencer would slump in the backseat and immediately fall asleep, while I'd be stuck in the front making the most inane small talk ever to the person driving the car. I mean, I can talk, but even I have limits. I think I even asked one poor guy what his favourite colour was, like we were on the worst first date ever.

Spencer and I got into a huge fight one day after staying in this farmer's barn in Cumbria. We were bickering about the direction to go in, both hopelessly out of our depth. I got my own way on the directions, and marched off with confidence, but after 12 miles of trudging about in the middle of nowhere, I saw a house in the distance and realised it was the farmer's place – I'd taken us in a complete circle. Spencer was furious. It didn't help that we were on constant alert the hunters would find us – we even chucked our untraceable burner phone off a cliff because we were convinced an approaching car belonged to the hunters. Obviously it just drove right past us. I began to get sick of Spencer fully checking out of the experience and leaving me to do the talking, so I said, 'Right, next time, you're making conversation', and he promised he would.

Our next stop was the house of a lovely lady who was an actual fan of *Made in Chelsea*. She made a huge fuss of us, telling us how much she loved the show and taking a great interest in what we'd been doing, and where we'd stayed. It turned out the woods we'd just come from were the same place she was taking her husband the following week for their anniversary – a surprise camping trip, so all very hush-hush. She was so sweet and we bonded so well. When it came time for us to leave, her husband arrived to drive us away, and the lady came along too. We were all in the car and I was chatting, but then I nudged Spencer to remind him he had promised to step up.

He rather awkwardly shifted in his seat, and patted the husband on the back and said, 'So, mate, I hear you're going camping next week?' Oh my God. No. I wanted to die. First thing out of his mouth. Obviously the husband was oblivious and asked what he meant. Rather than change course entirely to avoid blowing the surprise, Spencer prattled on. 'Next week. Your wife . . . said she's taking you camping. For your anniversary.'

Mortifying. Eventually, the poor wife had to own up, and that was the surprise wrecked. After that, we agreed Spencer probably shouldn't speak again. I bet he did it on purpose.

The best thing about our relationship is that we can make fun of each other and we know how to laugh at ourselves. I remember once when we got word that Spencer was going to appear in *Heat* magazine, as Torso of the Week. Sounds a bit like an autopsy, yes, but basically in every issue *Heat* used to select a male celebrity to be their pin-up. Usually the photo is shirtless, or at least sexy. Clearly this was very thrilling – we were jumping up and down with excitement.

'You're going to be in a magazine! You're going to be in a magazine!' You see, being in a magazine was a big deal, it meant you'd made it. On the day it was supposed to come out, Spen and I hopped down to the newsagent, opened the magazine and found it. Oh. Oh, no. Oh, dear. We had a problem. First of all, they'd put him across two pages, so you had to turn the magazine on its side to see him standing the right way up, so it was a huuuuge picture. And he looked . . . well, as I said, we weren't really looking after ourselves at that time. Partying, eating badly, sleeping off hangovers rather than going to the gym. It was a swimsuit shot, massive, across both pages, and the only way I can describe it is that Spencer looked like a hippo emerging from a mud bath. We were both laughing hysterically. Spencer was baffled. 'Why the *hell* would you make *that* torso of the week?' he cried. 'And have they stretched it to make it wider?!' Gutted.

It's funny, but I always thought Spencer and I would be the last bachelors standing. We speak every single day, and maybe what Spencer doesn't know is how much he's guided me. He has such a strong mental approach. It's incredible. More than anything else I admire his ability to just get through things. That's the power of a brilliant friendship. A true friend will inspire you and guide you; they'll tell you when you're doing great, but also pull you up when you're making mistakes; they'll stick by your side through thick and thin; and through it all they'll make you into a better person.

When he met Vogue, I liked her a lot, but I thought she would be just another girlfriend for Spencer; I didn't realise it was serious. It was like I'd lost a teammate. I soon realised it was meant to be: he and Vogue are made for each other. They're so in love, it's amazing. He's left his wild days behind him – and looks pretty terrific these days too, I begrudgingly have to say – and has an amazing family and is a terrific dad. I even get to have a little role all of my own: Spencer and Vogue asked me to be godfather to their youngest, little Gigi. I was thrilled. I'd always had this fear that nobody really liked me because of all the mistakes I'd made, but it made me realise people did actually care for me. I struggle with that sometimes. I was so honoured too, that they'd put their trust in me and knew I'd always be there for Gigi; it showed the love and respect and loyalty they have towards me. I was overcome! I feel so close to Gigi, and Spencer and Vogue's little boy Theo too; I literally love them. It's kind of cool how your love and admiration for a friend can also be transferred to their children, it's pretty special. Like a little bonus.

Chapter Six
Rising Star

A lot of people dismiss reality TV, but I'm really proud of *Made in Chelsea*. Seriously proud. It's a cultural phenomenon. In the early days, few would have predicted it would last, but it has – it's seen off plenty of contenders. I must admit, at first, I couldn't see the attraction. As I said, I wasn't in the first series, and when my friends told me they were doing it, I said they were mad. 'A bad decision,' I said. Huge. I mean, think about it, we were just kind of staggering out of a horrific recession. People had no money, and this show was about posh kids going around drinking champagne and having parties. Imagine people working all hours of the day to come back and switch on their telly at 9 p.m. and watch young kids driving around in Bentleys, talking only in vowels. I mean, it seemed an awful idea, I thought. Terrible idea. How could it be popular? Well, I was soon eating crow, along with the rest of the haters. I guess I was the perfect fit for it, in a way. I was this young hyperactive blond boy saying yes to everything, my eyes huge with wonder, so excited about everything. Plus, my dating history was already of interest to them – I'd dated Caggie before – and I was already friends with most of the cast. But I knew it was a risk, there was a bit of fear there. I'd seen some other reality shows chew people up and spit them out, leaving them unable to be taken seriously, so they'd never work again. I was worried about editing – I knew they could make you look like any kind of person they wanted. I was still in two minds about what to do right up until filming started. Remember that I had the wealth management job there ready to go, a job where I'd know what was going to happen every single day – wake up, go to work, that's it. Even though I knew it would keep people happy, the thought of having to do that filled me with so much dread. Or there was this other option, where anything could happen; no two days would be the same and I had no idea where it might all lead. Anyone who's been on a road trip will tell you that the roads are more exciting if you don't know where they're going – but of course there could be danger. I ummed and aahed about it for so long, I started to drive myself mad, but I've never been one to shy away from danger, so I thought I'd go for it. And I wouldn't be alone: my friend Oliver Proudlock, and some other girls I knew, had all signed up too. We'd be in it together. And there was strength in numbers, right? Great. Decision made. And then none of the others turned up for filming. They'd all backed out! Every single one. I was flying solo on this one. Shit.

On my first day and shaking like a leaf, I was sitting with some producers I didn't know, just waiting to start filming and still trying to convince myself this was the right decision. My mind was working overtime, and I was very aware that once the cameras started rolling, there was no going back. Anyway, I got through it and, pretty quickly, I settled in.

I think I almost expected to be famous straightaway. I mean, it was TV, everyone watched TV! But *Made in Chelsea* was pretty slow to take off – my friend Francis did the first series and went out after the first episode had aired and was shocked that absolutely nobody knew who he was. We live, now, in a viral age, where things are huge quickly but there's no longevity, the faster you go up, the faster you fall down again. *Made in Chelsea* was a bit of a slow burn. People treated it like escapism, a bit of a guilty pleasure, kind of having a little holiday from their own troubles and losing themselves in our dilemmas. It was a bit like lifting a curtain on a life that many people might not have seen. I certainly don't think they watched it because they liked us, not at first anyway. Maybe they watched us with a weird fascination, not quite hate-watching but . . . you know how it feels when you watch someone you don't like that much spill red wine down themselves? That kind of thing. Slowly, though, I think we worked our way into their hearts. They started to like us.

I didn't really think too deeply about it at first though. I used to wake up every day so excited because I didn't know what I'd be doing. Dashing out to do some filming, having a lovely time, what's not to like? It was thrilling. And then the first show came out. Remember I was very young, so I wasn't too interested in the story or anything like that . . . I was more interested in what I looked like, how funny I came across. I can't describe that experience of seeing myself on screen for the first time, but it was not how I imagined I looked. I'd never seen myself from so many angles before, it was like being trapped in a hall of mirrors. 'Oh my God', I thought, 'does my body really look like that in my trousers? They look so baggy on me! Why do I talk so fast? And so much? I never shut up! Oh no, my voice is really weird, I sound so posh.' I couldn't stop – I was just flooded with all these insecurities in an instant. It was a shame, really, because even though this was one of the most exciting moments of my life and, instead of just loving the fact I was on this amazing show, I was obsessing over negatives.

The way people watched and talked about TV was changing too. Twitter was starting to explode, and people would tweet along as they watched. And obviously, being 22 and desperate to be liked, I had to know what they were saying. Maybe I shouldn't have looked; I couldn't help myself. There it was in blue and white: 'Oh my God, who's this new kid Jamie Laing? He looks like a weirdo.' 'Ugh, how annoying is he? Get him away!' Ouch. Because Twitter hadn't been around that long in 2011, nobody had prepared us for this. Unlike now, there was no media training, or advice – people were only just starting to understand the power of social media. No one could warn you, we had to learn on our feet. I tell you, to go online and read stuff about yourself was a horrendous experience. I used to obsess. And even though I'm sure plenty of other people said nice things, it's the bad ones that stay with you. If you're a slightly self-critical person, you look for the negative rather than the positive. I used to go searching for mean comments, for people saying I was short, or ugly, or boring, or not that funny – because that's what I thought about myself, and this was the validation I needed. I assumed people were just saying nice things because they felt like they had to, or they didn't really know me. It's like we can't possibly think anyone is telling the truth unless they're saying something horrible.

I remember when I first realised I was famous. Actually, hang on, I must say: I don't actually think I'm famous. Not properly. You know, Brad Pitt is famous. J-Lo. People like that. I'm just . . . I don't know, some people know who I am, I guess. I can still walk down the street and nobody starts screaming. But the first time I had an inkling I was becoming a celebrity was when I was walking down the road and a car drove past then reversed with a screech and parked next to me. Kidnap attempt? Special delivery just for me? I had no idea. Anyway, a woman and her kids got out and they were very excited to see me. They screamed! They took photos of me! In fact, it was the first photo I'd ever had taken with a fan, I guess. I was mortified, though, so embarrassed. Obviously, I like attention; I've been chucking myself into the centre of things since I was a child, but this was different. I hadn't orchestrated this, I wasn't controlling it. It was just happening to me whether I liked it or not. I've always struggled with this kind of attention and when *Made in Chelsea* won the BAFTA, I stood on stage like a startled lamb. I was so uncomfortable. And this attention would come at the most random times. I was in Scotland once at my cousin's and walking down the road when a tractor drove past, pulled up, and reversed level with me – again! – and a guy opened the door and shouted out, 'I just named my two goldfish after you and Spencer!' But the thing about this attention was, it helped me earn a bit of extra money. I was glad of the perks. At my first solo personal appearance, I was so nervous and I didn't know what to expect. I arrived and my anxiety was through the roof, truly; I was panicking. I got out of the car to find four bouncers encircling me to escort me in. 'I haven't seen this since Peter Andre came,' said one of them, amazing! This is the level of fame we were dealing with. There were 2,000 people in there going nuts at my very presence, screaming my name like I was Drake. Everything I had ever wanted in my life – popularity, people loving me, all eyes on me, making people happy – it was all there in one room suddenly. It certainly laid to rest the ghost of the evening of the boos and the burrito with Spencer. And, reader, I liked it. Maybe too much, almost. All this praise, and validation, it became like a drug. A dream come true! But me being me, I couldn't just sit back and enjoy it. Just as I had with pretty much every good thing in my life, even while I was having a blast, I couldn't help but let the odd negative thought creep in: one day it might all be over. And then what?

Even when the show was at the very height of its success, when I was travelling all over the world having the best time, I was worried about what was going to happen. Always catastrophising about work. It felt like someone was going to figure out that I wasn't actually supposed to be one of the stars of the show, that I was going to be axed, or forgotten. I was always ready for the fall. And it's so pointless, isn't it, anxiety? It's impossible to live in the present because there you are worrying about hundreds of possible outcomes in the future, none of which might come true. I've never really lived in the past, I didn't worry too much about things that had happened – other than feeling mortified if I'd made an arse of myself, but I could always move on – but I was always scared of what was to come. My friends and family certainly didn't indulge any celebrity airs and graces I might have acquired. When I was on the show, my nearest and dearest kind of treated it all as a joke, like it wasn't real. I wasn't famous for playing the guitar or singing a song or writing a book or painting a picture, after all; they all thought it was ridiculous. All my friends were doing internships and trying to get jobs, while I was just wandering around the Kings Road drinking Bloody Marys at 11 o'clock in the morning then tootling off to nightclubs in the evening like I had no responsibilities.

I remember being with my mum and getting asked for a photo – she was incredulous. 'You want a photo of my Jamie? What on earth for?' This was probably a good thing, really, because it kept me grounded and made me realise, this wasn't real life, this couldn't be what I did forever. In a way, it gave me that work ethic to find other stuff to do, to make a living and make everyone proud, to show I had much more to give, and to keep trying to create stuff. I think a problem with lots of reality stars is you get a golden ticket into the world of entertainment, and you think that everything will be that easy, that you will just get given a show to star in and that will be that. I mean being famous is fun, but you're just famous, and there are absolutely loads of famous people out there now. The way I always looked at it, you have to do something extra to make it work for you, you have to work hard and get yourself a business, or start a podcast, or write a book – all of which I can now say I've done, yay! – you can't just sit there, thinking, 'Well I'm famous now,' and wait for opportunities to land on your lap. It doesn't work that way. And I guess that applies to all walks of life: we all have to be willing to drive ourselves forward to find success; nothing significant ever comes to those people who just sit around and wait for it. No one will give you a career on a plate. You have to go out and grab that opportunity with both hands.

But back to my early years in *Made in Chelsea*, and let me be clear: fame is fun. Oh, it is, despite everything. I got to go to so many parties. I could walk into any nightclub across the country and get free drinks and be treated so well. When you're in your early twenties, it's the dream! We were flown all over the world to film the show, or to do photoshoots for articles in magazines. We once got a free holiday to Barbados and free clothes, just for appearing in an article. That was one part I could never understand and didn't quite sit right with me. People work their socks off, as hard as they possibly can to get by, and they don't get anything for free. And when you become famous, you work barely any hours in the day – I mean honestly, what was I actually doing sometimes but talking a load of nonsense in front of a camera? – but you're given everything for free. I didn't understand how this was allowed. The idea that having a certain profile made people want to be associated with you was so weird to me at first. It was exciting, of course, and the attention was very welcome. I grabbed everything the world offered me with both hands, let me tell you. And I was always grateful to be there, never complained even when I was tired or we had long shoots or anything felt intrusive. I was never rude, or aggressive, or mean, or got into fights with people or anything; I didn't take a second of it for granted. I couldn't believe my luck, that it was still happening. We were just so silly all the time. I remember when a few of us did a *Come Dine With Me* special in the early days – me, Alex Mytton, Louise Thompson, Georgia Toffolo – we ran wild. I stripped naked – obviously, this was a common theme back then – and there was can-can dancing and so much wine we could barely see when it was time to give our scores. The poor director had never seen anything quite like us, and by the end, I think he was ready to change careers for ever. But if we were hard work, we didn't mean to be. We were never horrible, we just couldn't believe our luck; it was so much fun, to all be together and revelling in this magic world into which we seemed to have fallen. Complete freedom.

Even though it was a reality show, I know people wonder if we were being our true selves. Me especially, I suppose. It was tricky for me because I only knew what people thought of me by reading the tweets and the posts – everyone else, who didn't tweet or whatever, had no idea what others were thinking. I do believe I was always myself, but it's like everyone: we all have different personas or sides to ourselves, and the dominant persona changes in certain situations. Even putting it simply: you dress and act differently when you go to work from how you do when you're at home. My mum says to me sometimes when I call her, usually if other people are around, 'Ooh, you've got your radio voice on' – no, Mum never lets me get away with any celebrity ego! So while I was myself on the show, I definitely turned the volume up. I wanted the show to be the most entertaining and interesting version of myself, I wanted people to carry on watching and, of course, say fewer horrible things about me, so I amped myself up a bit. I told more jokes, I was louder in some situations, I tried to make sure there was never a dull moment, like I taped over my off-switch and was just on, on, on, all the time. And sometimes that filters into real life, because you know that people like you when you're on TV, so maybe you need to be like that all the time. The tricks that make a good scene, for example, might not work as well in real life one-to-ones. I remember one of my very best friends saying to me once, when we were catching up, 'You're not on Channel 4 at the moment, Jamie. Why are you interviewing me?' I was acting like a producer on the show, but almost in my own head, producing my conversations in real life. So while there was no 'persona' or 'TV Jamie vs. Offscreen Jamie', I did sometimes have difficulty adjusting between the two. You do, after a while, start to wonder who the hell you really are.

And I guess sometimes it got in the way of my having fun on the show. I wanted to make the best TV possible. I was always the one who asked what the viewing figures were, or how well we were doing on socials. Life became a leaderboard. I think it stemmed from school, where our grades were put in a leaderboard from the age of eight. I thought everything was a race. And actually, I know now, it's not a race, you just have to enjoy the present. Stop. Just enjoy what you're doing right now. But it was very hard to say that to the 24-year-old Jamie. I wanted the world. And for a while, I thought I had it.

Chapter Seven

Superhero

The one superpower I would love to have is the ability to freeze time, so that I could spend more time living in the moment. I've had so many wonderful times in my life that I wish I'd spent a bit longer enjoying them – not just the wild parties or meeting famous people or travelling, but the little things. Playing rugby when I was younger, or being a teenager and having no worries, or before social media took over our lives. Just being young and free and flirting a bit at parties – I hardly got to do any flirting at school because we hardly had any contact with girls, so maybe this is why I made up for lost time once school was over. All that naivety, and innocence, and fun, and to be so overtaken by all the excitement that you can feel it bubbling in your throat. All those firsts you experience in your life, they never quite hit the same high when you do them over and over again. Life speeds up so much as you get older, things get more routine. I like my life now and don't want to be a kid again or anything like that, but I definitely miss that feeling. There's nothing more exciting than the sensation of your first kiss – do we ever feel such a high again?

Other than being able to catch literally anything in my mouth – although, if you see me in the street, please don't randomly throw something at me; I have to know the object is coming – I suppose my one superpower I do have is being able to make people feel comfortable. I love talking to people, I'm genuinely interested in them. I suppose that's why I started my podcast *Private Parts*. I like listening to people's stories, I like being curious. Is that a superpower? If a superpower is something you feel lucky to have, and that makes you feel like you're making a difference, then maybe it is.

We've had a lot of great guests on *Private Parts*, and we've had a lot of fun. What's really interesting about doing the podcast is that sometimes the most earth-shattering moments come when you least expect them. After doing the podcast for so long and also after dealing with my own past anxieties, I guess I have this sixth sense when I'm talking to guests; often I can kind of tell if there's something going on beneath the surface or if they've had similar experiences to me. You know the signs, I suppose, from how they carry themselves and there are little clues in what they say. I remember when Max George joined us. Max and I were on *Strictly* together, and he's probably best known for being in The Wanted, for having huge No 1 hits, touring the world and generally living his life to the full as a popstar. But of course, The Wanted eventually broke up, and he was telling us about what that was like; and while some people might have been tempted not to let things get too deep and give media-trained answers, Max started to open up about what a difficult time it had been for him. So I started asking a few questions, based on my own experience, because I could see flickers of my own situation in his. I guess it took a while to get there, but my attitude to this kind of stuff now is 'better out than in'. Keeping it all in is *definitely* not my style anymore and here's the book to prove it. I approached the subject sensitively. I wanted to make sure Max was absolutely comfortable with sharing, and this led to him speaking publicly about his severe depression for the first time. I totally got where he was coming from, and it was an honour that he decided to share that moment with us. It was such a moving and powerful conversation; I was honestly in awe of Max's bravery. You know, men don't speak up about this kind of stuff enough and the statistics can't be ignored: around 75 per cent of people who take their own life in the UK are men. And although Max had chosen to open up on *Private Parts*, talking about something so personal with Francis and me, well, that was one thing, but broadcasting it to the world – well, okay, not the whole world, but we do have a lot of listeners – that was quite another. So even though it was an inspiring conversation, we offered to cut it out, wipe the lot from the podcast, if that's what Max preferred. Initially, I think he was a bit embarrassed that he'd spoken so openly. And again, I totally got this; I knew about the shame of feeling that having anxiety was something you had to hide, or a confession you had to make. It's all very well to talk about 'breaking down the stigma' but when you're the person and you're sharing your story, it can feel like a lonely place. You can't un-say this kind of stuff, you know? After Max had given it some thought and decided that everything he had said should stay in the podcast, we kept it in as he wished and I think that really helped him. I know he's spoken about his depression elsewhere since then and I appreciate, from my own experience, what a relief that can be – and also how you kind of get a kick out of knowing you've helped others.

Maybe it's a side of me people aren't aware of, but because I've been open about my problems, whether it's tinnitus or social anxiety, my friends often come to me for advice and they know I won't judge them. I'm a safe pair of hands and a discreet pair of ears. Not only that, but I find having these conversations, whether in person or on the podcast, quite rewarding. On a personal level, they help me learn about people and to grow, and professionally, it means I can give something back – every single month on *Private Parts* we donate money to individuals, communities, charities, people who are unsung heroes, those who deserve it most. Maybe it's a selfish thing, but it's good to know you're here for a reason, that your existence is having a positive effect on others. It was important to me that the podcast had a purpose. I suppose when it comes to advice, I'm quite practical; I've had my ups and downs, but I got through them. And in a way, I wouldn't be without them.

I'd say life is like a heart monitor, it has to go up and down in order to survive – if we flatline we're dead, right? So we need these moments in our life, the peaks and the troughs, and the lows help us appreciate the highs.

I think that's why I like doing nice things for people. I want to avoid as many flatlining moments in life as I can. I want to make people feel good. I'm well aware of how ridiculous my fame is, and, still, how nuts it was that I was flown around the world and paid thousands of pounds to pop in and say hello to people trying to get on with having fun in a nightclub. That desire to make other people happy has never left me and I don't think it ever will. Obviously, it has its bad sides, when I end up promising too much and letting people down, but usually it works out okay. I honestly get such a thrill out of it. I've always wanted people to experience the cool stuff with me; I don't want to do things alone. Sometimes I'd be at some beautiful place and having a great time, but I'd start thinking, 'This would be even better if my best friend were with me,' or, you know, 'Mum would really love this.' If ever I manage to earn a decent bit of money, the first thing I do is think about how I can spend it on someone I love, on how much fun can we have. Letting people down, though, that's the worst. Oh, I can't bear it. In fact, I have such a fear of letting people down that I actually end up letting people down more, because I end up leaving it until the last possible second before telling them I can't do whatever it is I've promised to do. Does that make sense? No, of course it doesn't, let me try to explain. So I don't like disappointing people; it plays into all my insecurities. It makes me worry they're going to dislike me, or that I'll lose them as a friend, or I'm going to be abandoned, and they're going to forget me. I get so anxious and worried I lose sleep over it. I know! But I still can't help myself. So, for example, if someone asks me if I want to go for dinner, I'll say yes. I won't check a diary, or my phone or say I'll get back to them, just yes, yes, yes – because then I'm not disappointing them. It would be easier to check my plans and say, 'oh I can't', or say, 'maybe', and it would probably be fine, but I don't see it that way. My view was always, if I don't tell them I can't go until the last minute the disappointment will be shorter, and they'll be less upset. Yeah, reading that back now it's written down, my logic does seem a little off, because obviously the disappointment is heightened, because they're all set and I've dropped them in it. Trouble is, I got a reputation as a flake, so I stopped getting invited to stuff because people thought I wouldn't turn up, which – ding, ding, ding, here comes the warning bell of anxiety – is exactly what I didn't want in the first place. So I'd make 100 different plans because I didn't want to let anyone down, and would end up doing none of them, and then not getting invited to anything ever – my ultimate nightmare!

So let's talk about the time I tried to do a nice thing, gave the superhero role a go, and it all went a bit wrong, basically the time I fulfilled my own prophecy. My little sister Emily is an actress and she's amazing; she's written her own play and songs, and she's a brilliant musician too. I love her to death, but I haven't always been a very good big brother to her. When we were kids, I just didn't really take much notice of her. Remember, I worshipped anyone who was older, and poor Emily was . . . not. We got on okay, but we were never close. We just didn't really hang out much together. And then as she got older, I was tough on her again. It came from a good place; I was always trying to motivate her and push her – she's so talented, and I know one day she's going to be hugely successful. I just wanted to do everything I could to help her get there. Maybe it's because I wish someone had done that for me more. I ran kind of wild at times, and I suppose I just wanted others to have that guidance.

Anyway, fast forward several years and it's clear what a brilliant actress Emily is, and my mum tells me she's got a part in a Broadway show. Obviously, I am thrilled for her, so proud – she so deserves this break – so I say to my mum, 'Look, how about I take you there, we go and watch Emily on Broadway, just me and you? All expenses paid. I'll take us there, business class and we'll stay in an amazing hotel. I know all the cool places to go from when I lived there; it's going to be amazing.'

I really wanted to do something nice for my mum – and for my sister, I wanted to show her how much I cared, how excited I was for her. But let's face it, it was Mum I owed. I had probably caused her tens of sleepless nights over the years. This was my big chance to treat her, and, you know, show off a little bit maybe? Perhaps show Mum that I was a responsible grown-up, and had great taste and was kind of worldly, you know? Show her the benefits of my ridiculous lifestyle and career? Mum was thrilled. I mean, yes, she could probably afford to buy herself a little trip to New York, but she wouldn't ever do it, that's the thing – she's not flashy, prefers to save for a rainy day, doesn't blow cash on herself, ever.

I was feeling so pumped about doing this for Mum, and then I went on the airline's website to book the tickets. I had done absolutely zero research into this trip, and I don't know if you've ever flown business class but . . . I was pretty shocked. These tickets were £2,000 or something. More! I kept checking to see I hadn't selected first class or private jet by mistake. I love my mum but couldn't afford to drop all this money on flights – that would blow my budget before I even booked a hotel. What could I do? I couldn't let Mum down, I just couldn't, so I thought I'd just book economy and worry about it later – maybe I could blag us an upgrade or some other miracle could happen. I booked what looked like a fun, decent hotel in Soho – I had insisted on staying in Soho, because it was the coolest place and I couldn't wait to show my mum around.

We arrive at the airport and it transpires I've forgotten to check us in online so, not only are we very much not in business class . . . we are actually sitting on different sides of the plane from one another. My mum is such a trooper, she didn't even mention that we weren't actually in business class, and said it was fine. We get to New York and arrive at the hotel and it's . . . well, it's probably a little bit livelier than the kind of hotel you'd want to stay with your mum in. It was the sort of place where you'd pay for a room by the hour, and I don't mean to go for a nap. So this might be why, when we were checking in, the hotel staff don't realise we're mother and son – we have different surnames – and they think I'm my mum's toy boy. My mum is a very beautiful lady, and any man would be honoured to have her on his arm, but this is my *mother*! Come on! We get given these orange wristbands – apparently there is a huge party on the roof and if we want to join in, we flash our wristbands. My mum and I look at each other. Uh-oh. What *is* this place? It's very weird. Kind of glamorous, but . . . not. Everyone's drinking tequila. We get into the lift, standing there tired, the scuzzy feeling of the plane still all over us, when suddenly a wave of shirtless partygoers join us, getting in between us and cramming us into opposite sides of the lift. They are very clearly off their heads, and one of them is trying to twerk with my mum, and I am beginning to have my usual 'hang on, maybe this is a bad idea' moment that always comes far too late into a disaster to be any use at all. But we soldier on. I tell Mum I know an amazing place for lunch round the corner, and that it's my treat, so we arrive and there's a gigantic queue snaking round the corner. Not another fail! I can see my mum can't be bothered at all but I'm desperate to impress her and show her the finer things in life.

'We have to do this; it's going to be amazing.' Famous last words.

Mum relents and we queue. When we get in there, we're given the shittiest seats – like, we might as well have been sitting in the dumpsters out the back, and the meal is a set menu, which is just about okay. So much for 'amazing'. The arrival of the bill is the one highlight, and when it's placed in front of us with a flourish by a waiter, we see this below-par experience has cost us $400. Gulp. So the let-down continues: 'my treat' turns into 'going Dutch' and I have to split the cost with my mum. Ever the saint, she doesn't protest.

But I know there's something genuinely amazing round the corner that will make up for all of this – we get to see Emily in her Broadway show, and we are very excited. My mum tells me the theatre name and we're tramping along Broadway and I'm wondering where on earth this place is. I give in and get on Google Maps and . . . this can't be right. I type it in again. And again. The only theatre with that name isn't on Broadway at all, it's . . . well, it's off-Broadway.

Quite far off, as it happens. I turn to Mum and she looks a little embarrassed. She'd clearly zhuzhed things up a little – Emily doing a play in New York became Emily doing a play off Broadway, which became . . . Emily's in a Broadway play! So we're now marching up and down the streets of New York looking for the right theatre.

'Mum,' I said, with all my own letdowns still whirling round my head, 'We've come all the way to New York for this . . . to go and watch my sister in a show, which is most definitely not on Broadway.'

I didn't have a leg to stand on, did I? Mum knew it. 'You brought me to New York to stay in a crap hotel, and as for our business class tickets . . . we had to sit in economy, aisles apart. So I don't know what you're complaining about.'

We had a minor back and forth about how crap this all was before getting ourselves together. To show there was no hard feelings, and that I was having an amazing time anyway, I made her stop for a selfie with me. It's such a funny photo because we are both clearly over it.

And then we get to the theatre and it's just some random theatre, but the production is incredible, and Emily is absolutely amazing. Yes, it wasn't exactly the heady razzmatazz of Broadway I'd been expecting, but it's super-cool, and my sister is terrific, and we're so proud. Out of pure mischief, however, I lean into my mum and whisper, 'Yeah, Emily could've just filmed this and sent it to us, to be honest,' and am met with a sharp elbow-dig from Mum. Well, at least we can see my sister afterwards, have drinks with the big (not) Broadway star. Except . . . my sister is doing her own thing, and wants to hang with her cool NYC friends, not her mum and brother who she could see anytime. So Mum and I schlep back to our bizarre, gaudy sex-hotel, flash our wristbands and try to have a drink on the balcony, which has been taken over by what looks like a sex party. Needless to say, I forget to check in again on the way back, so we have to sit apart once again. Maybe it was for the best. We laugh about it now, the famous 'Mummy and Jamie go to New York' story. On paper it sounds legendary, but in reality it was a disaster.

It was a reminder to me that even though my cape is always ready to go if I get the chance to play the superhero, maybe sometimes I'm better off leaving the heroics to someone else. Someone who can remember to check in on a bloody plane, for starters.

Chapter Eight
Bad Guy

Right, okay, first of all, before we get into it, I need to make you understand that I'm not a bad guy. I don't feel like one. I'm a good person, I am kind and always polite. I have lovely friends, and people who work with me always say it was fun and that I'm pretty easy to get along with. I know all this is true, and yet . . . well, sometimes you get an idea in your head about what people think about you, and you look at some of your past behaviour and you wonder . . . hang on, maybe I'm not a nice person, after all? Maybe I've been wrong all these years and I'm actually secretly evil? Self-doubt thrives on making you feel bad about yourself. But even though I am pretty confident I'm not in fact an evil mastermind who's set out to ruin as many lives as possible, I have to admit, like even the most wholesome person must, that there have been times when I've come off as the bad guy. I'm no saint. I've made bad decisions, and I've been thoughtless. In the past, I've put my own feelings above others, I've misled people into believing I thought one thing when in fact I had entirely different plans. While I have never intentionally set out to hurt anyone in my life, sometimes I have ended up as the villain of the story.

Often, usually, okay . . . very nearly always, it's stuff that's happened in my relationships that have let me down. And, yes, I know what you're thinking, there have been plenty of them. Jamie Laing, with his string of exes, a trail of broken hearts behind him longer than the queue for the toilets at Glastonbury. And, okay, while it might be true that I haven't exactly lived like a monk, I took my relationships very seriously. Maybe too seriously at the time. And there haven't been *that* many exes. But part of growing up and moving on is admitting when you have been the bad guy, and I suppose there's no time like the present – and no place better than the pages of a book, so it's all official, there in black and white – to atone for some of my behaviour. I'd like to start by apologising to all of my ex-girlfriends. I'm sorry, really sorry.

See, trouble is I struggled with monogamy from an early age. I mean, even at primary school, I was sneaking off with Eliza behind Hannah's back – aged six! There was no hope for me really. I thought that dating people made me cool, so I had to do it, and I suppose the more I did it, the cooler I would be. And I was obsessed with being cool; I always felt like I didn't fit in, even though I did, just fine – but I couldn't shake off the feeling. So I would get myself into these ridiculous situations. When I was 17, my girlfriend Lucy came to my school to watch me play rugby, and no sooner had I dropped her off at the train station to go back home, than I was off to meet Caggie, who I was also dating at the time. We were going away for the weekend and went to get the train . . . only to find Lucy still standing there, on the opposite platform, because her train had been

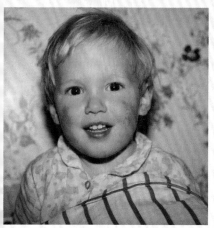

Me, aged three. Already perfecting my photo face.

Me, aged four, dressed as a pirate. Clearly I've always been a fashion icon.

Me, aged seven, with my brother Xander, aged eight, and my sister Emily, aged four. I'll admit, the wellies were excessive.

Spitting image. Me, aged eleven, with my mum Penny on holiday in Turkey. I think we know where I get my good looks from.

A young Usain Bolt wannabe running for Summer Fields in the 4x100m relay. I always ran the first leg and we generally won!

I lived and breathed sport as a child. I used to dream about captaining the England rugby team. Rain or shine, Mum came to cheer me on.

Dad on holiday sailing. He loves sailing!

Remember when eyebrow piercings were cool?
On holiday with my parents in Portugal, aged eighteen,
rocking a new look. Do I pull it off?

With my brother Xander, aged
19 and Emily, aged 14. Candid.

MIC squad goals. Playing a spot of tennis. Doing my best impression of Björn Borg in
the middle.

[L–R: Spencer, me, Proudlock, and Alex Alfud] Jet skiing on the Hudson River when me and Spencer were tearing it up in New York.

Spencer and I had an unhealthy obsession with Minions when we lived in New York. No, I'm not inside the costume.

Selfie with Mum after our disastrous trip to New York to watch Emily's 'Broadway' theatre production.

My doomed foray into stand-up comedy at a charity gig at The Comedy Store. Got up on stage in front of 400 people wearing a T-shirt saying 'As seen on E4'. If only I'd learnt my lesson then.

My 'merinj tower' from when I appeared on the 2018 celebrity special of *The Great Celebrity Bake Off for SU2C*.

The last scene me, Proudlock and Francis ever filmed together in 2015 (series 10 of *MIC*). In London, baking cakes, and reminiscing about the good times when we all lived together.

One of the first ever Candy Kittens pop-up shops at Latitude Festival in July 2014. *MIC* partner in crime Jess Woodley sitting on my shoulders.

Ed Williams, my Candy Kittens business partner, being forced to wear a tight-fitting CK T-shirt on his stag do in Hvar, Croatia. Could have been worse!

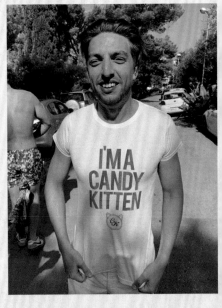

In 2012, I got the Candy Kittens logo tattooed onto my hip bone. Sadly, the logo has changed since then!

Me and Francis Boulle, my *Private Parts* co-host. This was one of the original promo shots for the podcast from 2018.

The first ever photo taken of me and Sophie together in 2019. We were filming *MIC* and had just told everyone we were dating.

Sophie during lockdown, always on-brand with her Candy Kittens facemask.

L–R: Me, Toby (black cap), Proudlock (drinking), and Robbo (pouting, as usual)]. Watching Lewis Capaldi at Glastonbury with the boys in the 2019. Happy days.

Don't let the smile fool you. I felt totally out my depth before performing the Charleston in week three of *Strictly*. You can't deny, I rocked that Hercules outfit though.

Rehearsing the Samba in week four. I had no idea what I was doing so thought dressing up as Karen might help me out.

It was back to school for musicals' week when we did the Jive to *Everybody's Talking About Jamie*.

[L–R: Bill, JJ, Me, Max, Jason, and HRVY] The *Strictly* boys of 2020.

delayed. My survival instinct, and innate fear of getting into trouble, kicked in, so I sent Caggie off to the shop to get provisions for the train journey while I skipped over to the other platform to see Lucy. Looking back, I cannot believe the sheer audacity of this absolutely shocking lie, but when Lucy asked me who Caggie was, I said, 'Oh, don't worry, that's just my sister.' Never mind a train, I think I got my first one-way ticket to Hell that day.

That mindset, that I had to be in relationships, never really left me, but I struggled to commit. As I've said, I hated letting people down, so things would just escalate from mild indiscretions into huge devastating bombs that would go off and hurt everyone involved. I think the first time I got my fingers burned was the most formative and something I've never forgotten. It set the tone for the next few years, and even almost repeated itself and, I hold my hands up, at first glance I don't come out of it too well.

We're going back in time. It all starts when I'm still at school, aged 14, at Radley. I have a best friend, let's call him Fred, and we are close. Thick as thieves. We spend loads of time together, he comes on holiday with us, this is 'brother from another mother' territory. Yet somehow, we were about to become rivals, and I blame myself entirely. You have to understand that we were in an all-boys school, and opportunities to meet girls were limited, which only served to make us more curious about love and sex, and more excited when we did actually have any contact with girls. All we had to rely on were socials, like these micro-organised events where we'd be bussed over to a girls' school, or they'd come over to us, and there'd be some kind of mingling – Scottish dancing, or games, or sports, or something. Think of the Danbury Ball in *Bridgerton* except with more fizzy drinks and crisps, much less facial hair, and only slightly less chance of social disgrace. We would meet girls at these socials, and exchange numbers. I remember the most exciting part of my day used to be getting back to my dorm after lessons and seeing whether I'd got a text from a girl. Sometimes, through friends, we'd be given numbers of girls we hadn't even met. I chatted to one called Lucinda for years without ever laying eyes on her.

Anyway, through one of these socials, I meet a girl I'm going to call Beth, who has briefly dated a friend of mine before. Of all my text buddies, she was the *one*. Beth was mysterious, she never gave anything away and, while I couldn't understand it, I found it appealing. I'm a totally open book, so when someone doesn't quite give me what I want, or I have to earn their friendship or their respect, I admire it, I find it intriguing. My girlfriend Sophie is a bit like that, she's guarded. I think it's a good thing – it means you can work out whether they really like you, once they let their guard down.

Beth and I used to text all night. Seriously, way past our bedtimes. I remember I was so worried about running out of things to say, and so anxious to keep the chat going, that I'd write notes in my phone as kind of prompts, to remind me what to talk about. Movies we'd seen was always a good one, or funny stories from my already quite large collection of misdeeds, mishaps, and misunderstandings. It was a bit like honing a stand-upj act. I remember one of my bits was, for some reason, claiming I had a good singing voice. I suppose

I thought being able to sing might make me sound sexy – girls pinned photos of singers to their walls, after all. I used to have this anecdote which would somehow lead Beth into saying, 'Wait, you used to sing?' whereupon I would very nonchalantly and modestly say something like, 'Oh yeah, I used to sing a bit, you know the song "True Colors"?' And Beth, or whichever girl I was spinning this nonsense to, would be really impressed. Amazing. I am cringing so hard remembering this right now.

One day, we were having a sports day at school, where I was due to pick up a prize, and I invited Beth as my date. She came along, although I didn't spend all day with her because I was very busy being a prize-winning sporting hero, but she had friends to hang out with. That night, though, she comes back to stay at my dad's house with me and I make my move. Well, we make a move on each other. Hang on, I'm jumping ahead . . . so, no sooner am I back through the front door with Beth, than my pal Fred calls me to say he had kissed Beth at the sports day earlier. Now, hang on a second here – I invited her as my date, what the hell was Fred on about?

'I just wanted you to know I really like her,' he said.

'Bizarre,' I thought. Maybe I should have talked it out with Beth and got to the bottom of it, but we were horny teenagers and we had a packet of condoms – now was not the time for a deep and meaningful conversation about the complexities of sexual politics and morality. Perhaps it was the universe trying to slide into *my* DMs and warn me I was on shaky ground here, but that night was a disaster. I had no idea what I was doing at all. I was just rubbing on top of her, and she kept asking me, 'Have you done this before?' and I answered, breaking yet another condom with this high intensity, sexless frotting, that of course I had, 'absolutely loads'. We did not quite seal the deal that night but carried on texting with a view to actually managing to complete one day.

Fred then came on holiday to Portugal with my family and confessed to me that he was messaging Beth too. He was pretty blasé about it, actually, saying that she had told him she really liked him. But she really liked me too, she'd said. Had those friction burns and massive embarrassment all been for nothing? Surely Fred could see that Beth and I were meant to be together? I was going to win this, right?

A few weeks later, I was invited to a tennis competition in Hunstanton in Norfolk and was looking for a seat on the train when who should I see but Beth, looking as lovely as ever. She seemed glad to see me but there was a hint of something else there that I couldn't quite work out – although I was about to find out.

'Wow, Beth! Hey! How are you? What are you doing here?'

She was off to Hunstanton, she said, which . . . was pretty obvious, as that's where the train was going, but I was too happy to see her to reply with any sarcasm.

'Oh wow, cool' – trying to hide my confusion and excitement here – 'Are you? Where are you staying?'

She was staying the same place I was. This was shaping up to be an amazing weekend. I didn't know she knew this person, and she said she didn't, but someone else had invited her.

'Brilliant, so who invited you?'

I'll never forget this moment. 'Fred,' she said. 'We're boyfriend and girlfriend now.'

Now, please. Understand something. Allow me this. I was 15. Life was a movie. I was the main character. There had never been a moment as dramatic as this in my life. A dagger straight to my heart. Beth and I had been messaging for months. I had bared my soul, shared all my best stories and jokes, and my most intimate movie opinions. And now this? I felt betrayed, brutalised. But I was staunchly British about it: 'Oh that's great, I'm so happy for you both.' It was very telling, however, that Fred hadn't said a word to me about this.

And all weekend, I had to watch them together. It was so awkward. There was no arguing, or showdowns; I just spent most of the weekend glowering at them, or pretending I was ignoring them. The joke about this now is I look back and realise what an absolute ball I was having, some of the best moments of my life. But this was also very serious, and I had been wronged and Shakespeare had nothing on this dilemma of mine. But I don't say anything to Fred – he is with Beth now, and I had to concede defeat.

Fast forward to another party, and I bump into Beth again, but this time there's no sign of Fred. We have a few drinks, a laugh, it's like our old texting sessions come to life. Then she stops me and says, 'I think I made a mistake. I made the wrong choice.'

'What do you mean?'

'I chose Fred,' she said, 'But I should've chosen you.'

Oh, man. Come *on*. This isn't fair! I'd already stepped aside, pushed down my own pain and learned to live with it. (If this sounds a bit much for a 15-year-old's thwarted teenage romance, please remember this was before Netflix so every little drama in our lives was magnified times a million.)

I asked her what she was going to do, and she said she was going to break up with him, and I thought . . . well, what *did* I think? I thought it was sad for Fred, but that he might get over it, like I had. At least that's what I hoped. And to my shame, two days after that, Beth and I slept together. Like, properly this time; I actually managed to put everything where it was supposed to go. It was probably less than stellar, but at the time it was like magic had happened, like I had finally had my eyes opened to a whole new world of maturity, and manhood, and pleasure. Maybe this was my downfall. In any event, Fred found out from a friend what we'd done and . . . he cut me off. Completely and utterly blanked me, forever. If I walked into a room, he'd leave it; if I sat at his table, he'd get up and walk away. He wouldn't listen to my apologies, or excuses, he wanted no part of it.

I seemed to have swapped one tragic loss for another. I didn't understand why I couldn't fix this. Nothing worked. To make matters worse, my victory – if you can call it that – was short-lived. Beth then told me that I had been a terrible mistake, and went back to Fred, leaving me abandoned both by my best friend and the girl. Heartbreak. Man, this was raw. I'd lost everything.

This was the first time my idealised version of love had taken a bit of a battering. I'd always thought that bad stuff happened but always came right in the end. But there was no going back with Fred. I was dead to him. I still have dreams about it. It's one of my biggest regrets, that I had complicated things in this way. Life isn't meant to be complicated when you're younger, but I'd got involved and made a mess of it.

I swore then I would never again let anything get between me and a friend, so great was the loss of both Fred and Beth. But history has a habit of replaying itself and I am a repeat offender when it comes to complicating matters. And a couple of years ago, it looked like it was happening all over again.

I'd always vowed I'd never date anyone I met on *Made in Chelsea*, until I met my girlfriend Sophie – by the way, that's a massive spoiler for how this next part of the chapter turns out, sorry. Anyway, when I'd been in any relationship that was part of the show, I had always met the lady off-screen, or knew them already, and invited them to be on the show. Sophie, I'd never met until she joined the show. I admit, sometimes I don't like that the story of our origin sounds like so many other reality TV couples, as I feel we're much more than that, you know? She joined *Made in Chelsea*, and we were quite friendly, but not to any great degree; to me, she was just a boisterous girl who seemed pretty cool but no more than that. On a filming trip to Croatia, she moved out of the girls' house to stay with us boys and, apparently, she'd started dating Sam, but I didn't know that. Something weird was happening to me when I was around her. It was so strange. I couldn't be in the same room as her by myself. It felt too awkward. I couldn't look her in the eye, didn't know what to do with my arms, couldn't even sit still. I felt like I needed to impress her for some reason, but I didn't know how or why. Was I already attracted to her and couldn't quite process it? Possibly. All I know is this had never really happened to me before. But we became great friends; she was fun to be around – in a group, when I wasn't acting like a weirdo! I remember saying to my friend Sam, 'You're onto a winner here. Try not to let this one go.' Sam could be a tough person to lock down, I think, but he noted that I'd said that. Thing was, I then started to notice that Sophie wasn't really that into Sam. The spark wasn't there; they were drifting. But Sam didn't really understand it, and the more Sophie pulled away, the keener he became. I warned him he was going to lose her – which might seem odd now given what happened, but I was genuinely concerned for Sam – and he thought he could turn things around.

I invited Sam and Sophie to my 30th birthday party, and that night Sophie told me she wanted to end things with Sam. Now, I know what you're thinking: there are scenes like this on *Made in Chelsea* all the time, but this was not on camera and in no way meant for the show – this was a private moment. I told her she had to tell him.

Sam was devastated and I felt sorry for him. At this point, I had no feelings about what this might mean for me. I had no idea what was going to happen, and it never entered my mind. Sam said something to me then that has stayed with me; I wasn't quite sure what he was getting at. 'It's a shame,' he said, 'But she needs to be with someone like you.'

I remember when I did my first stand-up gig Sophie messaged me to wish me luck, and I thought it was so sweet. None of my other friends had done that, and I remember feeling it was so nice that she was thinking of me, that she was going out of her way to send me a message. (Sophie is still adamant that at this point she didn't fancy me, by the way; but what do you think?). At this point, I was genuinely just happy to be friends with Sophie – nothing else entered my head.

Things changed when we headed to South Africa to do some filming for *Made in Chelsea*. I'd caught up with Sam before I left, and he said to me, 'Make sure you don't hook up with Sophie.' I don't know whether he'd seen a connection that I hadn't, or was just wary of my reputation – which I felt was a little unjustified, even then, if I'm honest – but I was baffled. 'Of course, I won't,' I said. And I meant it.

We had a ball in South Africa, and nothing happened between us while we were out there. I'll confess: we were flirty. But I flirt, it's what I do. It doesn't always mean there has to be a goal. I guess flirting was my way of making myself feel at ease. It's natural for me to lay on a little bit of charm if I want someone to like me, but, okay, this did feel a little different. On the plane home, Sophie and I sat next to each other, still kind of lost inside that holiday high. You know how it is, you don't want the good times to end, so maybe you get a little bit tipsy on the plane, and act like there aren't any real responsibilities waiting for you once you land. So maybe we got a bit carried away. So maybe we forgot ourselves a little. So maybe we kissed. Actually, no maybe on that one – we definitely did.

Then we landed, and got off the plane, and I sobered up, and I thought: 'Shit.'

Sophie and I started seeing each other, but we kept it a complete secret. Usually on the show when there's a bit of romance, it turns into a big storyline, but I didn't want that to be the case here. This was different. I shocked myself, really, because I actually liked her. I had fallen for somebody on the show; this wasn't how I usually operated. This wasn't me meeting someone in a bar, and then laying on the charm, and pursuing her. I was always driving those situations. I could usually see how they were going to play out. But Sophie? I couldn't read her at all.

This went on for two months, neither of us telling a soul. Everyone was kind of guessing, noticing we hung out together a lot, but we always denied it. The lies soon stacked up.

It was always going to come out sooner or later, I realise now, and perhaps we weren't as clever and secretive as we thought we were. Sam must've got wind of it, because our regular tennis matches became less frequent and he wouldn't take my calls. It was like Fred all over again. When we did speak, he was very angry. He said some things that were hard for me to hear. I suppose he didn't realise how serious I was about Sophie, and I think I was still kind of reeling from it myself at this point. Maybe he thought I was doing it to prove I was the alpha of the show, or just for fun, but I felt a proper and meaningful connection with Sophie. I'd never felt like this before, never had a relationship start this way. We were friends first, so we already knew each other, there wasn't that period of discovery you get when you start dating a stranger – there was no chase, or me having to live up to some role and try to impress her with showing her as good a time as possible. She knew all the tricks, all my tactics, and wasn't interested in them. All I had to offer her was myself and, it seemed, that was enough. It was a totally new experience for me.

But I couldn't let my friendship with Sam go; I had to break this bad guy curse. I wouldn't repeat the mistake I made with Fred. I looked at it from Sam's point of view. I was always the older one, I was always hogging the storylines at *Made in Chelsea*, I'd mentored him, he was my friend's younger brother. I hadn't treated him as an equal, I'd belittled him and now I'd even started dating his ex. I hadn't taken his feelings into consideration, and this was a wake-up call for me. You can't expect people to be cool with something just because it makes you happy. Like with my little sister, I'd been tough on Sam over the years because I saw such great potential in him – so this must have felt like an extra slap in the face. I had to win him over. It was sheer persistence that did it in the end. I put the work in, unlike with poor Fred where I'd just accepted my fate. Friendships are important. At first, Sam wasn't having any of it. The first time we saw each other was on camera and he was calling me a dick, which I took on board, but I wouldn't give up. Some said I was being selfish still trying to get him to be my pal, that there was no point, that I should leave Sam alone, but I couldn't see years of friendship disappear like that. Nelson Mandela once said seeking revenge is like drinking poison and wanting the other person to die. It only hurts you. Eventually, Sam and I started to get back on track, and we're talking again. I'm not sure he's ever quite forgiven me, and maybe we'll never be exactly as we were, but I keep hoping that maybe one day we will. Whatever happens, I won't give up. True friends are always worth fighting for. I'm never making that mistake again.

Chapter Nine
Romantic Hero

Love is weird. Yet I love it. I love being in love, and have always been fascinated by it. But I realised from a young age that being too in love with someone was going to be a problem. Loving someone can give the other person such an advantage over you, can make you out of control. Love can send you wild and crazy, all over the place. To be too in love with someone is a really scary place to be, especially when the person doesn't reciprocate or, even if they do love you back, not feel quite as strongly as you do.

I know that to many people I'm known for my different relationships on *Made in Chelsea*, but that's the bit I've always found the hardest. I've never been fully comfortable with playing the romantic hero. I love romance, and I totally buy into everything it can do, and the joy it can bring, but I never used to be quite sure what to do once the wooing was over. Sure, I can play Prince Charming easily – that part comes naturally – but what about the happy ever after? That's the part that never quite computes. I can slay the dragon, find the sleeping princess, break the curse, and wake her up – but the next day, I'm like, and now what? When it's time to go off into the sunset, my reaction has usually been: 'Hang on a minute, I've still got loads of stuff I want to do. I don't want to go.' It feels so final.

It doesn't help that I used to fall in love very quickly. I didn't do things by halves. In fact, you might call it an obsession: I'd always wanted to be loved right from when I was a kid. When I was little, I used to imagine being in love, and how exciting it would be to have a girlfriend. It would be so cool, I used to dream about it, remember, and I was always chasing what was cool. I used to imagine taking this mythical future girlfriend on romantic picnics, or rowing her out to the middle of a lake in a little boat, or strolling hand in hand through museums making little quips about all the artefacts, or snuggling up in the back row of a movie theatre feeding one another popcorn. Nonsense, really, or at least a very idealised version of what love actually was, but I was so obsessed by the idea of falling in love. When I was small, this quest to adore and be adored was focused on my mum or other older women who would show me affection. I was always first with kisses whenever my mum's friends would come round, I never ran away from hugs and didn't need to be asked twice if I wanted a cuddle on their knee. I think I knew, even back then, the happiness that comes from affection – the need to be desired and needed and wanted. But I didn't just want to lap up this attention and affection; I wanted to give it too. My mum still happily recalls one of my earlier romantic gestures, back when I was four years old. I was calling a young girl called Sophie Burnett my girlfriend at the time – which in a way shows my commitment issues were kept in much better check when I was four than when I was 24 – and we were taking part in an important formative athletic event – that is, the egg-and-spoon race. I was in the lead, of course, but looked back to see Sophie B had dropped the egg from her spoon. Ever the gentleman, I did the chivalrous thing and ran back and helped her put it back on – can you imagine our chubby little fingers trying our damnedest, sooooo sweet – and then I helped her over the finish, no doubt breaking the heart of every mother watching. So, you see, the need to please, and show affection, was always there. It's just that as I got older, I got less great at putting the egg back onto the spoon.

When I went away to boarding school, there were the under matrons; I was always building connections with women, because I hated the thought of being left out in the cold. So when I was old enough to be in relationships myself, it would be the same principle. Meeting a girl I fancied, I'd be chasing the romance, hurtling towards love as fast as I could. I suppose, early on, I mistook attraction and kindness and that feeling of slowly getting to know one another – and maybe even lust – for love, that we must be in love.

You might be wondering why, if I adore love so much, I'm so bad at relationships. Well, why I *was* bad at relationships, anyway; I definitely think I'm getting better at them, but maybe you would need to ask Sophie about that. But to be honest, I often used to ask myself the same question, because I couldn't really work out what was wrong with me. Why chase, declare undying love, and pledge commitment to these women if I couldn't take things all the way? It was so frustrating, because it wasn't like I did this on purpose.

I've never wanted to hurt anybody. You know what it's like sometimes, you can be too close to yourself, almost, too involved in your own life to see what's happening with any clarity. I suppose this is why people go to therapy, to get a handle on themselves. I was talking about this with my friend Georgie, who's watched my successes and stumbles in relationships since we were teenagers, and she hit the nail on the head: I never used to like being alone. I'm better at it now, I can enjoy my own company, but historically, I've always needed someone there. It seems obvious, I suppose, given as a child I was always crawling into my parents' bed at night or waiting for my brother to finish his violin playing so we could go to bed at the same time. And because I was such a romantic, I thought I should be in a relationship, I thought that's what I should be doing. And as Georgie reminded me, I did meet and date some wonderful, clever, funny, beautiful women, so why wouldn't I want to be in a relationship? But . . . and this was the big revelation to me, I guess: I didn't actually *want* to be in a relationship. Not at all. I wanted to be out with my friends, having fun. Especially after *Made in Chelsea* started, and there were all the opportunities to be out and partying. I'd always battled against authority, like parents, and teachers, and rules, but in relationships, I was battling with myself – there was the version of me that just wanted to grow up and settle down, and be older, but there was another side of me, that just wanted to taste the freedom of being an adult on a TV show, with every opportunity that came my way. I tried to run the two lifestyles at the same time, and this was where it would all go wrong, because I would find ways to let my girlfriends down. I would stay out at the party, leave them to go home alone, I would flirt with other women. And because I have this pathological fear of letting people down, I could never just be honest with them, and have the chat, and say, 'Look, I'm not ready for this', or be honest with them about not being able to commit, so I'd make things worse and worse until, eventually, they would just cut me out of their life. Which, of course, would leave me devastated and desperate to make amends. And on and on and on, over and over. Now I look back, having a proper relationship and trying to do *Made in Chelsea* at the same time was an impossible task for me. I had been part of many love dramas on the show over the years, but not many successful relationships.

The prime example of this would be my relationship with Tara. She was younger than me, still at university, and we were in this cycle of being together, me letting her down, her dumping me, and me begging for forgiveness. When this happened, I went into what at the time I imagined to be full romantic hero mode. She was at university in Bristol so I would dash down there on the train and wander round the campus to see if I could see her, and if there was no sign, I'd go round the town just on the off-chance I'd bump into her, or sit on the doorstep of her halls waiting to get a sight of her so I could beg her to take me back. I remember I would sit there feeling so sorry for myself, in utter devastation. I had lost the love of my life, I was convinced. I would never feel this way again. Oh, woe! Woe was me, who had ruined everything *again*. If only she would give me one more chance to prove how much I loved her. Yes, very deep and meaningful, I'm sure you'll agree; and no, I'm not especially proud of this display. Anyway, with me being on the TV and quite a high proportion of students watching *Made in Chelsea*, word soon spread that the blond, posh guy off E4 was hunched up on the steps to the halls of residence waiting for his girlfriend. Sometimes, if I was extra lucky, students would call out to me, either by my name, or 'It's YOU!' or, less thrillingly, '*Made in Chelsea* wanker!' or 'Posh twat'. Always great to meet someone who watched the show, at least. Anyway, word of my humiliation would eventually reach Tara and she would find me there, and either very generously forgive me, or tell me to fuck off. The success rate varied. Looking at it now, I get a huge cringe. Can you imagine? Thinking I can fix everything by getting on a train, sitting on the steps to her halls and expecting my inability to leave her the hell alone would make her feel sorry for me? At the time I thought it was very romantic, but now . . . I don't know. Vaguely creepy? Certainly tone-deaf. I'd definitely say to any man reading this – don't sit outside someone's house waiting for them so you can beg forgiveness.

What made it all worse was I was trying to juggle being on the show with being in a relationship – my head could feel quite busy with it all at times. I loved her, but I also loved doing the TV show. And if I was in a relationship with her, I couldn't really do the TV show. So why didn't I just let her go? In the end, ironically, something I did on the show became the final straw. Okay, so this sounds quite bad, but you have to remember, filming so intensely alongside people day in, day out really heightens your feelings, so you find yourself more drawn to each other than you might if you weren't on camera. Where I'm heading with this is that I told a girl called Jess, on the show, that I fancied her. I told her I really liked her. Now, this was true, even though I didn't intend to do anything about it, and it was a very sweet and romantic moment, but probably not the best thing to say to someone, on TV, when you already have a girlfriend. It gets worse. There's a lag between filming and transmission of the episode – about seven weeks. Now, you might think I would take this opportunity, almost two months, 49 days, plenty of time, to tell Tara what I'd said. Wouldn't it be better for her to hear it from me, so I could calm the waters, explain what I'd done, tell her it meant nothing, that I was lost in the moment? Yes, I agree, it would. Does that mean I did? No, I did not. Don't worry, you can't think worse of me for this than I already do myself, and my head goes straight to my hands whenever I think about it. But that's what happened; I didn't say a word, and instead Tara watched me tell her friend I fancied her – oh yes, she and Jess, btw, were friends, I kept that part back until now because I didn't want you to throw the book away in disgust. I know! I still feel bad. Nothing about this is romantic, or heroic.

So, I had to race off to Bristol for forgiveness and this time she was adamant she never wanted to see me, ever again. I was gutted. I'd always thought I could win her back, but this felt different. I must've left hundreds of messages for her, and quite rightly, she ignored every single one. I don't do well with heartbreak and I guess I made a fool of myself. One morning I woke up and saw a missed call from her, and I was distraught that I hadn't picked up. Looking at it with a clear head and no romantic notions, she had very probably sat on her phone, or her dog had dialled my number by mistake or something, but just in case she called again, I slept with my headphones in my ears for a month afterwards, so I'd hear it go off straightaway. Sad!

You might assume that someone who has been in love quite a few times, and sees himself as a romantic, might be into huge gestures, like whisking girlfriends off to Paris in a helicopter, or releasing a hundred doves into the air for my lover's birthday. But I'm actually not that showy – and I also have no idea where I would even get two doves, let alone a hundred. Hang on, actually, I did once take a girlfriend off to New York using my student overdraft, but that's a story for another time. I'm up for having fun and going out on dates, but that's not the side of love I'm interested in. I'm always attentive and caring, but if anything, the soppy side of me only really comes out when it's over, that's when I go full rom-com ridiculous. I remember, when I was 16, getting my heart broken by Daisy. It was possibly both the most romantic and pathetic setting for a dumping ever – we were in the middle of a bridge, in beautiful Oxford. Picture the scene: our star-crossed lovers are standing amid the dreaming spires, eyes locked on one another, as our Juliet quite definitively declares to Romeo that it's over. I reacted . . . well, I can say now as a man in my thirties that my reaction was somewhat over the top, okay. But, I felt this so deeply, I can still remember the electric charge of loss running through my veins, the tightness of my chest and the choking sound in my throat as I begged her to change her mind and . . . fell to my knees. Oh, yes, forget restrained devastation or a stiff upper lip, I got down on my knees and cried hot, salty, floods of tears at her feet. I can even remember my tears splashing onto her plimsolls and the pavement around us – actual waterfalls, like a cartoon character. This felt like the most romantic, crushing moment of my life, but even as it was happening, I could see this was like a low point for me, seriously uncool. It was also pretty useless, as Daisy was utterly unmoved. I realise now, of course, that I wasn't crying because we were madly in love, or had the most amazing relationship that was supposed to last forever. I was crying for myself, because I hated change, and things had been taken out of my control, and now I was going to be on my own. I was putting all that above what Daisy wanted – which was, essentially, to not go out with me anymore – even though I too knew it wasn't working.

This is the problem with thinking you're in love; it can make you selfish. I remember my girlfriend Lucy, the one I was devastated to leave at the airport before South America – I thought it would be the most romantic thing in the world to go to the same university as she did, which is part of the reason why I convinced Leeds University drama department to take me on their course despite my underwhelming results. Young love, inseparable, living together like proper grown-ups, enjoying all the freedom of going away to university . . . except, well, that's not how it works, is it? I think about it now, and I'm, like, why the HELL would you want to go to the same uni as your boyfriend or girlfriend? You are 19. Live your life! If the relationship survives being apart for three years, then excellent! And if it doesn't . . . oh well, the bar's always open.

That first year, we really isolated ourselves, spent time only together. So romantic, we thought then – but on reflection, a bit weird and obsessive and, even worse, we must've been such a pain to be around. We argued a lot, like a hell of a lot, and we clearly didn't want to be together at all. We weren't even having sex, just lying next to each other thinking that we would rather be anywhere else at all, which at that young age is just ridiculous – our parents were probably doing it more than we were. Yuk, what a horrible thought, but it's true!

And yet, predictably, even though all I wanted to do was break up with her, when she ended it, I was destroyed. Suddenly, I was on my own – a very small fish in a large pond, and I didn't have the usual stuff going for me that helped me attract girls. I didn't play sport anymore because of my knee. I wasn't a DJ, or someone with a promoters' list to get people into nightclubs. I didn't smoke weed like everyone else did. Yes, I was everyone's friend, and I was the small, cute, funny one, but not the kind of guy people wanted to date. It became a running joke at university that I wasn't kissing anyone, or sleeping with anyone at all. Everyone else was at it constantly, but not me. It was a huge blow to my confidence, and I didn't really know where I was going in life. I think this period is what influenced a lot of my behaviour on *Made in Chelsea*. Not that it's an excuse in any way, but it was like a chance to make up for those years when I'd felt a bit lost and unsure of what I was doing. Suddenly everything became accessible. But what happened was all my old insecurities came out, so I would try to date anyone and everyone. When I went into relationships, I would sabotage them, even if they were incredibly nice and wonderful and lovely, because deep down I didn't really want to be in them.

Yet I never gave up trying. I remember being very excited when Lucy invited me to her 21st birthday party. Even though it was definitely over, there was still a little light on in my head as I was thinking, 'Well maybe she wants me to go so we can get back together.' After all, we'd had some amazing times together, she was funny and sweet and one of the coolest people ever. I decided to make a romantic gesture and show her just how much she meant to me. I bought her a beautiful book by the famous photographer Mario Testino. I was sure this would show her I was thoughtful, right, and a grown-up, and not that silly kid she used to be with. I mean, it cost a fortune and I was still a student – my mum's emergency credit card was but a distant memory. So I arrive and place the gift on the table, proudly. I remember thinking how desperately I wanted to get back with her, how I couldn't accept it because she had broken up with me. Lucy's nowhere to be seen but her mum is there and greets me warmly. She notices the book.

'Oh, whose is that?'

'Mine,' I say. 'Well, Lucy's. I bought it for her birthday.'

She smiles genuinely. 'Oh, how lovely of you, that's so sweet.'

And then I notice Lucy's mum has a box with her, and she places it on the table, on top of my book. It's another present for Lucy. It's a shoe box. Within, some very special shoes. Louboutins, to be exact. Not exactly plimsolls, and certainly not a book. The truth is staring me in the face, but I choose to ignore it and ask Lucy's mum. 'Are these for Lucy? Are they a present from you?'

'Oh no,' she says, matter-of-factly. 'They're from Lucy's new boyfriend.'

And I look from her, back to the box of Louboutins, which are on top of my book. Those shoes are basically dancing all over it, in fact – it's like those spiked red heels are tip-tapping away right on my own head, into my eye sockets.

I am crushed, totally crushed, but instead of making a fuss, I say something trite like. 'How nice,' and pretend I knew about the new boyfriend all along. I've never been able to look at Louboutins the same way since.

I'm different now. I finally met someone I wanted to grow up for. Sophie is a proper hero to me, she's like a rockstar; there's never been anyone like her in my life and a day doesn't go by when I'm not constantly wowed by her. I am in awe, honestly. She gives me butterflies in my stomach, still. I remember someone saying to me, 'Do you want to be the last one to leave the nightclub, or do you wanna be the first to leave with your best friend?' The answer for me hasn't always been clear in the past, I've been torn. But now I know for sure: I want to be the first to leave with my best friend. She's stuck by me through everything and I would be absolutely lost without her – my world only makes sense because she's in it. I know I'm a better man these days because of Sophie; she's driven every positive change within me, and being with her makes me strive to be the best boyfriend I can possibly be. Am I the luckiest man alive? I think so.

Because before Sophie showed me the meaning of love, I struggled with it, I couldn't get a handle on what it was. I thought love was about being obsessed with someone, about thinking about them non-stop and always wanting to be by their side. Like, that feeling where you can't live without them. Not being able to live up to that was tough – especially as I also struggled with the concept of monogamy. I've always fought against rules and I hated being restricted. Love and monogamy felt all-consuming, they scared me a bit. I spoke to my dad about this once – he's been married three times – and he said there are pluses and minuses about monogamy, but life can be lonely if you're not with someone. I find that being in a relationship gives you balance. I thought life was about pleasure, all the time. And sometimes it is, but it's also about learning and growing and being balanced, having a job you love to do, having an impact on someone's life, having friends and family you connect with and speak to every day – and a monogamous relationship. Love isn't about not being able to breathe without the other person; it's about being content and bringing out the good in each other, and being able to bring up the bad things and deal with them. I used to think love was a feeling, but I see now it's almost like a situation you find yourself in, made up of so many different things that all come together. It's like a puzzle that Sophie has helped me solve. I'd jump in front of a car for Sophie if it came to it, and I think that when you love somebody, you put them above yourself without even realising that you're doing it. Whether it's saving their life or even something pretty simple like dividing up some cake and automatically giving them the larger piece – Sophie comes first, always.

As for romantic gestures, you can flash the cash, but I've found it's the little things that matter most. I remember when Sophie lost one of her precious earrings she'd had made from her grandmother's engagement ring, and I decided to get a replica made for her. Now I am generally the worst person in the world at surprises, because when I have an exciting idea all I want to do is tell everyone about it. But I held this one in, got these amazing replica earrings made and gave them to Sophie just before our second anniversary. It's a small thing really, and it wasn't a big flashy moment – I didn't even give them to her on our actual anniversary – but it was a very romantic moment and meant so much to her. Grand gestures can be fun, but they don't mean that much – it's the personal touch that make things special.

Chapter Ten
Entrepreneur

I have lots of ideas. While I've never had a typical job, as such, I've always had an eye for enterprise. I started young: when my mum asked me to dead-head the dying daffodils in the driveway, I negotiated a dead-heading fee of ten pence per daff. I was six years old, and already business minded. And, boy, did I go for it; I wanted to meet my targets. I brought Mum so many beheaded daffodils – some of them taken way before their time, now I think about it – that she didn't have enough money on her to pay me. I must call in that debt, actually. My head for business carried on at school too: I designed commemorative rugby shirts for anyone who was leaving and sold them on, making hundreds of pounds. My friends used to joke about LAT – Laing Added Tax. If there was an opportunity to be had to make a bit of cash, and show off my flair for ideas a bit, I was there. Sometimes my small businesses weren't entirely wholesome: I had a sideline at Radley College where I would acquire booze for my schoolmates and sell it to them. You know me, I like to be liked, and there's not many people a teenage boy will like more than someone who sells them booze underage. I remember one job I had for a catering company, handing out canapés at swish fashion events. Man, it was dull. I had to stand there, looking pretty, totally still with a huge gold-fish bowl in my hand, within which were some actual live fish, swimming about, and on top of that bowl . . . sushi. I mean, talk about being insensitive to the poor fish; it was like getting married in a graveyard. Have to admit, though, I only lasted a few days holding this heavy glass bowl, sushi right under my nose, for about £30 a shift.

The thing about having lots of ideas is you have to share them to make them a reality, and this is where you come across people who say 'No', that it can't happen and that you're crazy. I don't give up easily, though. I remember when I launched *Private Parts*, my podcast, with Francis, the first episode was recorded in a cupboard in my bedroom in the south of France. People told me podcasts were over, that nobody would be interested, what could I possibly have to say that was of interest, but Francis and I knew there was something there. A place to share our experiences and talk openly about issues affecting not just us, but everyone. One thing about me is that while I will happily give anything a try, I never expect it to work. I hope it will, obviously, but I never walk into a project thinking, 'Yep, this is going to be huge.' So, when something does work out, I'm always surprised. I mean, *Private Parts* has been hugely successful, has run for nearly five years and shows no sign of slowing down. We've attracted some huge star guests and bared our souls but, more importantly, we've helped a lot of people along the way. It has absolutely blown my mind that our little podcast is not only doing the numbers but genuinely making a difference. That's what it's all about and as much as Francis and I drive each other crazy and make fun of one another, we both know we're doing a good thing.

So, ideas? I have plenty, but when it comes to running a business, like the actual day-to-day . . . I'm not so hot at that. Cash flow, staffing, that kind of stuff, nope, best leave me out of it. I'll only make a mess. In fact, frankly, I think of myself as unemployable. I am! I just can't do what normal people do, and go to work every day and do set hours, in a suit. It feels so restrictive and, going on my past record, I would drive employers mad, asking too many questions, not focusing enough, skipping all the boring bits. In a way, I'm lucky that I have instinctively known what I'll be bad at – saves a lot of time and tears all round. Plus, while I had plenty of drive, it didn't extend to working for anyone else. I wanted to be my own boss. I never understood the concept of making someone else successful. It's not like I haven't tried, though. When I was a teenager, after I received my disappointing A-level results, my mum bet me I couldn't get a job. If there's one thing I like, it's a challenge, so I marched down to my local burger restaurant, and found a guy who looked like he was probably the manager – Adam, I think his name was, but it doesn't matter too much as he doesn't crop up in other chapters, this isn't a Batman origin story. I told him I wanted a job, and, to my surprise, instead of laughing like a drain, he asked me what I wanted to do. What were my skills? I thought about this. Did I have any skills? Well, lots, but how many of them would be useful in a high street Byron? Then I remembered a movie I'd watched recently where someone had said they worked 'front of house' and it sounded cool, so that's what I said. To my disbelief, Adam said, 'Great' and told me to come back the next day. So, I went home, crowed a bit about my amazing new career in hospitality to my incredulous mother, and rocked back up at the burger place the following day to find Adam wasn't there, and wasn't coming back. It turned out he'd quit, and my hiring was like his final joke before he sacked off the company for good. Nevertheless, the actual manager, who was not called Adam but let's not get into that again because who cares, put me to work as front of house and . . . well, naturally I was terrible at it. I had no idea what I was doing. Trying to remember how long someone had been at a table, managing queues, dealing with diners' questions and complaints sent me into a panic, I'd just walk off in silence – I was so out of my depth. I might as well have been handing out canapés in the ballroom of the *Titanic*. I lasted two weeks.

I used to really worry about not having a job when I was younger; I was very anxious about it. My friends were getting internships and moving forward but I had no clue what to do. Ever since Xander had told me stories about my imaginary adventures in Sweet World, I'd dreamed of owning my own sweet shop, but I wasn't sure how to make that happen.

Most success stories start with a kindly stranger taking a chance on a plucky kid, and mine was no exception. Thankfully, I don't suppose many are about a kindly stranger who buys a pornographic magazine for a primary school aged kid. But mine does and mine did. When I was little and on holiday, a man saw me staring at a copy of *Playboy* and asked if I wanted him to buy it for me. Now, this is all kinds of inappropriate because I was about seven, but maybe he didn't realise what the magazine actually was or maybe he thought I was a very short, young-looking grown up? I'd rather not dwell on that. Anyway, mortified, I said no, and ran out of the shop. But later on, after this man had left the resort, I found he'd left a copy of the magazine on my bed – yes, I agree, this doesn't sound totally normal – so what else could I do but flick through it? You might think that this was the first intimation of the reputation I now have as a ladies' man – that's haunted me for years – but I don't think it's that deep: I just liked the beauty and the glamour of it. And yes, there were naked women, but it wasn't hardcore pornography; it all seemed so stylish and aspirational. I hesitate to say tasteful but that's kind of what it was. This imagery really stayed with me and began blending into my existing fantasies about being a grown up.

In my very first interview for *Made in Chelsea* – in which I look and sound weird, by the way, total radio voice, as my mum would say – I said that I wanted to open a glamorous sweet shop and have my own version of playboy bunnies, the Candy Kittens, and become the Hugh Hefner of London. Well, I guess it's good to have ambitions, even if they are absolutely bonkers. And, like I said, even though I always aimed high, I've never expected to get that far off the ground.

But before we get to *MIC,* I had tried to get a proper job. I had interviews; I wore suits. I didn't realise then that I wanted to be an entrepreneur. I had no clue you could go and do stuff other than work in an office all day. I was always told you had to earn money in order to survive. And my catastrophising brain told me if I didn't earn money, I'd live on the streets and become an alcoholic. I had this interview for a financial company. I put on the suit and everything and I did a test. It was incomprehensible, going on and on about oil prices. I just kept staring at it like the words would magically change into something I knew about and understood, but they didn't. In my one-on-one interview, they were talking about the FTSE and my mind was whirring, like 'What the hell?' So I said to the interviewer that I thought footsie was something you played when you were flirting with a beautiful woman and . . . well, you can guess how all this ended.

Then *Made in Chelsea* came along, and it was a great diversion from having to think about the real world, but right from the beginning I knew I didn't want to be just another reality TV star, so I revisited my idea for a sweet shop. I imagined it like a cool sushi bar but for sweets, with a conveyor belt full of goodies and people paying top money for this amazing confectionery. I'd seen one in New York run by Ralph Lauren's daughter and I thought, 'Right, I have to do this,' especially when I saw how much people were spending at the till. My main concern was that it had to be cool. I wanted it to be very aspirational and stylish. I was obsessed by Abercrombie & Fitch at the time. As a teenager I used to lie to girlfriends and say I was an A&F model, and once I even got scouted by them in the street. They didn't make me a model, though; they shoved me into the stockroom. I wasn't even allowed to use the front door to get to work. But there were no hard feelings on my part and I couldn't deny how sexy and cool the brand was. That's what I wanted Candy Kittens to be. After all, sex is cool, and sweets are even cooler in my book. I wanted to combine the two. I wanted my sweets – which I already knew should be shaped like tiny kittens – to be like an accessory, a must-have that would look good in your hands or in your flat, and the shop had to be a must-visit destination. How I was going to make money out of this, I had no idea – I didn't even have any cash to get it going – but I knew it was my big chance to make something of myself.

Reality came crashing down hard on me – I discovered the cost of renting a shop would be about £3m a year. Three million. THREE MILLION. For just one year, and that's before you've done anything else, like . . . made the sweets, kitted the place out or hired your glamazonian assistants. I only had £3,000. I was feeling a bit lost until I met a guy called Nick Higgins when I did a PA at Loughborough nightclub – see, those PAs were a brilliant move, Spencer was right all along. He ran a business that made T-shirts and suggested we made some branded tees to get Candy Kittens out and into the public consciousness, and I thought 'Yes, what a great idea.' It was a way to make it feel like I was one step closer to achieving something. He introduced me to his flatmate Ed Williams, who had just graduated in design. The first thing Ed said to me was a pretty big truth-bomb: I should give up on having a sweet shop and sell sweets online instead. I wasn't sure – it had been my dream, and I thought it was important to never lose sight of my dreams. But then he showed me the designs he'd done, of the sweets and the packets and, honestly, they blew my mind. I'm good at imagining stuff, I can visualise in great detail, but I'm not great at getting things down on paper – I can't draw or anything like that. It was like Ed had somehow seen inside my mind; the designs were perfect! A beautiful relationship was born, and my dream became a shared goal. Ed and his friend Warren packed up and moved to London and for a while they both slept on my floor while we made this happen.

Now, I didn't want to go at this half-arsed; I really wanted this to work, so I realised it would be a good idea to start mentioning my plans on *Made in Chelsea*. I talked about it on the show and even got filmed meeting my bank manager. I really wanted this to get off the ground. I wanted to make the best sweets possible, so Ed and I trooped off to a huge annual convention of the confectionery industry in Germany, our heads full of stars, thinking we were going to walk away from the place as the next Haribo. For our first move we went up to the biggest sweet manufacturer we could find and asked if they could make our sweets. Now, let's put this into perspective: you know when you're a kid and you make what you call 'perfume' by mixing rose petals with water in an old jar? Well, this is like going to Chanel with a grimy jar of stagnant rose cologne and asking them, 'Please will you make this perfume for us in your factory?' It could've been a straight no, but I think they kind of admired our pluck: here were two kids just starting out and taking a chance, so instead they said, 'Well, just to let you know, our minimum order is 300 tonnes of sweets, about £4 million, a year.' Oh, okay, we have a bit more work to do, we thought.

Then we talked to another factory, who said they would do our sweets – we were thrilled! – but then they said it would take them 18 months. What the hell were we supposed to do now? We had all this energy, and drive, and momentum, and sheer determination to make this happen. A year and a half was way too long – plus we needed to get the money together, and I had already nearly messed the whole thing up by going off to do a PA in Ireland, missing my plane back home (hungover, yes) and not turning up to an investors' meeting. It was awful – Ed was so cross with me he didn't want to be my partner anymore, and my mum and stepdad marched down to my agent and demanded they take control of me otherwise I was going to fuck up everything. Luckily, I pulled it back, but I was aware, if I wanted this to work, I was going to have to get my act together. It was time to get serious.

But we really were lost: a sweet company with absolutely zero sweets. So what about the T-shirts? We had some great designs, with either 'I'm a Candy Kitten' or 'Candy Kittens Team' on them – just in case anyone didn't want to be objectified by a T-shirt slogan – so we decided, why not just launch the tees and, I don't know, magic the confectionery company into existence? Worth a try, right? In the new series of *Made in Chelsea*, I gave my cast-mates free T-shirts, and talked up the company. Then, after the first episode had aired, we launched our website thinking we might drum up a bit of interest and maybe sell a few T-shirts. Boy, was I in for a surprise. That first night, we sold £25,000 worth of T-shirts. Twenty. Five. Thousand. Can you believe it? I *still* can't! We didn't even have the money to make them – we had to get Nick to do them for us on credit. Now that we knew there was demand, our next move was to open a pop-up shop on the Kings Road in the heart of – where else? – Chelsea! It was over two floors and, just to remind you, there was not a single Candy Kittens sweet in existence, not even a branded grain of sugar to be had. But what we did have was tons of branded merchandise: pencil cases, jumpers, tote bags, all sorts of things – just, no sweets. We had a smoothie maker in the corner but that was about it. We decided to go big on this, and have a glitzy press night. I wanted to look the part, so I donned my most hated type of outfit, a dreaded suit. I never wear a suit. Everyone came for the press night; it was incredible. Well, it was incredible until we noticed at the end of the night that people had been helping them-selves to the merchandise because they thought it was all free! Most launches have a goody bag of free stuff, I know, but this was ridiculous; they'd stripped it just like piranhas at an all-you-can-eat buffet.

As we were locking up that night, some girls arrived and said they were camping out all night so they could be the first to get inside the shop on opening day; they'd come all the way from Surrey, specially. I was, like, are you serious? You're going to sleep outside my shop, even though there are no sweets in there? It was like a Harry Potter book launch or something. But even then, I don't think I realised what was happening. That night Ed and I went out to celebrate and the next morning, feeling deathly hungover, I woke to my phone ringing. It was Ed. Uh-oh, what had happened? He was calling from the shop, as he'd gone to open it up.

'Jamie,' he said, sounding mildly spooked, 'I think you need to get down here.'

I was living only a few streets away back then, so I got ready and kind of shuffled in the vague direction of the shop. As I approached the Kings Road, I could see a gigantic crowd of people. I thought, 'What the hell is this?' Is the Queen here or something? Turns out it was a queue. Can you tell where this is going? Yep, it was the queue for the Candy Kittens pop-up. It was wild! We were . . . a phenomenon? People were really interested in a brand we had created. I like to be liked, true, but this was validation I'd never counted on. Amazing!

People really wanted our stuff – I remember being there at opening time on another day and watching this girl who was the first person in the place, running in like she was being chased by a tiger. She didn't know what to do first, so she just started grabbing things, like she was in a panic. We were bowled over by this success; we felt like such amateurs, we didn't even know what on earth we were doing – but the public didn't care. I've always said that naivety is the biggest weapon you'll ever have. It's a Blake quote, I think: innocence is broken by experience. If we'd been experienced businessmen, we'd have done it all differently; maybe it wouldn't have been as good. If we'd calculated and schemed a bit more, and had had really precise business plans with all kinds of projections, it would not only have been less fun, but maybe people who liked us would have seen through it, and not got on board with the brand. We wouldn't have done a pop-up shop, we would've just sat on our hands and waited the 18 months to make the sweets, we wouldn't have done these jumpers and T-shirts, or anything. But I think our naivety – or you could call it stupidity, if you want to be harsh, but how dare you – showed how genuine we were.

We took a chance. Being innocent is a marvellous thing. That's why children are so truthful; they haven't yet been tainted by the consequences of being dishonest.

I remember once walking down the street and seeing a guy coming towards me who was wearing a T-shirt that looked vaguely familiar. Actually, the closer he got, the more familiar it looked. There was no mistaking it, his T-shirt said 'I'm a Candy Kitten.' I looked at him, he looked at me, I looked down at the T-shirt, he looked a bit more intently at my face – I saw the connection spark, and we obviously telepathically decided that the best thing to do was just nod, walk on, and go about our business. It was mortifying, but hilarious. It never really occurred to me I'd see my brand out there in the wild like that. When Ed got married, and we needed an embarrassing outfit for his stag do, can you guess what we selected? Yep, a good old, very tight-fitting 'I'm a Candy Kitten' T-shirt. And we didn't let him take it off even for a minute. Hey, free advertising is free advertising, right?

Anyway, after two weeks, our amazing pop-up adventure was over and in that short time we'd had made an impressive £80,000. I didn't even have a proper business bank account. I was just transferring money here and there from my own current account. But now we could pay to get the sweets made, and get going, and Candy Kittens in its true form was realised. It was a bumpy road and we made some big mistakes – I still remember hiring these swanky lawyers and not realising how expensive it would be until we got the £15,000 bill, around five times the money we actually had to launch the business. But we made it work.

My friend Rory always says, don't follow logic, as it always brings you back to the same place as everybody else. Instead, you should go against the grain, and we certainly did that. As an entrepreneur, naivety is often your greatest weapon. I'm not saying don't take advice or listen to the opinions of others, but you should trust your gut. When you're building your own business, or following your own ideas, you will nearly always make mistakes, and you will often feel like a failure, but I'm a firm believer that 50 per cent of success in anything is about turning up, giving it a shot, working hard and trusting your instincts. I ignored advice from lots of people when I put all of my savings into Candy Kittens. There was a moment in the early days when things weren't going well – because most businesses never do that great at first – and we had a meeting with my stepfather, who's chairman of my company, and he said, 'Look, I don't know what you guys are going to do.'

Ed and I walked down the road feeling kind of despondent, and I said, 'Ed, please don't leave me. Please don't go anywhere.' Gotta love my abandonment complex, right? And Ed said back to me, 'If I have to sell sweets from my bedroom, I will, don't worry.' And he meant it. We were only kids, about 23 or 24, and I adore him so much for that. He stuck by me, and he stuck at it. We both did. We turned up every day and we worked incredibly hard.

I'm so glad we did it, because I've always felt I had something to prove. All my life, people around me have wondered what the hell I was going to do with myself – when I left school, after university, after my travels, *Made in Chelsea*, whatever, and now I have something that says, 'I did that!'

And now we're the fastest growing confectionery brand in the UK so, I guess I did something right, yes?

But, seriously, Ed, please don't ever leave me; I still have absolutely no idea what I'm doing. Like, ever.

Chapter Eleven
Horror Movie

Nobody's perfect, I know that. We've all got our little hang-ups about the way we look, or how we speak, or act. We all wish we were a bit thinner, or more ripped, a little more confident, maybe. I suppose the difference for me was that, unlike most people, my imperfections and hang-ups were right there for everyone to see on a TV show every week, for a decade. Every little flaw, every doubt I'd ever had about myself was being broadcast to the nation, sometimes on very large screens. I've told you how I remember watching myself on *Made in Chelsea* for the first time and thinking, 'What the HELL?' Seeing my head from all angles, what my body looked like in relation to others, how clothes looked on me. It was like finding out my bedroom mirror – and every mirror or window I'd looked in to see my reflection – had been lying to me. I even considered a nose job at one point, and went for a consultation, but all the noses they suggested for me would've made me look like I should have been on *Made in Whoville*, not *Made in Chelsea*. And, yes, I did have Botox once. It didn't really work out too well for me; I had the permanent look of someone who's just stood on Lego in bare feet. I was desperate for it to wear off – I even spent every day in a sauna for 45 minutes because I heard that helped it deactivate quicker.

My face, well, I've just had to learn to live with it, I guess, but I have a bit of a love-hate relationship with my body. I'd always been quite athletic as a teenager, but when I couldn't play rugby anymore, back when I was 18, I put on quite a bit of weight, because I carried on chomping my way through my rugby-player diet but wasn't working off the energy. I remember someone saying to me I looked 'stocky', but I didn't even notice at first – I looked in the mirror and thought I looked good. This was before camera phones, so you wouldn't often see photos of yourself all over the place, but then one day I did. I don't know how to explain it, but I didn't look like me. There's nothing wrong with being bigger, I know that now, and I believe body positivity is really important, but I just didn't look like me – this was not the body I'd been living in. I just remember this strange feeling of shame, of seeing how my body must look to others, and that was the beginning of my weight issues. I would try not to eat too much, and aimed to cut as many calories out of my day as I could. When anyone offered me food, I would lie and say that I'd already eaten, and I'd buy things like reduced fat houmous, but hide it so nobody knew I was eating low-fat food. I saw booze as empty calories, so I stopped drinking alcohol entirely for about a year and a half. I barely ate and was so conscious of every little thing I put inside my body. I convinced myself skinny meant attractive, skinny meant people were going to fancy me. Gradually, I stopped obsessing – and I started loving myself, and stopped caring so much about how I physically looked – and a bad break-up also soon had me back on the booze. I suppose I had even bigger things to worry about than my body. I know now that if you obsess over what you look like, and think about it all the time, it only takes you down a negative dark hole, but I also know how hard it is not to obsess over it – and I must admit I still have my self-conscious moments.

I mean, I've always known my limits: you're never going to see me on a catwalk, and I may not be an athlete, but I'd always kind of thought I was okay in the looks department. More than okay. I'm cute, right? I have a nice smile. I'm not super-tall – five-foot-nine – but everything is in proportion. I'm, what? An eight out of ten? Nine on a good day if I'm on a red carpet? Four if I'm hungover. Nobody's a ten, are they? Except maybe Zac Efron, or Brad Pitt? Sophie, she's definitely a ten, yes, but me? Eight. I was happy with that. But on TV, I saw my score plummeting. *Why* was my head that shape? From behind I looked like a completely different person. What machines did I need to use in the gym to make me look like myself? It was like staring at my own evil twin – well, at his arse, anyway. Horrifying. It didn't help that of all the little hang-ups or whatever, I had two big ones. Two things have always bothered me. One, I've already touched upon. My height. Five-nine. I know it's not that short but I've always wished I could be taller. So much taller. I've never liked being small. It was handy when I was little and needed to be cute so I could get my own way or talk myself out of trouble, but as I got older I always found myself wishing I could have a bit more height going on.

And there's not a lot you can do about it, if you're short. You can wear heels, I suppose, but people would probably notice my height even more if I arrived everywhere tottering in on three-inch heels. And I probably wouldn't be able to walk in them; I may as well wear stilts, or just have a big neon sign saying 'five-nine, actually' flashing above my head. What you might not know about TV is that people tend to look much taller than they actually are. I've met a few famous people now and most of them are tiny, and there's always that reaction when I meet someone for the first time, where they go, 'Oh', as if they were expecting a giant. I've only tried to do something about my height once, and it taught me a valuable lesson. When I was first asked to be on *Strictly Come Dancing*, in 2019, I was very excited, but immediately conscious that *Strictly* is watched by millions of people across the country, most of whom would have no idea who I was and would be seeing me for the first time. And it felt like . . . well, there wasn't that much of me to see. The sets on *Strictly* are huge, and some of the other guys taking part that year had a decent bit of height about them. I mean legendary goalkeeper David James was on that year, and he's six-foot-four – what if I ended up standing next to him for some reason? I wasn't exactly panicking about this or anything, but it was on my mind. Then someone told me about 'lifts' – no, not the kind that take you up to Soft Furnishings in Peter Jones, I mean little blocks you can put into your shoes that make you seem a little taller without actually making your shoes look higher. Seemed like a foolproof plan – all I had to do was slip these miracles into my dancing shoes and I'd be . . . well, okay, I wouldn't exactly be towering above everyone, but at least I'd have a couple of extra inches of confidence. I know people always say size doesn't matter, but in this case, and to me, it definitely did.

It was going pretty well right up until we began filming the launch show, where we had to do a big group dance. I'll talk much more about *Strictly* in a bit, of course, but that day I was so excited, I just couldn't wait to get going. When it came to my big moment, I was supposed to pop up in front of the camera and then do a kind of slide across the dance floor, which I did, but . . . uh-oh. Ouch. What the . . .? Whatever had happened had really hurt. I felt something go in my foot – turned out I'd given myself plantar fasciitis from these stupid lifts. I couldn't believe it, both that my *Strictly* hopes were dashed, and that my vanity had been the cause. Well, maybe calling it vanity is too strong. There's a fine line between vanity and insecurity, isn't there? And that's what it was. I've always wanted to be the best I could possibly be, look the best, and have the most fun, and be as confident as possible. The lifts in my shoes gave me a bit of a boost, and I don't just mean in measurements. I know it's silly, but just feeling that inch or two taller gave me extra confidence. I was so embarrassed that I didn't tell anyone what had caused it. I went to scores of doctors trying to find someone who would give me the all-clear to appear on the show. Only one guy said it might be possible but he warned me that if I tore the ligament any further I could end up with something called 'floppy foot', which sounds just horrible, doesn't it? So I had to pull out, and watch all the fun from home, nursing my torn ligament and my bruised ego.

There's another thing I have a hang-up about too. Well, not so much now, for reasons that will become obvious, but it's my hair. My crowning glory, my gleaming halo, my all-things-bright-and-beautiful blond bombshell look. For many years now, I've been a little worried that my hair may well turn out to be just like I used to be when faced with commitment – keen to do a runner. I only have to look at my dad – as a family we've been monitoring his encroaching baldness since we were kids. Poor Dad always had to deal with us shouting out about his 'bald spot'. So I've always been on my guard and a little self-conscious about how my hair looks. I suppose I can laugh about it now, but it's a serious matter for many men. Sixty-five per cent of men experience hair loss and one of the most visited sections of the website for the men's mental health charity CALM – Campaign Against Living Miserably – relates to hair loss. It's a big deal, and not just about vanity. Losing your hair changes your whole look. My friend Francis always says to me, 'We're not losing hair, Jamie, we're gaining face', and it always makes me laugh, but I'm perfectly happy with the amount of face I've got, thank you very much; I don't need any more right now.

I'd always flirted with the idea of doing something about my hairline. I used to take supplements and medications that would encourage hair growth or help hold on to what I already had, like Propecia, these drops you can take. They seemed to be doing the trick, but then when I was suffering with anxiety, I became convinced the anti hair-loss drugs were messing with my hormones, attacking them in some way and sending me haywire. I mean, I was in denial here:

it was much more likely to be down to the fact that I was hardly sleeping and partying too much but, no, in my head I was certain it was the hair drops. So I stopped taking them, and watched as my hair slowly but surely began to make its long drawn-out exit.

Then I met my friend Rodney. Well, Rodney was more a friend of a friend, to be honest, but we bonded because he was in a similar situation to me, in that his hair was going on a round-the-world tour and not taking him along with it. He asked if I'd ever considered a hair transplant. I had, as it happened. I'd done a bit of research and seen that they were mega expensive, and to make it even slightly affordable you would have to fly out to Turkey to get one done, and even then they were over £12,000 – not the kind of money I had lying around at the time (or indeed any time – I am not the McVitie's heir, remember). But Rodney had a solution: he'd found a place in the UK that could do it and, best of all, if we both went to have it done, we could get a deal. A discount. Alarm bells should have been ringing, shouldn't they? Think about it, someone offering you a 2-for-1 or a buy-one-get-the-other-half-price discount on something like a McDonald's or a sandwich in the supermarket is a pretty good deal and not that unexpected – but surgery? Really? 'Oh yes, just drop in with a friend and we'll offer you mates' rates on a very complicated hair transplant' – sounds legit. So just a tip for you here: if someone offers you a special deal on a bulk buy of hair transplants, have a think about it first.

More alarm bells should've gone off when Rodney mentioned that he had already had a hair transplant before. The signs were not good if he needed another. And yet, me being me, Mr 'What's-the-worst-that-could-happen?', first place in the world championships of delayed regret, I say yes!

On the way up there in the car, I begin to have doubts. I badger Rodney for reassurance, and he's cool as a cucumber.

'Will it be okay, Rodney? Are you sure?'

'Absolutely, dead easy. You've got tattoos, right?'

Indeed I have.

'Well,' he says, 'It's just like getting a tattoo, very chilled.'

What could I do? Do a jump and roll from the moving car into the middle of a motorway? I suppose I could have asked him to let me out at the next services station but instead I choose to believe him, and we carry on. We get to Nottingham and arrive at the place where Rodney says the transplant is going to happen. When Rodney told me we were getting a discount, it's true that I wasn't exactly expecting a top-flight, glamorous Swiss clinic in the mountains, which is good, because we appeared to have pulled up outside someone's semi-detached on the outskirts of Nottingham.

'Rodney, this is a house.'

'Yep, this way. It's gonna be fine, relax.'

I now know for absolute sure this is not a good idea. A woman named Tatiana opens the door and ushers us through to a back room, via her kitchen. My stomach is churning. I've done it again, haven't I? Got myself into a right mess. Worst of all, I've already paid – I had to hand over the money when confirming the appointment. So I walk into Tatiana's makeshift surgery and she's very friendly, which is great, but isn't really giving off professional vibes.

'Let's have a look at you, then,' she says.

I stare back, searching for the words. 'What?'

She points at my head. 'The cap. You need to take it off. Can't do much with it on.'

She looks my head over. 'Hmmm,' she says. 'You don't really need it, do you?'

'Don't I?'

'Well, no, you're fine, really, but we're here now, so let's do it anyway.'

I could've backed out at this point, but I'm too scared and also, I don't want Tatiana – a total stranger – to think I'm rude or get cross with me. I might as well do it, I tell myself, Just do it. It's like a tattoo, remember, Rodney had said, totally chilled.

So I start to relax a bit and ask a few questions. Now seems the right time to mention that I have a photoshoot the next day; I'm doing a cricket campaign with Stuart Broad and it's kind of a big deal. That'll be okay, surely, I'll be all better by then, yes?

Tatiana shakes her head. 'You can't do that.'

'I can't? What do you mean?'

She looks at me like I might be insane. 'You'll need to rest, afterwards,' she says. 'We don't know what it's going to look like. It's worse than getting a nose job this, you know.'

And then I am imagining all sorts of horrific outcomes. Stitching all over my scalp like Frankenstein's monster, or all my hair falling out, or being unrecognisable. And yet, *and yet*, no, I still don't back out.

She draws a line on the front of my head to show where my hairline will be. If I'm honest, it still looks too far back to me, like I'm still receding, but I am gripped by terror and in no mood to argue. She gets me to lie face down on what looks like a massage table, my face squished into a hole to hold my head steady. Rodney also settles into his, a few feet away. When he said we had got a deal for getting it done together, he was serious; Tatiana will be flitting between the two of us during the procedure, like a bluebottle between two frittatas at a barbecue. She numbs my scalp with a local anaesthetic. Well, numbs is too strong a word – she dulls it a bit. And then she starts drilling. That's right, drilling. Okay, don't faint or freak out, she's not actually drilling into my head with a power tool – she's taking a very sharp implement and gouging out the hair follicles from the parts of your head where they always grow back, the back and sides. And she does this 2,000 times. I'll write it again, in words, so you can see this isn't a mistake: two thousand times. TWO. THOUSAND. It's not a great sound, I have to admit; it sounds like someone is crunching onto freshly laid snow, and it feels kind of crumply and rough in my head as she roots about for these unsuspecting hair follicles, all two thousand of them. She plonks the extracted follicles into a little petri dish beside me. And then? Well, I have to turn round, lie on my back and she has to implant every single one of them back into my head, at the front. A big day for these follicles. *Fuck.*

Spoiler: this isn't like getting a tattoo. It's like having a tattoo, but using the nose of a fighter jet as the needle. And this takes seven hours. The last hour is agony, as the anaesthetic is wearing off and Tatiana can't give me any more because I've already had the legal limit – suddenly laws and regulation are important! My whole head and face just hurts, hurts, hurts, like it's on fire and someone's trying to put the fire out with cricket bats. I am very miserable by this point. 'This can't possibly get any worse,' I think; I am in excruciating agony, but at least it's over, it is done, and soon I will have a lustrous mane. And then I catch sight of myself. I look . . . this is not good. It's a vision of horror. I look like a bloated corpse, like I'm having a very unhappy Hallowe'en indeed. My scalp is a mass of dried blood and tangled wisps of hair, also soaked in blood. I turn to Rodney, who also looks like his head has been blow-torched.

'This is not like getting a tattoo! Why didn't you warn me?' I look like I've been dunked in boiling oil. Tatiana bandages me up, and hands me a little spray bottle.

'What's this?' I ask, shell-shocked still.

'Salt water. You have to spray it on every two hours.'

Spray it on? What has she planted in my scalp? Hair, or cress?! 'Every two hours? What about when I'm asleep?'

'Set an alarm. Every two hours.'

I daren't ask what happens if I don't spray it, so I take the bottle.

She hands us two valiums for the pain, and we leave. Rodney is driving, which probably isn't safe after anaesthetic and two tranquilizers, but it's hard to see how things could get any worse. My head, my poor head. My hair! Will I ever look normal again?

'Look Rodney,' I say, 'you can't tell anyone about this, okay? It's a secret. I don't want anyone to know I've had this done.'

Quite how I hope to hide this from people is anyone's guess, but at the moment keeping this quiet is my top priority.

'Yeah, Jamie, no problem. Won't tell a soul, don't worry.'

We pull into a service station for petrol. We're all mummied up, like, covered in bandages; we look ridiculous. But so far nobody is looking, miraculously. Rodney fills up and I start to walk into the shop. Then I hear shouting. Uh-oh. I turn, to see Rodney hasn't put the handbrake on, so the car is rolling away, and Rodney is trying to stop the car but also deal with the petrol pump in his hand. Swarms of people emerge from their cars and from inside the garage shop to witness this spectacle, all shouting 'Whoaaaaa!' And then one person says – and it only ever takes one person to notice you before the onslaught begins – 'I know you.' I keep quiet. He goes on. 'Yeah, you're that bloke off *Made in Chelsea*.'

Great, the one kind of attention I don't like. And here I am standing in a petrol station forecourt looking like I'm auditioning for *Saw*. 'Um, yes, that's right, hi,' I reply, meekly, as if that is going to make everything go away. The next question is inevitable.

'What you done to your head?'

Before I can make something up, or feign a heart attack or something, Rodney for some bizarre reason decides now is the time to pipe up. 'Oh, he just had a hair transplant.'

What the fuck, Rodney?! I can't believe it! Maybe the valium has made him forget that about 20 minutes earlier I said this was a secret. We travel back, my head throbbing both with pain and anxiety about this getting out. I have to tell my agency to push the campaign back for a day, which is the right decision: my head the next day looks like a bag of meat.

Just when I think I've got away with it, disaster strikes – my agency get a phone-call from a tabloid. They know about the transplant. They have photos! They're going to run a story on it. This is awful; how the hell has this happened? I feel like I have no control over this, I need to take it back. I decide to swallow my pride and announce on *Made in Chelsea* that I've had the transplant. That way, the story will be worthless, I will show I have nothing to hide, and, you know, maybe it will help other people out there with hair loss to know that I've had problems too. So that's what I do, I go on the show and I talk about the process – and I feel so powerful! A man renewed! I've beaten the media, I've played the system, I don't have to live in fear anymore, I've taken ownership of my life. Yes, I get a bit of a ribbing from the press for doing it, but who cares? At least I wasn't exposed as having a dirty little secret.

And then I speak to Rodney. There was no tabloid calling the agency. It was him, just as a little joke, pretending. So my hair transplant was now public knowledge, had been broadcast to hundreds of thousands of people, for no reason, and I hadn't wanted anyone to know, ever. Amazing.

But I have to laugh about it now, because it could have been so much worse, and I have learned to live with how I look – more or less. I was reading that two-thirds of men at some point in their lives feel like they need to change their appearance to make themselves happy, or to fit in, and that's a sad statistic. As I've got older, I've learned that you love yourself when you feel comfortable in yourself. Like my hair, and my height, most people are so focused on themselves, they don't care if you have a receding hairline or if you're really five-foot-nine. The less you care about yourself, the more free you'll feel at the end of the day. I mean, I've got this hair transplant now, and it looks fine, but there's a very real chance it will start to look ridiculous in time. The hair follicles that Tatiana so lovingly chiselled into my scalp will never die – they're here for the long haul – but my hair further behind my hairline is my natural hair, and that could recede further, or even disappear altogether, so I'll be stuck with hair round the sides and back, and a little fin of hair at the front, like the world's most pathetic unicorn, or Jedward after a fight with a lawnmower. But I suppose I'll deal with that when it happens – or not, maybe I'll just learn to live with it.

It's what's inside that counts though, right? This is what I keep telling myself.

Chapter Twelve

Clown

Anyone who knows me will tell you, I'm a bit of a joker. Okay, I'm a *lot* of a joker. Almost all my friends and pretty much all my family have been pranked by me at one time or another. I don't know why I love playing tricks on people so much – but I've always had a naughty streak and although I have a serious side, I do like to have fun. It's the reactions, I think, that I love most. You never quite know how it's going to go, you see. Obviously, you hope that whoever you're playing a trick on will quickly see the funny side and laugh along with you, but . . . well, sometimes it's even funnier if it takes them a little longer to get it. Those excruciating moments before you reveal it's a prank just have me doubled up with laughter. I prank Sophie all the time and I think I must drive her mad, although I do get her laughing eventually. You'd think she'd be used to it by now, but I still manage to catch her out every now and then. The element of surprise – there's nothing quite like it.

My favourite person to prank, though, and probably the one I play the most tricks on, is my lovely mum. Hasn't she been through enough having a wild child like me in her life, you might ask? Well, yes, probably, but she's such a good subject to prank. Her reactions are always priceless. She gives it everything, really falls for it and then . . . when the payoff lands, she never disappoints. And then we both laugh about it – usually just in time for her to remember that I'm her son and she loves me and that, as much as she wants to hit me over the head with something for pranking her, she probably shouldn't. The thing with pranking, though, is that you always want to top your last joke. I'm all about pushing the envelope, seeing how much I can get away with and, because a mother's forgiveness is . . . well, it's usually automatic, I save my best ones for Mum. The most successful pranks play into little doubts or annoyances that people have and I know for a fact that my mum hates tattoos with a passion. I have quite a few of them already, and every time I've shown her a new one, she's been annoyed with me. 'Why would you want to do that to your lovely skin?' she always says. Honestly, she acts like I've had it tattooed on her as well! Worst thing you can do to a prankster is show them your weakness though, right? So that's why I decided if I was going to get Mum, I needed to get her good.

I decided I was going to tell Mum that I'd got my then-girlfriend's name tattooed across my chest. Actually, I wasn't just going to tell her I'd done it – I was going to show her. I had a special transfer made up with the name in massive letters and had it applied to my chest. This was . . . big. If it had been real, it would have been pretty life-changing. The letters were very big. I was already chuckling to myself when I saw the result. This was going to be good, unmiss-able. If my mum freaked out at my tiny tattoos – which she did – she was going to go nuclear when she laid her eyes on this beauty. So I did what any other normal son would do and set up cameras in my Candy Kittens office to film her reaction. What, you don't think that's totally normal? Speak to my family – that's an average day when you're with me. I knew Mum's reaction would be absolute gold content and, look, we've all done it, we've all thought something would be just perfect for Instagram or our YouTube channel, haven't we? Right? Exactly. So, we're all set, the cameras are in place, and I am ready to film this gold content. Everyone at work is in on it and is keeping as straight a face as possible.

It was like a military operation, with texts and messages going back and forth. 'She's on her way in. Get ready.' I was excited.

So in comes Mama and I can tell right away that this is not going to be straightforward. I know my mum and I can always tell when she's not in a very good mood and let's just say on this particular day she looks like she's in absolutely no mood for any of my shenanigans. But I've come this far, I've got the cameras set up, everyone's in place and I am practically vibrating with excitement at the thought of this huge transfer under my shirt. I can't back out now.

We have a little bit of the usual chit-chat, but I can't hold it in any longer. So I said, 'Hey Mum, so . . . I got a new tattoo.'

Well, she didn't like that at all. An eye-roll. Tutting. A cross look on her face. She began her usual protests.

'No, but listen,' I said, 'it's really nice. I think you'll like this one. Let me show it to you.'

The rest seemed to happen in slow motion. As I carefully began to unbutton my shirt, I kept my eyes on my mum's face and . . . okay, so I've seen my mum disappointed before, but this was next-level. At the first sight of the ink peeping out from my unbuttoned shirt, her face began to drop, her whole demeanour totally changed. And the more I revealed, the worse it got. Instead of raging at me like she usually does, her voice went quiet and kind of crackled, like she couldn't quite get the words out. I saw her looking over the tattoo, the colossal letters spelling out the name. Now, I had to weigh up my options here; I must admit I was starting to panic slightly because . . . this didn't look good. The plan had been for Mum to fly into a rage and hit me with a barrage of the usual 'How could you do this?' and 'Why have you destroyed your beautiful skin?' and 'You realise this is *forever*, Jamie?!' Usually I can hold out for quite a while, so I was hoping to keep this going for as long as I could and then reveal it was just a transfer. But there was none of that, just Mum, quiet and visibly upset, devastated in fact. I admit that even at this point, in my head, I was kind of thinking, this is fantastic content. But I was also thinking, this is my mum and I love her, and she looks like her entire world has collapsed and I don't think I can carry this on without emotionally scarring her for life. So I had to put a stop to it. 'No, look, it's not real, it's a transfer, honestly, it's fake, look.'

The relief on her face! But even though I'd revealed it was all a joke, she wasn't ready to let it go. You know how when you have a dream about your partner cheating on you, maybe, or you fall out with a friend, and then you wake up and even though you know it wasn't real, you still feel inexplicably mad at them, or a bit sensitive about it? That's what it was like for my mum. Honestly, a week later, even though she knew the tattoo was just a joke, she was still upset by it, at the thought that it could've been real. I realised maybe I'd gone a little too far this time, so I resolved not to prank her again, and I haven't done, and I won't. Unless . . . that's just what I want her to think . . . (No, honestly, Mum, I won't, promise.)

Even when I'm not purposefully pranking someone, I get myself into the weirdest situations sometimes, all kinds of scrapes. And they're not always of my making . . . Take the time my best friend Georgie and I went to the casino, for example. That should've been a very straightforward night out: two friends, a few drinks, a little bit of gambling. But as you may have noticed, there's no such thing as straight-forward with me, and especially not when I'm with Georgie. But I'm jumping ahead. So, after my little trial of casino lifestyle when I was 17, when I'd won and lost a few hundred pounds, I'd been dabbling ever since. Nothing too huge, no megabucks bets with the McVitie's millions (not real) or anything like that, just a few trips to the blackjack table every now and then. I used to go with Georgie when we were at Leeds University together. There was this slot machine there that Georgie loved to play, called Lucky Lady – it was her favourite ever, she loved it more than anything. So while I was off playing blackjack, she was sinking her cash into Lucky Lady. One time she got so into it that she ended up getting arrested. Basically, we were in the casino having a 'few' drinks and she'd been having a very good night on the

Lucky Lady and had won all this money. She remembered the high of winning and collecting the cash and then she had one of those moments of drunken clarity, like when you sit bolt upright in bed after a dream and can't work out what's real. Suddenly, she had no money and was convinced someone had stolen it. They hadn't of course; she'd just lost it on the machine but had blanked it out because she was so hammered. But she became quite . . . well, maybe we'll call it tired and emotional because she couldn't remember losing the cash at all, and the police had to come and, you can guess the rest. Luckily in the end we managed to smooth everything over. This experience might put some people off but, as you will have worked out, we are not *some people*.

Back in London, Georgie was working on the doors of various nightclubs. One evening, we wanted to relive our heady casino nights out, so after a few drinks in one of Georgie's clubs, we zoomed off to a casino in South Kensington, near the Natural History Museum. As soon as we get in there, we peck each other on the cheek like an old married couple and go off to our usual stations: me downstairs to the blackjack table and Georgie off to play her Lucky Lady machine. I'd played a hand or two, when I noticed there was this taller guy to the side of me, standing and watching. I don't know what he was looking at, as I wasn't having a particularly lucky game, but I kept looking back to see if he was still looking at me, and he was. I thought maybe he just likes watching very boring games of blackjack – the same way my little brother could watch endless YouTube videos of kids flipping water bottles. I just kept on playing, aware of my audience of one. Well, you know what I'm like with a bit of attention. So then I start making jokes to the table and turning the volume up a bit. Then, from nowhere, this other big guy comes to stand at my other side and I'm like, okay, fine. If I'd been more sober I might have panicked a bit more, because this was all getting a little bit *Casino Royale*, but instead I just shrugged and carried on playing, quite badly by this point.

Then, I hear giggling behind me that I recognise, and I turn to see Georgie, holding this colossal cocktail with mounds of fruit and flowers and all sorts of things coming out of it – it's like a rainforest in a glass, and by the looks of her, she's had more than one of them. She is with a shorter, older guy. Like, much older. Grandfatherly, I suppose, except he's not smiling at us like my granddad would've.

'Jamie!' trills Georgie, excitedly, 'have you met my friends?' She motions at the older guy and the other two men who've been standing and watching me. Now, if I *was* in a James Bond movie, I might be tempted to call these two guys henchmen, but I wasn't in a James Bond movie – I was in a Jamie Laing one, and anything can happen in those. I say a polite hello to Georgie's alleged new 'friends' and get back to my hand, which I promptly lose. I'm wiped out. Oh well, nice while it lasted. Suddenly, Grandfather puts his hand on my arm and says, 'Don't worry, here you go' and hands me a hundred quid's worth of chips. He just gives them to me like it's nothing, like he's offering me a pound coin for a shopping trolley or handing me a Werther's Original for being a good boy. I look down at the chips. I can't take this, can I? I look at Georgie for reassurance or even a hint of what I should do, but her head is buried in her cocktail.

'Erm,' I say, 'Don't you want me to pay for these?'

He shakes his head. 'No, you just play with them – it's fine.' I didn't need telling twice. £100 is £100 and I'm a student and don't have a penny, so if he is willing to lose it, I am more than happy to help him out. Yes, yes, yes, I look back now and realise this was a stupid thing to do, but it wasn't then, and it was about one in the morning, and . . . Drinks! Casino! Fun! Georgie! Just going with it is in my DNA.

So I start playing with these chips, and, much sooner than I would like, they get away from me. I lose the lot. Shit.

Grandfather smiles and tells me, 'Don't worry. Here's some more.' Again, £100 worth of gambling plastic.

I'm, like . . . What? Are you sure? I look at Georgie. 'This is amazing. This guy's given me all this money to play with.' She laughs loudly, and takes another glug of her cocktail, which I see is actually a different one now. And then Grandfather takes us to the roulette table.

At this point, with someone else's money and so literally nothing to lose, Georgie and I feel like we're VIPs in Vegas. So young, and free, where anything can happen – but, in a good way. The atmosphere is electric. Georgie is in full cheerleader mode, shouting, 'Let's put it on red. Let's bet on red.'

Grandfather looks at me. 'Well? Which one?'

'Red.'

We win. It's amazing. We're overjoyed. And then he says I can keep the winnings.

Now, okay, I imagine for most people, alarm bells would be ringing by now. We have met a benevolent stranger, who is plying my young, pretty female friend with cocktail after cocktail and is handing over stacks of £100 chips to me like they are *nothing*. But, look, I'm a very trusting person. I like to see the best in people, and I believe in fate smiling upon you and all that kind of stuff. I just thought this was some good Samaritan trying to show two kids a good time, and the fact he had two henchmen in black leather jackets was just . . . well, he obviously had a lot of money so needed security, no big deal. I know!

After a few more rounds of this, and some more wins and losses, Grandfather says to us, 'You two seem like fun, why don't you come back to this party with us?'

Now, Georgie, who has sunk enough of those cocktails to float a barge in her belly, is very much up for this. 'Yay!' she shouts, in a voice loud enough to lift the paint off a radiator, 'Let's go! Let's do it!' But, me, well, I admit, this is starting to feel a bit odd now. Betting with his cash in the relative safety of the casino is one thing, but leaving the place with them is quite another. But Georgie is keen and at least we're together, so . . . okay.

We stand outside the casino and a Rolls-Royce pulls up, so I'm thinking, 'Well, okay he's got a Rolls-Royce, this is quite cool.' He tells me to sit in the front, but as I get in, the steering wheel is on the wrong side. Now, I know a bit about cars – not much, but enough – and I know that a left-hand drive Rolls would be much cheaper than a regular one. So, as flashy as he is, he isn't super-rich, which makes his behaviour in the casino feel even stranger. I mean, super-rich people do weird shit all the time. I look behind me and Georgie is in the back, sandwiched between the two henchmen, having the absolute time of her life. She is dancing along to music in her seat and they're handing her drinks and she's knocking them back. So guess what happens next?

It comes. Finally. The realisation. The fear. Like a wave, consuming and crushing me. Oh, fuck, we just got into a complete stranger's car. We have no idea where we're going. Georgie is in the back hammered with these two men who . . . they are fucking massive. They could crush me with one flick of the wrist, I'm like a fly to them. And then there's this guy, this Grandfather. He's made me sit in the front seat and he's driving this car . . . like, he's loaded and chucking money at me, but he doesn't even have a driver. What the hell is going on? I feel the same terror I felt when I got held at knifepoint on the beach in Brazil. I am shaking, my head coming up with all kinds of scenarios, how this was going to turn out, and very few of them ended up with us still alive. Where was this realisation earlier, when I needed it? The carefree me of just half an hour ago, laughing as I chucked someone else's money down on a roulette table, seems like a distant memory, like it happened to someone else. I imagine the reconstructions on TV, the search for our bodies. Shit, shit, shit!

So we're driving, and I surreptitiously dial 999 on my phone in my hand, still talking to Grandfather all the while. He says we're gonna go back to some apartment, but doesn't say where it is. I don't say anything. We drive past Green Park, and I remember there's a casino nearby.

'I've got an idea,' I say, trying to keep the nerves out of my voice, 'Why don't we just go to Palm Beach casino, gamble a bit more, I'm feeling lucky.'

I remember the guy getting so angry; he really doesn't want to go. But I keep on, 'Oh come on, it'll be so much fun. Let's do it.' And then of course Georgie hears this in the back and starts chanting 'Let's do it!' So the man finally gives in.

We park up and as soon as we get inside the casino, I run to the bathroom. I'm trying not to hyperventilate, desperately working out what to do. As I try to pee straight, I notice one of the henchmen has followed me in. He stands, silently, near the door, blocking it with his foot, so nobody else can come in. This is bad. What is going on here? This is *really* not good. I smile, finish up, wash my hands, and the henchman opens the door and I go back out into the casino and take Georgie aside.

'We can't be here. We can't be with these men. This is not good.'

We're both pretty drunk, but she can see I'm being serious and I spot that little bit of clarity enter her eyes. She just manages to say, 'What do you mean?' when Grandfather comes up to us and says, 'Right, come on, we're going.'

Now is my chance. It goes against everything in my nature, but this is one person I don't feel the need to please. The night has been too good to be true so far, like a dream almost, but now I've never felt more awake.

'I'm sorry,' I say, voice shaking. 'We're not going. We're staying here.'

Grandfather isn't happy about this at all, insisting we come back with him. At this point, I have to ask: what the hell is this all about? Maybe I should've asked him this, I dunno, maybe two hours earlier, but I was caught in the moment. Now I am stuck in this one.

'You're coming back with me,' he's saying. 'We're going to make a movie. I've given you all this money, you have to come with me.'

Now . . . hold up. We're making a movie? Who is? What kind of movie? And then I realised. The endless cocktails, the £100 chips pressed into my hand, the Rolls-Royce, the promise of a party, the look on his face. He wants to film us, me and Georgie . . . having sex. Actually, doing it. Together. Me and Georgie. And he wants to watch. Now, I'm as keen to get my kit off as anyone. I love sitting around the house naked, and, yes, I've been known to strip off after a few drinks and I even once streaked across a rugby field. (That was a nightmare, actually. I did it for a bet and ended up getting chucked out into the streets of Leeds, naked, by the stewards. I had to knock on someone's door and borrow their clothes.) But all of those occasions had been on my own terms. Even without that, Georgie is like my blood; we are *not* about to be having sex, at any time, let alone be filmed doing it.

I stand firm. I hold Georgie's hand in the middle of the casino. 'You're not going with them, Georgie, don't leave with them.' God love her, she's oblivious, or doesn't care – even now, years later, she still says it was all fine, but it occurs to me later that there was probably something else in those cocktails. I shudder and turn to Grandfather. 'We're not going. I'm so sorry.' I remember being so embarrassed, because even then, when my life could have been in danger, I didn't want to let them down. I was trying to think of an excuse in my head. What possible excuse did I need?!

It starts to get nasty. People are looking. Grandfather has started kicking off. Security have to come and drag him away, his henchmen following behind. He is screaming wildly. 'I'll find you!' he warns.

All I can think as I watch him getting hoisted out of the place is how terrified I am, and how lucky. And, okay, a bit stupid. We could've been murdered! God, I can still remember his face, so red and angry. Boy, did we ruin his plans. Sorry, Grandfather, looks like you played a bad hand after all.

I suppose I can look back now and realise how insane that all was, and how lucky we were to come out relatively unscathed. And with hindsight, the lesson here is pretty clear to see: if something in life appears too good to be true, it probably is. That, and if a stranger offers you hundreds of pounds of free chips in a casino, proceed with caution.

It wouldn't be the last time I found myself being presented with a proposition I would struggle to talk myself out of, though. Once, Spencer invited me to a party at the apartment of two guys he'd met at his parents' hotel out in St Barths. They are, apparently, both called David, or at least that's what I'm going to call them here, and they're married. Imagine being married to someone with the same name as you. 'You have to meet the two Davids,' Spencer says, 'They're amazing, so much fun.'

So I go along to this party in their apartment. Now, let me tell you, this is no ordinary rich person's apartment. This is like something out of a movie, the most incredible apartment I've ever been in. It's unbelievable.

It's a fairly intimate party. There's me and Spen, and a few other people, and then the two Davids. We're having a pretty good time, the drinks are flowing, there's loads of laughs, and I'm doing my thing of amping up the volume and telling jokes and keeping everything going. I notice that one of the Davids keeps breaking away from the group and going into the kitchen, and then coming back after a few moments. He does it a few times, and I start to overthink. Oh no, my mind is going, he must think I'm so rude for not helping him clear glasses and refill the snacks – because that's what he must be doing, right, back and forth from the kitchen all the time? What else can it be? So, the seed has been planted, it's in my head, that's what he wants me to do. I wait until there are a few more empties, and then I pick up all these glasses and make my way through to the kitchen. I walk in. This is the most opulent, stunning kitchen I've ever seen. It has absolutely everything going for it: high-tech appliances, pristine surfaces, gorgeous wall-hangings, a plush dining area. It also has a naked man in the corner, masturbating, and looking right at me. It's David. Well, it's one of the Davids. I don't know which one.

What would you say in a situation like this? Would you scream? Laugh? Run away? I stopped dead. Oh God. Erm. What else could I do but say the first thing that popped into my head.

'Hi David!'

He is still looking at me, and still . . . well, he's still helping himself out, shall I say. 'Hi, Jamie,' he says, never taking his eyes off me for a second. 'Do you want to fuck me?'

Oh God. Oh God. Oh *God*. GOD. There are so many things I could say, all of which would be very valid reasons for not doing what David has just asked me to do. I've never been in a situation where someone was so overly suggestive to me, literally offered themselves to me like a tray of sushi. I've always been the one who has to try and woo someone; very few people have ever been quite so explicit and insistent about wanting to have sex with me. But I don't really know how to respond. I don't want to offend him, so I don't feel I can say, 'Oh, I'm sorry, I'm straight.' It would feel rude somehow, like I was being homophobic. Yes, not the best logic, but I'm dumbstruck here and the silence is deafening. So I say the only thing I can allow myself to say out loud: 'But David . . .' I stutter, 'What would the *other* David think?'

And with that I flash a smile and exit the kitchen and go to find Spencer. I feel so vulnerable in that moment. I don't want to cause a scene or upset anyone. I find Spen, chatting away, and tug at his arm. He turns to me.

'You look like a fucking ghost. What's up with you?'

I say, 'Spence, I'm really sick. We're gonna have to go, we really have to go.'

Not much ruffles Spencer, so he shrugs, and we leave. But he can see there's something not quite right from the look of terror on my face, and it makes him laugh all the way out of the place.

We manage to leave without anyone wondering what's going on, and once outside, Spencer turns to me and says, 'Well?'

I breathlessly recount the story. '. . . and, he was there masturbating in the corner, looking right at me, and then he said it – he asked me to have sex with him.'

'Oh,' says Spencer, as calm as a millpond as usual. 'And did you?'

Being confronted with someone else's naked body was one thing but having my own out there in public was another entirely, but that's what happened when an intimate photo of me got accidentally shared on Twitter. When I say intimate, I mean . . . well, you know what I mean. There was nothing hidden, everything was on show, and it was . . . ready to go. My girlfriend took it for a joke, as we were messing about. Twitter was just booming then, and somehow the photo got posted from my account – I'm not sure who posted it, and I don't want to get into a whole thing about it, but it certainly wasn't me, and it wasn't shared with the best intentions. This was someone being mean. I realised very quickly, after, like, minutes, and took it down. But the internet is forever. It was too late; it spread like wildfire, and people were screenshotting it and . . . I am not kidding when I say I think this might've been the worst thing that ever happened to me. I am liberated about my body and I'm not ashamed of it, but if I show any of it, it's always on my terms. This had been taken away from me. And there it was, my erect penis all over the internet, me just standing there, holding it. 'This is the end of everything,' I thought, 'my career is over, I'll be branded a pervert.' It fed into my imposter syndrome too. I'd always thought, 'Oh, someone's going to figure out what I'm actually like, someone's going to discover that actually, I don't deserve to be on the show at all. I'm never going to work in TV again.' Obviously, it got into the papers. I felt destroyed, like this wasn't who I was supposed to be, like I'd debased myself. I had done a lot of embarrassing things, but those are situations I've put myself in, and mostly ones I have been in control of. If I was going to lose my career, I'd have rather it was down to something I actually did – if it's my fault, I can handle it. I've made the mistake, I get it. But not like this, not because someone spitefully leaked a photo of me. I was so ashamed. My parents saw it! Everyone knew.

The interesting thing about it is that we go through life imagining the worst. I was convinced a moment like this was going to end everything, everything I had strived for and worked so hard to build. The truth is stories, pictures, comments spread fast online and on social media, but then they are quickly replaced by new stories and new pictures. Don't get me wrong, it was crushing in that moment, but I've moved past it. When you actually step back and reflect on disasters like this, you realise it's not that big a deal.

Not that it was a small deal either, you understand. It was a decent-sized deal, definitely. But still, after that, I covered up.

Chapter Thirteen
Disaster Movie

I can never quite decide if disaster follows me around wherever I go, or I just run into it, at every opportunity. I think it might be a bit of both. Whichever, I'm never really far from catastrophe. Now, yes, sometimes, this is my mind playing tricks on me and making me think things are actually worse than they are, but sometimes, on quite a few occasions, things really are that bad.

Cataloguing my various disasters, the calamities and misfortunes that have made up my life, would take a very long time. Where did it all start? I couldn't say. Sometimes I have been the victim of something beyond my control, a disaster not of my own making, but often – I don't wanna say how many times out of ten, but a fair few – have been my own doing.

Take, for example, Portugal, and the stomach-pumping incident at the grand old age of . . . 14. Portugal was the first place that I ever experienced many things. First place I reached second base with a girl – or whatever those bases are. Maybe it was third base? I kind of don't want to google it in case something I really don't want to see crops up. It was also the first place I realised that alcohol could kind of make any bad feelings or emotions disappear – temporarily, of course. So, on the day after I found out that my friend Fred was also messaging my one true love – or so I thought – I decided to give alcohol as anaesthetic a go. We used to go down to this place called the Praça in Vale do Lobo, basically a big square with a beach bar and a nightclub called Geckos. It was so much fun, especially at 14 years old, and especially if, like me, you thought you had been destined to be a grown-up all your life and childhood was getting in your way. There was a drink you could get down there called Gold Strike & absinthe. Absinthe! What a terrific idea for a mildly heartbroken teenager! The idea was that you would get a half a shot of Gold Strike and half a shot of absinthe, and the Gold Strike had little metal bits in it, like little gold flakes. The rumour was that the best way to drink it was to cut your throat and drink it through there, so the absinthe would then go right into your throat and make you drunk quicker. Now, I'd had my foolish moments but even I wasn't that dumb – no throat slicing happening on my watch, thank you very much. In a way, I might as well have done that, because one way or another I was ending up in hospital and at least that would've got me there quicker. I must have drunk eight of these infernal things. Being underage didn't matter, they served you whatever; they didn't care. The last thing I remember was thinking, 'Hmmm, this feeling's not good,' and kind of hobbling on a boardwalk toward the beach. And then . . . darkness, nothing, a void. My brother Xander, who was off being very sensible and responsible nearby, heard a rumour that there'd been some kid throwing up because they'd snorted baking soda – the teenage rumour mill just never stops being hilarious, does it? And so, woefully misinformed, knowing me as he does, Xander quickly worked out that whatever was happening, was probably happening to me, and he should get over there. By this time, there was no sign of me on the beach, because I'd been taken to hospital, so my poor petrified brother went to get my mum and stepdad, in hysterics, and got them out of bed. They tried to ask Fred what had happened, but he was passed out in bed, as wrecked as I was. They phoned round the hospitals and found out there was a posh, blond boy in one of them. Yep, me. Clearly.

I remember waking up and being in a hospital bed with a drip in my arm. I knew I had gone too far this time. I'd had my stomach pumped and I felt so awful, like death had me in a headlock and was punching me in the balls. My mum and my stepfather walked in, and Jonathan said, 'Hello, James Laing.' By calling me James, I knew I was in serious trouble. 'My drink was spiked,' I said straightaway, but my mum was ready for me, and knew that would be my excuse. I have only seen her that mad a few times, and this was bad with a capital B. I was taken home, shamefaced, and there was a huge row and my mum was so furious she banned me from ever going down to the Praça again. But my stepfather actually stepped in and said 'That's a terrible idea. Let them go out. He's made a mistake. He'll learn from it.'

And you know what, it's true . . . kind of. I went back down to the Praça the next night (hardcore!) and I tried to do one shot, but threw it straight back up again. I couldn't drink at all that night. So, yes, I did go there again and, yes, I did try to have a shot, but it made me ill and then I really got the message. I think sometimes having the freedom to make mistakes is a better way to learn your lesson than being forbidden to do something – as sometimes it just makes you want to do it all the more. Well, it did for me anyway. When I was younger, rules were like the protective casing over something much more exciting beneath: you had to break them to get to the good stuff.

You'll know by now that I've always been a rule breaker, but I've also always managed to keep on the right side of the law. Well, more or less. My first taste of legal problems came when I was a student. I know people might think I had a huge allowance and lived like a king in a grace-and-favour flat while I was at university but it couldn't be further from the truth. I got a bit of money from my dad every month to pay my rent and keep me in tins of beans and beers, and that was it. I was kind of sick of not having any spare cash, until someone told me if you went to the bank and asked, you could get free money. Now, before we get to the part where you shout at the page to warn me that this is categorically untrue, you're too late.

So I tottered off to the bank and was told about this amazing thing called an overdraft. It was just as that person had said – they literally give you thousands of pounds to spend and you don't have to pay it back. Ever. Or at least that's what I thought, or told myself at the time – the details are hazy, probably because the first thing I did when I got the overdraft was go to the pub, and then I took my girlfriend to New York and we had a brilliant time on someone else's dime. Then, when that was gone, I went to a different bank, to get another overdraft, but for some strange reason – can't think what – they told me to get lost. This is all sounding like the best idea ever, isn't it? Oh no. I didn't think much of it for a while and just carried on living my life, as the overdraft sat, accumulating menacing zeroes as far as the eye could see, with not a penny going into my accounts to pay it off. Imagine my surprise – horror, actually – when I was home at my mum's for a few days, and there was a knock at the door (while she was out) and some very stern-looking people standing there starting asking very official-sounding questions. They said they were bailiffs, and could I please hand over thousands of pounds, and if I didn't have thousands of pounds, could I please step aside so they could start removing my mum's furniture? I know this sounds ridiculous and I know I sound like I was born yesterday, but at that age I had no idea how overdrafts worked! Nobody had ever explained. I just thought the bank gave you overdrafts as a student, like, a helping hand. Anyway, now the helping hand was knocking at my mum's door and reaching for my throat. The debt had to be paid and they wanted me to agree to a payment plan as soon as possible to avoid having to take my mum's stuff away. I have never told my parents about this, by the way, so if they really do sit down and read this, I am in such big trouble you won't believe it. I'm a grown man and already terrified of the rocketing I am going to get for this.

So, I have to agree a payment plan, which feels like it is going to take forever, and every little bit of money that comes my way has to go towards paying off this mountainous debt. Birthday money from Granny, any jobs I do, any little pennies I come across never even get to feel the inside of my pocket – they're off paying the debt bit by bit. I felt so stupid and ashamed of what I'd done. Not only that, but my credit rating went through the floor, which meant I couldn't even get a phone upgrade. When my brick of a phone finally conked out, I had to get my mum to take out a contract for me – she did wonder why she had to come with me to get the new phone but I somehow managed to explain it away. This loss of independence and facing the consequences was a big eye-opener for me, the first time I'd had to be responsible and manage my own money (badly, as it turned out) and I quickly found out that the real world had some serious consequences if you fucked up. I have talked and smiled myself out of many a disaster, but if you're in trouble with the law, charm can't get you out of everything. It was scary because suddenly that safety net I'd always relied on was gone. Some might say it was long overdue – maybe I'd agree with you. I couldn't just 'Ooops, sorry' my way out of this one. Apologies don't matter when you've broken the law. Lesson learned.

Sometimes, of course, my disasters have been hilarious. Take the time Francis and I took the *Private Parts* podcast on tour. This was massive for me, going on the road, stepping out of my comfort zone a little and showing live audiences what I could do. No hiding behind a microphone this time – in fact, there was no hiding at all, because I had decided, in my infinite wisdom, that I would open every live show with me totally naked. Well, what can I say, there's nothing much funnier than a bare bottom bouncing onto the stage. Seemed like a good idea, until Francis pointed out to me that we had 28 live shows to do, so I would have to get my arse (and everything else) out another 27 times – as much as I love being naked, that was overkill even for me. And as if my problems weren't bad enough, on the very first show, I stood there and . . . forgot my lines. Whatever I had to say just flew right out of my mind. I stared at Francis, then back at the crowd, then into the beaming spotlight, then back at Francis. Silence.

Francis gave a little smirk and said, 'You've forgotten your lines, haven't you?'

'Nope,' I said, no doubt blushing because of my blatant lie and lack of clothes, 'I definitely haven't.'

What else could I do in this situation but . . . leap behind the sofa on the stage and . . . pretend to read a book? It made sense to me at the time, which is to say, it made no sense at all, but I didn't know what else to do.

'You got your lines in that book, Jamie?' called Francis, clearly loving it! Thing was, there weren't any lines inside the book, I wish there had been. Anyway, somehow I managed to wing it and managed to get through the rest of the show with only a slightly red face and raised heart rate.

One thing I thought might steer me away from disaster was getting an agent. You know, someone to look after my interests, make sure I wasn't making bad decisions. God knows I needed the help. I'd already been turned down by one agent because they had no idea what to do with me, which is probably because I didn't know what I wanted to do either; I just knew there had to be more to me than being a reality TV star. I was proud of the show, and what I'd achieved, but there was still loads of other stuff I wanted to do. So I was very excited when Storm said they would sign me. Now, Storm is famous for being the agency to lots of hot models and I thought, 'Wow, this is it – I'm becoming a model. How cool. Finally!' And then reality was waiting with its usual sledgehammer – for some reason . . . they didn't put me on their modelling books at all. Rude! I was on their 'special bookings' list instead. Special. Well, I liked the sound of that at least. I was excited, looking forward to seeing if there was any possibility that this fluke that had found me on reality TV could actually turn into a career. I'd been in the show for three years at this point and I was ready to show the world I wasn't just a posh blond boy who got himself into sticky situations.

And then it happened: my first big job, a deal with a huge brand. Now, remember, just topping up my cash from *Made in Chelsea* with personal appearances at this point, so this was a big deal for me. In fact, it was a very big deal for me. A really big fee. And this brand wanted to pay it to me? Just me?! Sign me up! It was set to be a huge publicity campaign for a well-known pizza brand, promoting a brand new type of pizza that didn't have a crust. Okay, sounds weird, but the selling point was that people who always leave the crusts of their pizza will love this because the toppings go right to the edge of the base – no doughy deadzone round the edges. Now, this might sound like a small thing, but I was so excited. I couldn't believe they'd asked me to do it. Surely this was revolutionary? People would be talking about this crustless pizza for decades to come; it was a turning point for pizza production, nothing would ever be the same again. Enthusiastic is an understatement. My first assignment as part of the deal was to be on a Saturday, at the O2. My then-agent Emily said it was all supposed to be a big surprise, that I would be doing something edgy and adventurous, and loads of fun. I didn't care, I would do whatever, I was just happy to be there.

'Just make sure you get plenty of rest,' she tells me. 'It's going to be a big day.'

Feeling overjoyed, and with the prospect of the very sizeable fee already burning a hole in my pocket – even though I hadn't actually had any of it yet – I go out to celebrate with some friends. I treat them to a lovely dinner, drinks in full flow, no corner of the dance floor left unstomped upon. This probably isn't the best idea, the night before my big day starting on the campaign, but at 25 I didn't really stop to think about hangovers. I barely get any sleep, a mass of excitement and booze. The next morning, I'm feeling . . . okay, a little fragile, but not like I need rushing to intensive care or anything. I head over to the O2, and meet my agent. Turns out the photo call is happening in the car park. Weird. Oh. There's a huge crane. And not just a photographer, but a camera crew. And, of course, pizza. Then the concept is explained to me. Because the pizza topping goes right to the edge of the pizza - hence the name, The Edge – I will be doing something edgy, on camera. I look up at the crane and realise the edgy thing I will be doing will be . . . plummeting from the top of it, attached to a bit of elastic. Yes, I'm bungee jumping. Suddenly I can feel every morsel I ate, every drink, every somersault on the dance floor, pounding in my stomach. But I'm a professional, so I grit my teeth. I have to wear this protective suit that's got cameras all over it so that every second of my terror can be captured on tape. But a job is a job, and I am lucky that I'm being paid a pretty hefty amount to be here, so I get ready and clamber into a cage that lifts me to the top of the crane. I look down. It's a long way. A hell of a long way. But I can do this. And then I am handed some pizza. I have to bungee jump, actually eating some pizza. At the same time, dressed like bloody Robocop. My stomach churns, seemingly tapping out 'Are you fucking joking?' against my large intestine in Morse code. Oh no. But I can do this. Just one little bungee jump. I get the thumbs up from the camera crew. I say my slogan. I take my bite. I smile. I jump. Stomach, don't fail me noooooooooooooooowwhoooooooooooooaaaaaaaa!

Okay, that wasn't too bad. I lived. I manage not to puke. I'm hoisted back up to the top, and await release.

'Yeah, can we do it again?' comes the voice of the director.

Really? I take a deep breath. One more. I can survive this. I don't know what I look like, but I feel green – greener than a courgette. But we go again. Slogan. Chomp. Smile. Juuuuuuuuump. Ugh. Okay. Again, not so bad. Back up to the top.

'We need to go again.'

I reckon at this point, a tear might have appeared in my eye. I am struggling to breathe. I can feel proper dread starting to cover me like fog round a mountain. But I think about what this means for my career. 'Sure.'

Chomp. Smile. Speak. Jump. Hang on, did I do that in the right order? Please tell me I won't have to . . .

'Can we go again?'

Panic. Cage. Lift. Smile. Slogan. Bite. Plummet.

'I think we need one more.'

Hyperventilate. Climb. Smile, with a thumbs up this time, because why not. Slogan. Eat. Jump.

'Can we do another?'

Breathless. Hysterical. Everything's a blur. Smile, eat, pray, jump.

'I'd like to see another.'

Eyes bulging in fear. Stomach a mess. Lungs have given up. But I still smile, say my thing, chew the pizza and jump. Aaaaaaaaargh. Okay, I made it. Surely—.

'Just one more?'

Man, I am really earning this enormous fee. I can't do it anymore. My body is wrecked. I feel like my soul left it some time ago. But I can't say 'Stop!', I'm too polite. I don't want to look like a huge diva, or be thought of as some air-headed, difficult celebrity wasting everyone's time. So, we go for take number eight. A broken man, I make my way back up to the top. But I'm still smiling, and I still eat that pizza like it's the best thing I've ever eaten and all I can think of as I hurtle toward the concrete is . . . 'Just think where this might lead, this is the beginning, this is it, remember they asked you to do this, they wanted you, and you are proving how easy you are to work with, what a dream hire you must be, not complaining.' And then I land, and I look at the crew, not saying a word. The man who owns the bungee jump pipes up: 'Look, I've never seen anyone do more than five, and we are on eight now; we'd better stop.'

The director scratches their chin. 'Brilliant, thanks Jamie. We've got it.'

Yes! I got through it. I say my thank yous and my goodbyes

and head off to Leeds, where I'm doing a personal appearance at a club that night. The hustle never stops! I sit on the train and give myself a little pat on the back. I am a businessman now. Career is on track. This will be the first of many promotions, once word gets around how professional I was, how I got the job done. The fact my stomach now lives permanently in my throat and that I'd rather have my mouth stitched to a horse's bottom than eat pizza again is irrelevant – I am on my way to the top flight.

The personal appearance goes great, and the next day I get the train back to London and call my girlfriend. We start talking, which progresses to a strong exchange of views, which escalates to a heated discussion, which then snowballs into a full scale, nuclear-threat-level argument. Now, I have a loud voice at the best of times, I used to pride myself on being the loudest at any party, but during this argument, I'm being particularly vocal. I was very well brought up and always told not to make a scene in public, but sadly on this occasion I forgot myself and this did, understandably, piss off quite a few people trying to enjoy a quiet train journey from Leeds to London. You know how you have one of those days that's going great and then one little thing happens, and it just seems to get worse and worse and you can't seem to control what's happening and before you know it, your good day is ruined and you can't work out how things got so bad? Well, I went from bickering with my girlfriend to being arrested on the train and hauled off it at Peterborough and shoved up against a wall by a police officer. This might seem harsh but . . . confession: I was acting like a proper douchebag, being way too loud and annoying and not taking too kindly to being told to shut up. I can admit that now without flinching – even *I* would have arrested me! So, I was mouthing off and thinking there would be no consequences, but the universe had other ideas, which is why I found myself cuffed and mortified in the train station. Obviously, people were taking photos and, yes, this got into the papers and, clearly, the pizza company saw it and told me, in no uncertain terms, that the deal was well and truly off. Luckily, I didn't get a criminal record, but at that point it felt like it was bye bye to my career, and it was definitely a very sad farewell to the lovely big fee. Disaster.

To add insult to injury, a couple of years later, I took part in a TV show called *Famous and Fighting Crime*, where I had to shadow cops on the job. I arrived at the station and said, 'Oh, this feels kind of familiar,' and one of the officers said to me, 'You don't remember me, do you?'

I had to confess that I didn't, but as I looked round the station, it slowly started to dawn on me. 'This is where I booked you,' she said, 'when you were arrested.'

Peterborough!

Chapter Fourteen
Action Man

I run on instinct quite a lot of the time. I like trying new things, am always chasing new experiences, and if I get a chance to perform, even better. I got the acting bug when I was very small. It all started with the school nativity play. Man, I really wanted to be in it, and I wanted the plum role. Obviously, Mary was out of the question, and an ugly, plastic doll had already secured the role of the baby Jesus, so I set my sights on the daddy of them all – well, not Jesus's daddy as it turned out, I suppose – Joseph! I was very competitive about it, because Joseph got to sing a song. Knock, knock, knock, any room at the inn? Still know all the words in case there's a TV adaptation. I wanted to be the centre of it all. I knew my mum and dad would be coming, and they'd be filming it, so I had to make sure it was worth it. See, my thirst for screen time didn't start with *Made in Chelsea*!

I carried this with me, going off to study theatre in Leeds, and then, obviously, *Made in Chelsea* happened. But, just the same as when I got an agent, and started working with brands, I was always looking for more. There was that side of my personality waiting to get out. I really wanted to show the world what I was like out of the *MIC* glare.

And I didn't want to just do anything. You might have thought I was never off the telly, but I have turned down so many things over the years. Thanks to my agents – first Emily at Storm, then Laura, Louise, and Flora at Independent – and people actually taking an interest in me, I've actually managed to keep busy yet still only do things I really want to do. I got asked to do *Big Brother* a few times. I said no, because – and this might sound weird – I didn't want to be known as a reality star. Even though I was one, I didn't want to be known for that; I wanted more, to be challenged. I turned down *The Jump* – Spencer did that, though, and met his wife Vogue on it. I said no to *Splash*, where you had to learn how to dive, and spend Saturday evenings shivering in speedos on live TV. Nope! There was one set in a hotel, I checked out of that one very easily, and one where I had to learn to drive. Francis Boulle did that one instead – he was furious that he had to be filmed, he just wanted to learn how to drive! I said no to *Celebs Go Dating* . . . I mean, I needed no more complications on that score, did I? I turned down a bonkers endorsement for a cushion that made you feel like you had someone's arm round you. I mean . . . no.

But what I did say yes to, I'm still very proud of. They helped me show another side to my personality away from the *Made in Chelsea* dramas. My first one was called *Famous, Rich and Hungry*. There was so much kudos attached; I was hugely excited. It was for the BBC, for a start, which was a big deal, and it was being made by Love Productions, who were doing *Bake Off*, so this is proper high-flying TV. The premise was that loaded people – or at least people who the public perceived to be loaded – went and lived with a couple of families who were having a tough time financially, to see what it was like. I know shows like this get a lot of flak for being 'poverty porn' and I totally understand that, but I went into it without any cynicism, and if I'd felt anyone was being exploited I wouldn't have done it. I'm always really interested in people's stories, what makes them who they are, so I was looking forward to it, but nervous. My first family was a single mum and her three kids, living in Croydon, and I was told their food budget was £1.24 per person, per day. I couldn't even imagine that. So I arrive, and they've obviously been told that some famous person is going to turn up to live with them. It's really exciting. I knock on the door, and . . . they have no clue who I was. Not big fans of *Made in Chelsea*, it seems. They're expecting like, David Walliams or something, and they've got me. I'll never forget one of the kids, who was about six, looking up at me with big eyes and saying, bluntly, 'Who are you?' Amazing! It was so awkward to be in someone else's house, I was talking my head off out of sheer nerves – I must've worn this poor woman out with all my questions. Their house was small and needed some maintenance doing to it. They didn't have much, I felt terrible for them. I asked her what she did for fun, and she told me her only sense of freedom was going to feed the ducks on the weekend with the kids, there was just nothing else. She had no money whatsoever. It was a tough life for them, but they were a happy little group. The kids were adorable and their mum did the best she could. It really opened my eyes to what life can be like if you're not as lucky as I was. Next, I was in Sheffield with a Muslim guy raising his sons after his wife had left, and he'd turned to alcohol to cope. Things were pretty miserable for them but above all, the father loved his two boys and would've done anything for them. It really brought home how important family is, how nothing else you have matters if you don't have people you love and can trust around you. I was young, and certainly naive, and it hit me like a truck. I could see what this father was doing for these kids, and the struggles he was going through with his alcoholism and his guilt and doing it all by himself. He shielded his kids from so much; they had no idea how much heartache their dad was suffering behind the scenes. I remember calling my mum in tears, because I'd never thought about how hard the divorce must've been for her, and how she just kept going and never showed how it was affecting her, and how she was always there for us, no matter what. I was so overcome with gratitude. When everything is lost, the only people who'll be there in the end are your family.

I was definitely ready for a bigger challenge. Although *Famous, Rich and Hungry* had shown another side to me, it was still about me being posh or rich or whatever – what if I could maybe move outside that stereotype a little? I mean, yes, I am posh and, compared to many people, I am from a rich background, but that wasn't the whole story. *Famous and Fighting Crime* came next, and it was an electrifying experience. I'm 28, and flung into the deep end, finding out what it's like to be a special constable, the unpaid volunteers who work in the police force in their spare time. Obviously they all took the piss out of me for actually being arrested in Peterborough that time, and I knew I had a lot to prove. I knew what they must be thinking, that I'm just some *Made in Chelsea* blond boy who wouldn't want to get his hands dirty. It was pretty intimidating, being out on patrol with these guys. Some of the calls you get are ridiculous, some people phone the police about the weirdest of things, like needing help to log off Facebook, or spilling food down themselves. But whatever it is, the police have to be there, they have to attend just in case. And then of course there's the hardcore stuff, like domestic violence, or getting involved in serious crimes. Sometimes you become the enemy because you're making a report, so you get sworn at all the time and threatened. I realised how these guys put their lives on the line every day. I was trying to build a rapport with them, but while they were polite and friendly, I could tell I was going to have to go the extra mile to earn their trust. One evening, we are called to a disturbance at a bar. See, 'disturbance'; I've still got all the lingo. So we get to this place, and there's a guy threatening people. He has a knife on him, some of the customers say, and he was swinging a sock with a snooker ball in it. Anyway, once he spots the uniforms and the blue lights, he darts off and runs up an alleyway. It's like this weird instinct kicks in. All three of us – so me and these two guys, who I've more or less just met – we start running after him. Now, remember, I was the sports hero at school. I can run, and I can run fast, and something just takes over me, some wild compulsion. This guy is dangerous, he can't get away. So I pick up speed and catch him, tackling him to the ground like I'm in the height of my rugby days, so these guys can arrest him. It's a turning point for me, my colleagues are really impressed and I even earn myself a nickname: Roadrunner! I love to belong and

I love to make friends and I love people to think I'm doing a good job, so this acceptance is amazing to me.

The boss wasn't so impressed though – I get pulled into an office and reminded that as a rookie, and a famous one at that, I can't just sprint off and bring down the bad guys like Batman – I have to get clearance from my colleagues first. It's not quite a rollicking, but I consider myself told. It doesn't matter though, I'm happy to play by the rules now I know I'm in the gang.

On our next patrol, we get a call to look for a guy suspected of some pretty heavy crimes. We head to his house at 11 o'clock at night to try to find him. His mum claims he's not there. Now, she is obviously fibbing, but we have to take her word for it – you never know what's really going on behind closed doors and she could be vulnerable.

Just as the guys and me are saying to each other that he is definitely in there somewhere, he comes running out the back door. Here we go again! We give chase, but I'm holding back my turbo power a bit, I don't want to get into trouble again. But that competitive edge . . . I can't escape it. So I look at my colleague George, who's running next to me, and I say, 'George, I can get him. I can catch him.' All I need is the go-ahead and this sucker is getting taken down. (Yes, I am really getting into it by this point.)

So George, still running beside me, tips me the nod. 'Go, Roadrunner!' he shouts, and I'm off. It was amazing, like something out of a movie.

I saw a lot of things in those two short weeks. It made me realise what a privileged life I'd lived growing up, what a small bubble I'd experienced.

I suppose I had never had to fully confront my privilege before. Obviously I knew some people made fun of my accent and my poshness, so I was aware I had it different, but I had never witnessed first-hand what life could be like for people less fortunate. I'd watched the news and read the papers and knew the world was full of inequalities, but until you experience it, until you find yourself in places where real life is happening, you have no idea. I had no clue what it was really like. I didn't realise how people live in poverty, true poverty; the people who can't afford food, or are beaten up, or sexually abused, every day, but that's just what happens. They're used to it and conditioned to believe they don't deserve any better, and feel like there's no way out. For a lot of people, life is really hard. The domestic abuse, the fear that some children live in. We arrested this one drug dealer who was 15 years old, and he said, 'What else can I do?' People who've been forced into sex work, people addicted to heroin, saying how they hate their lives, and they can't get off it. These people need help and support; it was a real eye opener. One of the police officers told me, 'It's just a game every single day. Us versus them. And it starts again every morning.' In the show, this Polish guy had nowhere to go to, he'd been kicked out of his house. It was freezing, and I said to the police, 'Where's this guy going to go?' They didn't know, said there was nothing they could do. So I gave him £20. He just started crying and held my hands. I got taken into the sergeant's office, though, and given a light bollocking again because you can't just give money out to people, but I didn't know what else to do.

So when I think about my big fear I had at the height of my anxiety, about losing everything, it's almost an insult to think, 'Oh, God, it could happen to me,' because obviously I had a huge safety net and am so much more fortunate than so many people. But, in my defence, anxiety isn't rational, and the feelings and the fears, no matter how outlandish and unlikely, still feel very real when I'm at my lowest point. I guess I'm lucky that when that happens, when I hit rock bottom, there is always someone there for me. So many people don't have that.

I'd done some terrific shows, but I was still looking for something a little different, something that took me out of that reality TV box, that showed me in a different context, made people think about me in a different light. It came along in a very unexpected way. *Murder in Successville* was immediately an intriguing concept. Comedian Tom Davis – who is an absolute genius, can I just say – plays a hard-nosed detective in a fictional celebrity-filled town known as Successville. Every week, a different famous inhabitant is murdered and Davis hires a new police recruit, played by a celebrity in a cameo role, to help him solve the crime. Just to make the whole thing even more surreal, most of it is improvised. There's a rough plot, and Tom knows where it's going and which scenes are coming up, but the rookie has no idea and has to make it up on the fly. I'd been talking myself out of, and into I suppose, tricky situations for years on *MIC*, so this seemed perfect for me. It was a risk, I knew that, but it was also an important opportunity for me. I knew some viewers might be seeing me for the very first time, and even those who recognised me wouldn't know this version of me. Here improvising in a comedy scenario, they'd be a seeing different side of me, and judging me on my acting talent. I'd always beaten myself up a bit about taking the 'easy route' into television, through reality TV, like I'd cheated somehow. But the thing about taking the easy way, is you then have to work harder than ever to get respect and prove yourself.

This was a big leap for me. And it went . . . brilliantly. It was everything I'd hoped for, it went down so well. It felt like this was the proper start of my entertainment career, and showed what I was really capable of. People I really respected were talking about the show, and my episode, really positively. They didn't even really know who I was, which is fine, but they had noticed me. I remember listening to Adam Buxton's podcasts, and he mentioned that it was one of the funniest things he'd seen. I felt this huge validation from it, that actual comedians and respected people in the industry had seen this and were being positive about it. It felt like I'd broken through somehow. This was the start of something.

This confidence boost may have been to blame for my doomed foray into stand-up comedy. Look, I will try anything once, and sometimes I'll try something twice – maybe this is where I've been going wrong, because sometimes once is more than enough. I have never been great at quitting while I was ahead. After starting the podcast and getting feedback from listeners about how funny I was – well, I suppose some people thought Francis was funny too, but there's no accounting for taste – I thought maybe a future as a comedian lay ahead. I was asked if I'd do a charity gig by a friend of mine called Tom Lucy. My default response to most things is, 'Sure, why not?', and it was only a ten-minute slot, so I decided to give it a go.

I took it very seriously and began to write my set. It was just stories, really, about weird stuff that's happened to me, and funny situations and the disastrous times when I'd slept with people. You want a sample of the kind of material we're dealing with here? Well, I suppose you had to be there, but one of my icebreaker jokes was about sex: I said that sex was basically pretty much like dancing – when you're sober it's awful and awkward and embarrassing because you've no coordination and you're a bit inhibited, but when you're drunk, you suddenly think you're amazing, pulling out all the best moves, giving it your all like you're Michael Jackson on the dance floor. I mean, comedy gold, right? Hmm, tough crowd. Anyway, I was very nervous in the run-up. I remember standing in the actual Comedy Store, surrounded by famous faces, wearing a T-shirt Tom had given to me which said 'As Seen on E4' written on it, waiting to go on and talk at 400 people for ten minutes. 'This is nuts,' I'm thinking, 'am I sure about this?' Then, boom! I'm on. I realise now that I had the luck of a beginner and the support of a crowd rooting for an underdog. It was my first ever gig, my nerves could be seen from space without a telescope, and it was for charity. Plus, okay, I was relatively funny. They laughed. They actually laughed, and I mean at my jokes, not just . . . me. The ten minutes whizzed by, and I swaggered off that stage like I'd just won Wimbledon. I thought, 'Well, this is it, this is my moment.' One hundred per cent, I was always meant to be a comedian, I can start selling out stadiums.

This is easy. I had found my calling.

Given I was such a hit, I was asked back to do another gig. I remember writing my jokes, and thinking they sounded quite smart and funny. Then the big day came, and I was suddenly aware that I no longer had the same safety nets that had protected me the last time. This wasn't for charity. It was a real gig, with paying customers, and expectations of a high-quality set from a world-famous comedy club. Plus, they wouldn't know, or care, that it was only my second gig. They weren't going to 'go easy' on me. As far as these strangers were concerned, I was the posh wanker from *Made in Chelsea*, deciding he was now a stand-up comic. There would be no second chances, or polite laughing; this was all down to me. At least, this is what was going through my head as I limbered up. But I'm not one to back out of anything, so on I went.

I don't know whether it was the fact my jokes were bad, or I'd lost my nerve or . . . actually, I do know! The jokes were bad. Not up to my usual high standard. And my delivery wasn't great. When you're standing in front of strangers, asking them to laugh at you, you can't show any weakness, you have to battle on. Sometimes all it takes is one laugh to pull you through. That's exactly what I got, too, one laugh. Worst of all: it was my brother doing the laughing. Xander was there giving me moral support, but had ended up being the canned laughter my material desperately needed. You hear comedians talking about losing the room and now I knew what that really meant. I looked at their faces and I knew it was over. There was no getting them back. Every joke I told pushed me further and further into Siberia. My mind was ticking over – if the jokes weren't working, what else could I do? What else was I good at? I could talk to people, right? I can bounce off others pretty easily. So I started asking the audience questions, seeing if I could hook a joke onto it. One guy told me he was originally from the Ukraine and without even thinking I asked him if it had taken him long to get here tonight. And then it came, a huge roar of laughter – my first actual hit. Except . . . it wasn't a joke. It was a serious question. I suppose having them laugh at me rather than with me was better than nothing but, you know, it would've been nice if they could've lost it at one of my actual jokes and not a perfectly reasonable question. This sent my nerves into overdrive and all I wanted to do was get off the stage and sit in a darkened room with big headphones on and pretend none of this had ever happened. But I still had ten minutes to go. Nightmare. I couldn't last that long, so I decided to tell the rest of my routine at warp speed. I rushed through it so much that my ten-minute routine became a six-minute one, and nobody could hear the jokes. Not only that, but as I was telling the jokes, my mind was working overtime and assessing how likely it was that the jokes I hadn't yet told would get any laugh at all, and coming up with blanks. The one joke I had coming up that I'd thought was the jewel in my crown – the one that was going to have them rolling in the aisles and offering me comedy specials on late-night TV – I now realised was about as funny as a verruca. I had nothing else to replace it, so instead of styling it out, I kind of mumbled over it. Now, most hecklers will tell you you're crap, or to get off the stage, but I was probably the first person on the stage of the Comedy Store to have a heckler asking me to tell the joke again because he'd missed it.

'Sorry,' he shouted out, not unsympathetically; he sounded genuinely interested. 'What was the punchline?'

Terror took over. I could feel sweat dripping down my back. In fact, even my sweat was sweating. 'What?' I managed to squeak.

'Um, a punchline,' he said. 'Was there one?'

Oh my God. I just couldn't. But I did, I repeated this shockingly bad punchline slightly slower than I had before. And, just like the first time, nobody laughed. This was torture. After six minutes, I called it a day, and went 'Thank you very much, I've been Jamie and . . . that's me', before walking off. A few people clapped and maybe there was the odd cheer, but it was definitely out of sympathy more than anything else.

I look back on it now and laugh, because I had thought I was so incredible and amazing that first time. How could I possibly fail? This would come to trip me up on *Strictly* eventually, too – more on that later. It was that blind confidence, the 'I'm gonna be selling out the O2 with my stand-up set' type of energy. Who the hell did I think I was? If anything, my failure was funnier than any joke I told. As good as it is to identify your strengths, you shouldn't be afraid to admit your weaknesses too. No one can be good at everything, and on that day I learnt that some things are best left to the experts. But at least I got to have a go. No regrets. Okay, some regrets – I should've made sure there were at least two family members in the audience, for a start.

Chapter Fifteen
Loser

It's strange, but even though I always say I wanted to be older when I was a child, I loved being young too. My twenties were, on the whole, an absolute blast. Obviously, there were ups and downs, but I was having the time of my life, and always grateful that I got so many chances other people might not. I knew it couldn't last forever, but that didn't stop me wanting it to. If life is like a party, I'm the guy at five in the morning begging everyone not to leave, suggesting we open another bottle. I was aware, as I was getting older, that people I knew from outside the show were starting to grow up and get proper jobs and even settle down, but I was happy to exist in this little bubble. They call it reality TV, but if anything, it's like reality is on hold. Sure, your situations and your emotions are very real at the time, but it's not normality; there's no way you could live like that all the time. For me, amid the trials and tribulations and the tears and tantrums, *Made in Chelsea* was like a party, and a rollercoaster. There is something about being a part of it that makes you feel untouchable and immortal. You exist through the lens of those who are watching you. Knowing there was an audience out there drove me forward, influenced my decisions – good and bad – and gave me that validation I'd always been looking for. On *Made in Chelsea*, I was celebrated for being me, people liked me for who I was, even if I wasn't always the best version of myself. Sometimes that could make things complicated. I wouldn't go as far as saying I was pretending, or playing a part, but there were things I'd done and said that I might not have said if there hadn't been someone watching – maybe I wouldn't have felt that pressure to perform, or to have the argument, or to make the mistake.

I remember one new cast member coming to me and saying, 'Why is the story always about you? Why do they never focus on anyone else?' They didn't see any point of being on the show because, more often than not, I would find a way to pull focus onto me. Hey, I'd been bouncing around in front of the home video camera since I was a toddler – I knew what worked. It was the same on *Made in Chelsea*. I went through it all: I could relay every emotion. I could be funny, I could be sad, I could be angry, I could not be calm, I could be challenging. I didn't sit on a fence. I gave them everything. When I went into scenes, I was very honest, I didn't lie about the way I was feeling. I'd also been in the show so long that I started to have ideas about what might work, not just to get more screen time, because that wasn't necessarily important to me, but to make it the best show possible. I wanted to feel like part of a winning team, part of the show everyone was talking about. They knew they could put me in any situation, and I'd deliver. *Made in Chelsea* was like the animal kingdom, everyone playing their part in the food chain, everyone with a role to fulfil within the hierarchy. Quickly, through screen time and years spent in front of the camera, I ascended, until I was, basically, the lion.

When I was first on TV, it was like there was a reset button, where I could do almost anything and I'd be forgiven – something that was probably already wearing thin for anyone who knew me in real life. On *Made in Chelsea*, it was part of my character, who I was on camera. I'd fuck up, and the only fallout would be, 'Ah, it's just Jamie, it doesn't matter; it's just what he does.' When I was still new and exciting, I got away with murder. People loved me. I'm not being big-headed about this; I saw the fan-mail, I read the tweets. The producers told me I was doing a good job. At the time I suppose it felt great, but looking back now I can see it was quite an alarming amount of power for an impetuous young man like me to have. And for everyone else, it got old. And so did I.

I could feel things were changing. When I first rose to popularity the future was so bright. I had loads of meetings with production companies and got offered different shows, but now *Love Island* had come along, and there was a new strand of celebrity coming through – the social media stars on Instagram and YouTube. My shtick started to look old hat. It was becoming routine. My friends started leaving the show too; they'd had enough of living under the microscope for all those years. They wanted to get on with their lives, control their own narratives, I guess.

This was hard, watching the gang break up. I looked around and felt quite alone. I wasn't as attractive a proposition to TV companies now that *Love Island* was creating loads of new stars overnight, and there were tons of people who were better looking than me and younger than me and had more followers. My YouTube channel wasn't doing as big numbers as everybody else, and my self-doubt was kicking in. Nothing seemed to be going to plan, and my relationship wasn't working. Even though I had come out of my depersonalisation era, I was becoming this person that I wasn't comfortable with; I was wondering what I could do to stay relevant, starting to feel like I was failing. It's funny, I had dreaded this day for years, catastrophised in my mind what would be, and how it would feel, and yet I still didn't feel ready for it. The feeling that my star was fading, that the party was over, was still a huge punch to the gut.

The cast was getting younger and younger, and I suppose I felt like these new cast members were after my crown. I didn't get the same energy from it anymore. I stopped being funny and started using fear instead. Whereas before I might have taken them under my wing, now I was being more intimidating, maybe. After all, I was the eldest, I knew how the show worked better than anyone, and who the hell was going to challenge me anyway, right? My ego was in bad shape, but it was about to get worse.

There was a bright light in the form of Sophie. Meeting her probably saved me from some even darker times at that point. But I'd always promised myself I would never actually fall in love with someone on the show, so I used to lie sometimes, saying that I knew her before the show, but I didn't at all. I was so scared of being toppled from that alpha male podium. Meeting on a reality show just wasn't exciting to me; I wanted our story to be so much more than that. So, although I was very happy with Sophie, there were still so many doubts in my mind about being on the show. Then *Strictly* came along.

Strictly was supposed to be the lifeline. My first huge prime-time experience, a million miles away from the dramas of *Made in Chelsea*. This was a much-loved national institution, and to be asked to do it made me feel there was still some respect for me there – not that many reality TV stars had been contestants. It was going to be amazing! My mood lifted, and everything seemed to be going right. And then . . . well, you know how this one goes. I screwed it up royally by injuring my foot, leaving me back where I started. Yes, lucky, still, to have a job and a profile, but I didn't feel like I was moving on with my life. For me, if I'm going to do any job, whether it's working in a café or being a Formula 1 driver, I need to feel like I'm achieving something. I have to have goals. And make progress. Day in, day out, doing the same old thing – I know plenty of people do it with no complaint, but I'm not one of those people. I have only one speed, and one direction I can go in: fast, and forward. But I was wading through quicksand. This brought me crashing back to that moment when I was 17 years old, and I'd damaged my knee playing rugby. Stuck. Stifled. Hindered by one of those bloody boots they put on you when you hurt your leg – like a grounded astronaut.

I'd been in and out of that series of *Made in Chelsea* in case I was supposed to do *Strictly*, but now I was back full-time, unexpectedly, so I flew out to Buenos Aires to join the others for filming. To complicate matters Sophie and I had got into a huge argument because I had been texting someone, and she got really upset and brought it up on the show. Obviously, this wasn't the first time my misdemeanours had come to light on camera, but this felt different. I really cared deeply about Sophie by then – well, I loved her, in fact – and our relationship didn't feel like an on-camera thing, probably because we'd hidden it from everyone at first. Plus, the dynamic between me and everyone else on the cast had completely changed. This group wasn't full of my old buddies who'd tolerated my behaviour or backed me up, and they weren't scared to go up against me now either. Nobody cared whether I thought I was the lion or not, nobody thought, 'Oh it's just Jamie being Jamie.' They didn't give a shit, and they were all hungry for a piece of the limelight I'd been hogging for quite a while. This had always been a bit of fun to me, but to them it was their job, a career – a stepping stone to bigger and better things. So they let me have it with both barrels and gave me a severe roasting. I remember sitting in a hotel waiting to shoot a scene, and I was so restless that I couldn't really sit still. I felt so uneasy and agitated. Going back to Buenos Aires should have been an amazing experience, reliving my travelling days back when I was 18, but all these years later, it didn't feel the same. *I* didn't feel the same. What had happened to that happy, gung-ho boy I'd been then, with his whole life ahead of him? I just felt restless all the time, I didn't have the same power that I used to have, and I was convinced nobody liked me on the show anymore either.

We came back and I felt gloomy. No other way to describe it. I was still so restless all the time, and my mind felt foggy. Nothing was going my way. I decided to stop drinking on my birthday – 3rd November, if you want to send me a card or a birthday message – because I thought perhaps it was the booze making me feel this way. We finished filming on the show and I headed off to spend Christmas with my dad and my brothers skiing in Morzine in the French Alps. After years of not turning up to stuff, or letting them down at the last minute, I don't think any of them could quite believe it when I arrived, but I remember them being so excited. It was, like, 'Yay! Jamie is finally coming on holiday with us.'

And even though I was excited too, something happened to me on the way out there. I suddenly had this wave of sadness. It just hit me so hard, like I was feeling the pressure of a full-on tidal wave, pressing against my chest. Now, I knew this wasn't anxiety. I could deal with that. I mean, it was still terrible, obviously, but at least I knew what to expect with anxiety – everything was heightened, and I'd be on high alert and full of nervous energy. This wasn't the same. I still felt anxious, but also epically sad at the same time. Just heavy. I pushed it to one side, thought it would pass. After all, I still had so much to look forward to. Sophie was out there skiing at the same time with her dad, and our two families had never met before, so we all got together for Christmas. It was a lovely day, it truly was, but I couldn't shake the sadness. I was laughing and joking, and full of Christmas cheer – although I wasn't drinking at all – but sadness was still all over me. Like a weighted cloak surrounding me, an inescapable heaviness. I think

I knew that when the celebrations were over that I'd feel really low. Maybe I was already dreading it in advance, like I had a couple of years earlier, when my depersonalisation started. I've always had a huge fear of that happening again. One night, the sadness got so bad that I phoned Sophie up and asked if she could come over to our chalet. She wasn't keen – she was very well brought up and didn't think it was appropriate to be sneaking into my dad's chalet at night like a teenager.

'I really need you,' I said. It was hard for me to admit that. This was a newish relationship; I didn't know if I was ready to show Sophie how vulnerable I was. I knew I loved her at this point, but I was worried about scaring her off. I remembered how my anxiety had been a constant menace with previous girlfriends, and I didn't want anything to get in my way this time. She did come over, though, and was very caring and understanding – even though, and I think she would say this herself, she probably didn't really understand what was going on, because neither did I.

I can't describe how frustrating it was to feel this way – but I probably should try because I'm writing about it in a book. I knew I didn't want to have these feelings, but I also didn't know how to change it. It was like my mojo, or my motivation, was gone. I had my ups and down, but mostly it was just this heavy sadness, like being wrapped in the worst kind of bear hug. I didn't have it in me to be upbeat and entertaining anymore – I'd always thought of myself as an 'always-on' kind of person, but now I was really having to use a lot of energy to even feel semi-enthusiastic about anything. This wasn't me. All I wanted was to be my old self again.

Eventually, I realised I had to address this, so I found a therapist who understood me, the amazing Maleha Khan – I call her Mal, and we've got to know each other pretty well. I tried to explain to Mal what was going on.

'I don't know what it is,' I remember saying, 'It's anxiety, but it's not. It's this . . . sadness.'

But Mal knew what it was right away. 'Jamie, you have burnout,' she said. I had no idea what this meant. 'You've pushed yourself to a place where you don't love what you're doing anymore. You've exhausted all of your energy on everything, and you are totally and utterly burnt out.'

Candles burned out, I knew that, but what did it mean for me?

I suppose I felt frustrated, because I was caught between a rock and a hard place. I loved the show and the lifestyle it gave me, but something was still making me unhappy. In a way it was a relief to have a name for the feeling, and I thought to myself, 'Okay, while I may not understand the concept, I guess now I know what I'm dealing with, it's all going to be okay.' But this was a bit like when I was younger when I went to therapy a couple of times and thought, 'Yay, I'm fixed!'

And at first, I tried to just kind of ignore this feeling, like it was a headache, and carry on. We were back filming, so I was just putting everything into making sure the onscreen me was like I used to be. I tried to just get on with life. And I was juggling everything: my social media, running the business, podcasting, but I'd lost the love for everything. I felt so empty. I just didn't want to do it anymore. I remember thinking, 'So what's the point of all this?' And that's when I started taking anti-anxiety pills, something I'd always refused to do. I've never told anyone that before. It can be hard to admit that you need help, that you can't always be in the driving seat. Sometimes you have to put your faith elsewhere.

But I was still so socially anxious, I found it really hard to be around people, and the sadness was still all over me; it was horrendous. Things came to a head when Sophie and I went to a wedding for one of my closest friends, Toby; I was drinking for the first time in a long while and when we got back, I just had a total anxiety meltdown.

It was a shock for Sophie, I think, and she very honestly said to me, 'I don't know if I can be in a relationship like this. I don't know how to fix you; I don't know how to give you the help you need to fix yourself.'

Obviously, I completely understood her point of view, but this was like the rug being whipped away from under me. I remember rushing to my therapist the next day, crying, terrified that I was going to lose Sophie, the person I loved more than anything, and Mal was clear on what I had to do: I had to start fixing myself, and doing that meant eliminating the things that were making me unhappy.

I finally realised that I'd come to a point where I had to let go of my past. I couldn't cling on to what I suppose I still thought of as my glory days, doing this reality show, where I'd thought we could all be friends together, and it could last forever. It was time to get real.

I'd always thought if I wasn't driving everything all the time, if I wasn't constantly on the go, that I'd lose it all. But this time, I put the brakes on. It wasn't just my health I was worried about; it was losing Sophie. I felt so guilty too, like maybe I'd deceived Sophie in some way, that I hadn't been the kind of boyfriend she'd been expecting. I told myself that Sophie would only be interested in the fun, always-up, enthusiastic Jamie, not the man I was becoming. I remember saying to her, 'It's like you took out this contract, and you were expecting your walls to be painted beautiful and bright pink, but instead everything's been painted dark.'

I have to say, while I know it was hard for us both, Sophie's loyalty was unwavering. She had my back the entire time, even when I pushed her to the absolute limit with my anxiety and self-doubt and feeling of helplessness. It must've been terrible for her. Her poise, her strength, her level-headedness – she didn't leave my side, and always encouraged me, and reassured me that she was there no matter what, and that this wouldn't last forever. She helped me see what I had to do to make a change.

And so I took a backseat for the first time. I started to slow down. I didn't try and be the most fun person in the room anymore, sapping my energy levels. I didn't try to argue or fight or create the drama, like I had done on *Made in Chelsea* for so many years. I rested, and took the time to rebuild. And I realised that it had been so long since I had focused on myself.

If people took my 'throne', so what? Did it really matter? I remember during this time, one of my cast-mates Olivia saying to me, 'Jamie, you're so much nicer now. I like this version of you.' I wasn't fighting to stay on top, or in front, anymore. I was letting someone else have the spotlight, and it was making me nicer to be around. I had always prided myself on being good company, and loads of fun, but the person I thought I had to be in order to stay on top wasn't actually the nice person; I drove people away. So now, my real sense of self, the old me, the *true* me, was starting to come out again. Realising that, and embracing that, made me feel much better.

I carried on with the therapy too, acknowledging that I couldn't be fixed overnight. I was so lucky to be able to go to see my therapist Mal every week, that's something I know isn't available to everyone. I really feel for those who can't get the help that they need, because sometimes it can take years for you to face your problems, and even longer to rebuild. Speaking out and having the space to be open about what's happening to you is so important, especially for men, because we bottle things up, think we have to act a certain way, so we won't be thought of as less of a man. But when you open up, you make a connection, you realise you are not alone in the world and often you find out that lots of other people are going through similar things. If you internalise your issues, they eat away at you from the inside. Admitting to yourself that something is wrong is always the first step. You have to say it out loud. So, if you're feeling lost, or insecure, or like life has become too heavy, try and find someone to talk to. It can be anyone: a friend, a family member, a therapist. In my experience, it helps so much. The world would be a much better place for everybody if men were more open about their feelings – that's why I don't try to hold things in anymore.

I thought I had to play all these different roles so people would like me, or love me, but this wasn't the case at all. It's so revealing that once I took a step back and came back to me again, that's what people liked. The reason why I had the friends I had, the reason I'd been liked, the reason I'd got the role on *Made in Chelsea* in the first place, is because I was being me. And the reason why I wasn't liked as much on the show, or was becoming a pain, was because I wasn't the real me anymore. My personality was changing because of how others reacted to me, and the image I thought I had to portray. I was influenced by stuff on social media, which can be so dangerous. So gradually, even subconsciously, I suppose, I'd started behaving a certain way to create entertainment to get me the screen-time that kept me at the top. And then when everyone else left, my protective barrier, the people I knew and joined with, was gone. I felt like I was kind of leading it on my own. It's like I was a gladiator, and every new person that came in, I had to attack and fight off. And everyone else was bored of fighting, but there I was, still fighting. So now I was taking that step back. I'd let the other version of myself dominate for too long, when all I needed to do was remember who I was in the first place. Being that kind, gentle, funny person was what made people like me.

But still I was too afraid to quit the show. I thought if I quit, everything I was working towards would just stop. Everything would disappear. Maybe I wouldn't be as popular so I wouldn't get any work ever again. I was very conscious of how I got my fame – in my head I'd come in through the back door. It always seemed very temporary, of less value somehow than true fame, that comes from putting your nose to the grindstone and trying to get your talent noticed. I thought I'd never get the chance again.

And then lightning struck twice, a rope ladder slowly dropped from a hole in the sky – *Strictly* came calling again.

Chapter Sixteen
Entertainer

I've appeared on lots of terrific TV shows – and some bad ones, okay, okay – but I really would do them all over again. I don't just love being on TV, I love being involved in it too. A lot of people find working in television a drag, because when you're not actually filming, there is a lot of waiting around, and stopping and starting and all that kind of stuff – but I love it. Seriously, love it. No complaints from me, ever. I love the bustle of a TV set, the different people you meet, all the things going on behind the scenes to bring you this hour, or half-hour or whatever, of TV, everyone focused on one goal and one goal only: entertainment! I'm honestly just happy to be there!

While the TV shows I had done before were great, there are some shows that are the Holy Grail, aren't there? Actual national institutions – proper icons that everyone tunes into, or, even if they don't watch, they know about – they'll have seen at least one, and will have an opinion on it, even if it's to say they hate it. *Strictly Come Dancing* is one of those shows. Another would be *Great British Bake Off* – I was lucky enough to do a celebrity special for Stand Up To Cancer and that was huge. That was a big risk for me as I'd never baked anything in my life before. I remember when the instructions came through for what I was going to have to bake on the show, I asked my mum for help.

'Mum, what's a "merinj"?'

You should've seen her face. 'A *what*?'

'It says here I have to make a "merinj tower". I've never heard of it.'

She grabbed the piece of paper from me, rolled her eyes, and handed it back to me, sighing. '*Meringue*, Jamie. Meringue tower.'

Well, I'd never seen this word written down before; I thought it rhymed with 'fringe'. Not the best start, but I was thrilled to be asked on. This was a proper TV show that people had grown up with, that mum and my sister watched. I wasn't doing another reality show that my mum couldn't really relate to or, more importantly, tell people about without them asking her what she was talking about. Everybody knew *Bake Off*.

Unfortunately, I wasn't very good at it. I didn't really understand the abbreviations on one of the recipes, so I confused teaspoons with tablespoons, and let's just say my banana loaf cake was less than stellar. Although I did score one accolade: Paul Hollywood said it was the worst cake he'd ever seen in the *Bake Off* tent. Quite impressive when you think about it. The dreaded meringue tower actually turned out brilliantly for me. All I did was copy exactly what Tim Minchin was doing; he seemed to have it all worked out. It was quite funny actually because when we first started filming, Tim Minchin walked on set and said, 'I thought it was supposed to be celebrities' – ouch! When it came to the meringue tower, though, Tim's kind of melted and disintegrated while mine managed to stay put. How did I do it? I have no idea! Poor Tim.

If anything, though, *Strictly* is a bigger deal than *Bake Off*, bigger than anything, maybe! Millions of people dedicate their time to watching it, every Saturday and Sunday night for about three months of the year. I was over the moon to be asked to go on it the first time, but, as you know, it wasn't meant to be. I was partnered with Oti that first time, and we got on so well, but I do wonder if she might have got a bit sick of me if I'd stayed on the show that year. I think I mess around too much. Anyway, we never got to find out because, of course, I'd worn those lifts in my shoes and given myself plantar fasciitis and in my very first show there was a twang and a pain and . . . that was me back at home on the sofa watching all the fun happen without me. I'm not ashamed to say I cried when I found out I couldn't do it. My big chance, a proper TV moment – gone!

Fast forward a few months later, and the world has much bigger problems going on – the pandemic hit. Such a frightening time for everyone. Once it looked like things were turning a corner and restrictions were easing, the possibility that a series of *Strictly* might go ahead for 2020 looked increasingly likely and I was absolutely thrilled when they asked if I'd like another go. It was the best thing in the world! I was so, so excited. In fact, I was a little *too* excited. Maybe it had been the collective buzz of the pandemic looking like it might be over (my, how that would change pretty quickly), and everything being open again for summer, but I wanted one last hurrah before I went into isolation for the show. Around two or three weeks before *Strictly* was supposed to start, I went to the pub and then back to a friend's garden for a few more, Covid-secure but still ill-advised, drinks. I was very pumped for *Strictly*, and when I'm excited there's always the danger I might act like an idiot, I'm afraid. Cut to me at 3 a.m., having races against my friends in the middle of the street, stripped down to my boxers when, suddenly, TWANG. Oh no. Noooooo. I felt the snap of my hamstring right there. I went straight to a specialist – well, after Sophie had picked me up to take me home for some very anxious sleep – and had to have an MRI. The specialist warned me if it was a grade three tear, there was no show for me. Grade two, and I'd be okay. Tense is not the word. Good news – it was borderline, but I'd probably be okay. So for the next two weeks before *Strictly* I had to have physio done in secret. I didn't tell anyone on the show, or any of my friends. I was mortified, and also desperate not to miss out on this chance. So, can we just keep this between us, yeah? Nobody needs to know.

So, *Strictly* is like no other show. It's an incredible experience but it's also the most mentally tough thing I've ever done. Ever! Sometimes it feels like you're climbing Everest, and it's impossible. Let me take you through a typical week, so you can see for yourself. Now, as a celebrity on the show, it's up to you how many hours you do, but if you want to do well, you have to commit. I wanted the full experience, and look, I wanted to win this thing, so I was up at seven every day for training.

So you get there Monday morning, bleary-eyed, and your partner tells you what dance you've got to do. I was with Karen Hauer this time – she is a powerhouse, truly an amazing dancer and incredible person. We became such good friends. But here she is, on a Monday morning, telling you, okay, you have the foxtrot or the jive, or whatever. Now, I have no idea what any of the dances are at this point. I vaguely know a ballroom dance means you'll probably be dancing quite slowly – not always the case, as I discovered – and that Latin is quite a sexy dance – again, definitely not always the case. But that was it. Everything else, I learned from scratch. The only way I can describe it is, it's the difference between skiing and snowboarding. You look at snowboarders, and what they do kind of all looks the same – unless they do a flip or something, you can't tell how good they are. A skier though, well, you can easily spot someone who's crap at it, and good skiers look amazing. But snowboarding is much harder as a beginner. With skiing, you get into your skis and kind of snow-plough down the mountain – congrats, you're skiing. But once you get the knack of snowboarding, it's easier to do well. Skiing is much harder to perfect. It's the same with Latin and ballroom. Latin is much harder to get because of all the steps, but once you get it, even if you're not that good, you kind of make yourself look good. At least this is what I told myself. It's much easier to get the basics of ballroom because the steps are much slower, but it's impossible to perfect. For me, anyway. It's so hard. Wow.

So on the Monday you train, train, train, all the time. And because everything is so new, you literally spend the entire day figuring out how to do one thing. Yes, ONE. So maybe you're doing a cha-cha – you'll spend the whole day learning the Cuban break. One step. Samba, it'd be understanding the bounce in your feet. For a full day. Jive, it might be a leg extension or something. For a whole day! That first day of the week is hell.' I was always thinking, 'I can't get this, no chance in hell. I'd get frustrated and frightened. I remember thinking, almost every Monday, 'Oh great, I'm gonna be the only person ever in *Strictly* history to go onto the dance floor and not be able to do it at all.'

Other celebrities would be training in other rooms at the same time. Max George from The Wanted was next door and we would pop in on each other, and I remember one day hearing him cheer so I rushed in to see what was happening.

'Oh Max, don't tell me you learned your entire dance already!'

Max looked back at me. 'What do you mean?'

'Well, I heard you cheer like you'd just won a billion pounds!' I was panicking a bit, worried I wasn't as good as the others, you see.

Max just laughed. 'Jamie, I was cheering because I have learned one step. Just one! So I cheered.'

It felt better knowing we were in it together. So, by seven or eight in the evening, after twelve hours or so trying to do your one step – with a fraught break for lunch – you go home. And now you realise how hard it's going to be, you're cancelling all your plans for the week, even your phone calls. 'Nope,' you think, 'I have to focus on this, this dance is impossible, and come Saturday, I'm totally fucked.' That's a totally normal feeling.

By the end of Tuesday, you're understanding things better. Like having a ball thrown at you again and again and finally catching it. But I was still a wreck. I remember thinking to myself, 'Right, I now sort of see how to do it, but, still, this is gonna be terrible.'

By the end of Wednesday . . . you're kind of running it. You can do it. But, well, you're running it in the way that a baby might run a nativity play, or a frog might drive a car. You wouldn't really want to sit through this play, or be a passenger in this car, but . . . good luck to them.

Thursday comes around and you're just about there in terms of knowing what you have to do – it's just a case of whether you're actually any good at it yet. But, seriously, this is ruthless, you're knackered. I was burning, like, 2,500–3,000 calories a day during training. And you're not just practising, it's full-on: you're doing the VTs for the live show so they can see what you've been up to, there's social media and behind-the-scenes stuff to do. And then we're up to Friday, and you have three tries at it and, normally, it's terrible. And then it's Saturday. The big day! And you come in and do two rehearsals and a dress run, and it's terrifying, and then of course it's the show. And if you're not onstage, and not out watching, then you're practising, right up until you come out and do the performance. If you're on first, then, great, you can get it out of the way, but if you're not, you just have to wait and it's nerve-wracking. You get about eight minutes to have a final practice just before you go on, and by this point I was usually just hysterical with nerves.

Anyway, you do your thing, the public votes, you either dance again or don't and, if you're still in, the whole process starts again!

What was interesting for me about being on *Strictly* and going through all this training and constantly taking on the new challenges, is that usually I work on instant gratification, as I've said. Quick fixes, instant results, natural talent – I've always just expected things to work out and fast, and if that doesn't happen, I lose interest, or get frustrated and give up. But with *Strictly*, I had to get over myself. I started to understand the process of learning, and the sense of achievement from working at something and nailing it – well, almost nailing it, just about enough of the time. By week five, say, I knew Mondays would be crap, I knew Tuesdays would also be crap in a different way, I knew by Wednesday I might actually get it. I knew what was coming, so I'd grit my teeth and get on with it, knowing I would get there in the end. In a way, it taught me to be patient with myself, and trust in myself a bit. It taught me the importance of resilience and always getting back up and trying again. There is this great Denzel Washington quote: 'Ease is a greater threat to progress than hardship.' I kept thinking about that when I was training with Karen. It's one of the hardest things I've ever done, but I had to keep going and I had to keep trying. It was like I saw the bigger picture – that it doesn't matter if I'm having a shit time in the moment, because it can only get better, and then I'll reap the rewards. And I did! Making it through week after week was so satisfying.

Mind you, being on live TV every week? God, I mean . . . I absolutely shat myself, to be honest. I suppose I went in there a little blind. I assumed that most people watching had also seen *Made in Chelsea*, so they'd know who I was and, if they were fans of *MIC*, probably thought I was an alright guy. But I was suddenly in front of 13 million people every week, twice a week. *Strictly* is a juggernaut. I could sense there was a bit of a negative perception of me, and I get it, in a way. At first, on celebrity shows, viewers aren't keen on contestants they haven't heard of, or have heard negative things about. I already knew that my background wasn't very relatable, and that people liked to make fun of the poshness, but I hadn't thought it would make people dislike me. It was a bit of a shock to find anyone had strong feelings about me either way, but this is what happens when you're in someone's living room for weeks on end, you start to belong to the viewers. I didn't think I was as bad as I was being made out, and I wondered what I could do to turn it around, but I realised all I could do was be myself. Just be the Jamie who had started to find himself again after my burnout, and they'd see, hopefully, that I was a nice guy. In any case, I couldn't overthink it too much: I had dancing steps to remember.

The first show was so nerve-wracking. I did sort of think to myself, 'Well everyone is in the same boat, it will be fine,' but what made it even more frightening for me is that I was desperate to be great. I really wanted to win. Some of the contestants didn't care, they just wanted to get through it, but I wanted to win. That first week, we did the cha-cha and . . . oh my, I did my old trick again, like when I did stand-up, thinking I'd aced it. In rehearsals, I was brilliant; I thought, 'I'm a professional now, it's easy' – that instant gratification buzz kicking in. But: devastation! I was in the dance-off. I thought now, 'Hang on, this is way too early for me to be in the dance-off.' For some reason, it didn't occur to me that my performance had been that terrible – if anything I felt I was reining it in to stop looking *too* good – so I thought there must be a plan. Yes, that's right, a cunning plan by . . . well, I hadn't really thought this far, by the producers, maybe? Because you don't quite want to think you're the worst dancer, do you? Like if someone breaks up with you, or doesn't fancy you, or your team doesn't win, you always make an excuse, that it's some external force out of your control, to make yourself feel better. So I thought maybe they had a plan for me to rise victorious from the depths the following week or something. I mean, I don't know – I was kind of used to *Made in Chelsea* and there being a bit of a story arc to follow, but this was not the case at all. In the second week, where I hit the bottom again, I realised . . . nope, there was no plan; I was just . . . crap.

Obviously, I lived to fight another day, but I knew I was going to have to work at this. I'd watched that cha-cha back and saw for myself: bad. Then I remember when we danced the American Smooth, and Karen and I watched it back and she leaned into me and said, 'Jamie, *now* you're dancing.' I felt incredible.

Karen was terrific, by the way; I love her. We became terrific friends, but she really made me work for it, she put me through the mill in training. I used to call her 'Goose' because if I messed up a step she would hiss at me, sometimes quite harshly. She's quite guarded, and I really had to earn her trust, but that's a quality I like in people – I'm a bit of an open book, but I'm drawn to people who are more mysterious and reserved. My girlfriend Sophie is like that too. Mind you, it's not surprising I had to work for

Karen's trust – I remember in rehearsals for the Hercules dance, I had to pick her up, but actually dropped her. She turned to me, and in a very angry voice said, 'Don't you ever fucking drop me again.' I didn't need telling twice. I have such respect for all the pros on *Strictly* because they're incredible. The celebs get all the praise, but the pros have to learn two or three dance routines a week, and then stand with some stranger they've never met before and teach them to dance, week in week out, and then compete on the show! I never complained, but I'm sure many times pros have had to deal with star partners complaining, or getting upset, or bolshy, and they just sit there and take it. I honestly applaud all those pros. There wasn't a single challenge you couldn't throw at them that they wouldn't do amazingly.

My biggest challenge? Myself, obviously. My nerves. Oh, man. I spent most of my time talking myself out of thinking I wasn't good enough, that I'd be too nervous to compete, or that I was going to have a panic attack on stage, or that I'd forget my moves. In rehearsals, most days, I would be challenged, but fine. On the night of the live shows, terror would grip me that I'd let Karen down, or that people would think I was crap, or that I wasn't trying hard enough. One week, Mr Price, a teacher from my old school, sent me a message saying he was watching and couldn't even imagine how I was feeling, given how nervous I used to be during athletics competitions at school. He used to have to walk me round the track the entire time, because I was so nervous. Right before every dance, I would convince myself I couldn't do it, but somehow, once you're on stage, it clicks. I don't know how, it just does.

I was in quite a lot of dance-offs – 70 per cent of them if you care to do the maths, which I don't, really. My fellow contestants would call me the assassin, because even though my first dance was terrible, I'd always somehow bring it home in the dance-off. It's strange, but at the point of death I'll always be the one who can get out of the situation. The trouble is I end up leading myself there – if only I could work out how to stay out of danger in the first place.

I remember one week I was up against JJ Chalmers, who was doing 'Chitty Chitty Bang Bang,' and I watched it and thought, hmmm, it wasn't that great but then neither was my jive. Usually after every dance I would go up to the show's choreographers for their feedback and they'd always give me a thumbs up and positive comments like, 'That was good, you looked great.' After the jive, though, I got, 'Hmm, do you know what? Just keep it more controlled.' I thought, 'Well, if they were saying that to me, it was obviously crap' and I was going home. There was a bit in the dance where I had to do a move called the drunken sailor which seems very easy but is technically hard to do, and right before, I had to go to face the crowd and kind of run around. In rehearsals, me being me, I amped it up, and kept cheering at the crowd like I was auditioning for *Britain's Got Talent*. Karen said to me, very sternly again, 'Do not do that in the show, you'll lose control. Do. Not. Do. It.'

Now, Karen is pretty imposing, so I did as I was told . . . until the dance-off. It was going so well, and I really thought I could beat JJ because his dance-off performance wasn't great (sorry JJ, but I promised my readers I would tell the truth), so the worst thing that could possibly happen happened: I got overexcited. I'm dangerous in these moments. So when it came to that part, I went to the crowd, 'COME ON!!' and really went for it, before promptly messing up the drunken sailor move, as Karen had warned me. Oops. As I was messing up, I was laughing at Karen. Her face! When we came off, she couldn't even talk to me. But we got through, and she forgave me.

Being in the dance-off was always a disappointment, as I did genuinely try my best every week. It was strange to think something I was doing wasn't quite hitting it off with the public. I did get lots of positive comments on the show and from viewers, but it's always the bad ones you remember, isn't it? Maybe it's my own fault for going online and reading, but everyone did. Seriously, as soon as the live show finished, we all dashed to our phones to see what people were saying. And there'd be live blogs, and people writing columns, and comments everywhere – if you wanted to know what people thought of you, you didn't have far to look. I remember Oti saying to me once, 'Jamie, *Strictly* is an amazing show to be on if you don't look at social media.' She was so right. You try not to take it personally, but people have their favourites, and some don't like you for whatever reason. But it's a competition, and everyone wants to be loved – that's the whole point, the most-loved wins. I remember one time I thought, 'Right, I'm not going to look at Twitter, definitely not.' So I didn't, for my first two dance-offs. And then, just as I was about to go and perform in my third dance-off, I peeked. First tweet I saw?

'Jamie is like that turd that you can't flush.'

What a burn! Straight after reading that I had to race to the dance floor and dance for my survival. I thought, 'You know what, this doesn't matter. The comments will be there whether I read them or not. They don't change what I'm doing, or how I dance, I need to block out the noise.' I laughed about it in the end. In a way, they were right, I kept surviving, week after week; I really was that little turd that wouldn't flush. It did get to me sometimes though. I remember once, when we were waiting for the results, saying to Oti how worried I was about ending up in the dance-off again, and she said, 'Look, say you are in the dance-off, what happens?'

'Well,' I said, 'I have to dance again.'

'Right,' she said, 'but won't you still be the same person? You'll still be nice, and kind? You'll still have your friends, and people who care about you?'

'Um . . . yes?'

'Well, then,' she said. 'It really doesn't matter, the dance-offs don't matter. It's just a TV show.'

So I felt calmer, and thought, 'Yes, Oti's right.' Anyway, we go to stand under the spotlights so Tess can announce who's going through. Oti's partner Bill Bailey says, 'Well, I hope it's not me in the dance-off because I've had a couple of Bacardis.' Amazing. Miracle upon miracle – it's not me. And then Oti and Bill are told they're going through and . . . well, you should see Oti. She's cheering and whooping hard, like punching the air with her fist, like she just scored a deciding goal in a world cup final, won the lottery, and been granted immortality all at once. She is pumped! So after the show, I said to her, 'Oti, I thought it didn't matter? But you were cheering when you got through.'

She smiled and looked a bit embarrassed. 'God, I know. It really matters so much!'

But, honestly, after a while, and a few more bottom twos, I realised she was right in the first place. In my head, I just went, fuck it, it doesn't matter. Doesn't matter anymore. Who cares? What was I going to do, try and win everyone over, or make them love me? I couldn't. I just had to go out there and dance. Occasionally I still freaked out. I had an anxiety attack going on to do my semi-final salsa; I don't even remember doing it. But deep down I realised, if I lose, it doesn't actually matter. It's the same as when I thought if I left *Made in Chelsea* after ten years, that was going to be it, the end of my career. So I thought I had to stick with it. But now I've moved away and . . . surprisingly, the offers keep coming in.

I couldn't believe it when I made the final. I mean, I'd come to win, but there was no way I actually expected to go all the way, especially after all those dance-offs . . . When we were picked to go through from the semi-final over Ranvir Singh – who was an absolutely amazing dancer – Karen cried. The final is such a wonderful experience. You're exhausted, and mentally drained, but you get to look back at everything you've done and how far you've come with this montage, and you really get a sense of, wow, I've done all of that. You're not only doing it for you, you're doing it for your partner, because your partner tries so hard, and this is their career. They've got you to the final, made something out of nothing – this was very much Karen's moment too. I must admit when they shouted out, 'Welcome our 2020 finalists', I felt immediate imposter syndrome. I was like, this is ridiculous; I should not be here. I kind of felt embarrassed. How did I get here? I never expected this. What am I doing? I remember when they were calling out the winner and I just had that crazy last-minute thought: what if? This is the end of the journey! This is it! I've come all this way, I stayed focused and resilient, and I made it here. 'They're about to read out my name,' I suddenly thought, 'Shit, this is going to happen!' It was like I was fantasising about winning the lottery, but the odds were way better. I waited. I stood up tall. The silence was deafening. I swear I heard Tess take in that breath before she was going to say that name and I was positive it was going to begin with a J. Oh man, was I ready for this? Then, just as my heart was about to burst, Tess said the magic words: 'Bill Bailey'. And I thought, 'Oh, yeah, okay, fine. Totally. Yeah, that makes sense. Yeah, that makes way more sense. Oh well!'

What was really interesting about *Strictly* was not just the chance that I got to show off my entertaining skills, but how it brought me and my family closer together, especially me and my dad. I've always wanted to make him proud. My parents have always been quite tough when it comes to my fame, in a good way, keeping me grounded, reminding me I'm just Jamie, the same old idiot I've always been. When I started Candy Kittens, or did the TV shows, they never really said much about them, because for them it wasn't a very relatable career path. As far as they were concerned, I'd never had a proper job, and I never got a degree from Oxford. But *Strictly*. It was something so many people they admired had done, and you had to learn a skill, and achieve – I think they totally got that. Our whole family came closer together because of it. And yes, I was front and centre yet again, but there was a sense of pride for all of them that their brother and their son was doing this huge thing. And my sister was organising interviews with my mum and dad to talk about me – it was like a shared experience for everyone. I felt like I was representing us out there and they were my strongest supporters. It was a team effort. On those interviews, I could see my dad's pride for me for the first time; I could see it in his eyes. My little brother told me he'd never seen Dad cry, but he cried watching me dance. I think for him it was a big thing to be my dad at that moment.

The really great thing about *Strictly* is that maybe people realised I wasn't such a knob after all. I think a lot of people came round to me, and thought I was a nice boy. Not just some posh white kid pissing about on the Kings Road. Maybe they could also see how hard I worked, and how much it all meant to me too. With me being such a people pleaser, that was a very nice feeling. I'd taken it seriously and given it my all, and I hope that came across to anyone watching.

Apart from Candy Kittens, I'd never put this much time and effort into anything before – I never put much muscle into my exams, for example, I'd often be reading up on revision topics for the first time while waiting to go in and sit them. But this was a revelation: I realised that if I put my heart into something, stayed focused and determined, I could learn something new, and I would be rewarded. Before that I'd only really focused on my natural talents, things I was already good at. *Strictly* totally changed me: I'm now much better at putting time into things, pushing myself a bit more, investing in myself.

I can even do it without being hissed at now.

Chapter Seventeen
Leading Man

I've taken quite a long time to work out who I am. Nearly 33 years in fact. Some people never work it out, do they? They spend all their lives searching for the answer. Maybe I've not actually cracked it at all, but I definitely feel like I'm in the best place I've been for years. For the first time, I now have balance, and I understand how great that can be. Before, I was always wanting to have the most fun ever, to always be on this relentless rollercoaster. Always chasing the absolute highs, the definitive buzz, but the trouble with these ultimate highs is they come with devastating lows. Those pesky wasps, remember – just waiting to sting. Would I like to be in my early twenties again, spending the days sozzled and dashing from place to place looking for fun? You know what, yes sometimes! But it's not all I crave. The key with balance is that the mundane days don't scare me anymore; I don't back away from anything that's normal or downbeat.

My life was not real life for a long time. Now there are still some days that are going to be super fun, and they're terrific, but sometimes there will be downtime as well. And that's okay. Not everything has to be a high-octane experience. Accepting that takes a lot of the pressure off and has helped me find joy in the everyday things. I'm properly happy in my relationship, for maybe the first time ever, because I'm not chasing more, more, more, all the time. There's still plenty out there to do and discover but I've got Sophie with me now, and most of the pleasure comes from experiencing it together. Does that sound soppy? Okay, it does, and look, of course we have days where we're, like, arguing, or having a cry or getting pissed off at one another – usually when I'm pranking Sophie on Instagram, if I'm honest. But that's what a relationship is: good days and bad days, days of not much happening and days when it feels like the end of the world, or the start of one. That's okay. The best thing about it, though, and the essence of our relationship, is that I get to hang out with and talk to my best mate most days. That's a rarity; I know not everyone is lucky enough to have that. She annoys me and makes me angry sometimes – and I know I do the same to her – but she's far better than me in every single way. I mean, look, I have to get real here: there's no way Sophie wakes up every morning, looks at my crumpled face, tongue hanging out the side of my mouth, probably a bit of dried-up drool there for good measure, and thinks, 'God, I really have hit the jackpot.' I'm fully aware! But I'm incredibly lucky to have someone in my life who loves me. I've had that before, but I don't know if I've ever let the love in or known quite what to do with it. I used to think being in love was the answer to everything, but it's what you do with the love, how you process it, how it changes you – that's the answer.

So why the change? Why am I like this now? Why am I more content in a relationship than ever before? What's the magic formula? Well, I have to be honest here, don't I, in that every time something went wrong in one of my previous relationships, there was always one common denominator. All the tears and misery and betrayal and hurt had one thing at the centre of them: me. I have to take responsibility for that, right? My friend Alex Mytton used to say to me, 'Jamie, you know, I think you just love the drama,' and I got his point but that wasn't it at all for me. I created enough dramas to keep a show going for almost a decade, fine, but it was never intentional. I've hurt so many people – and myself – throughout my life and I knew I had to change. After letting go of doubts and insecurities, and feelings of being under pressure to have a relationship, I finally felt ready. It all happened in the most surprising of ways, that I didn't have to focus on monogamy; it came to find me. I realised how amazing it is to have a good relationship with your family too; it's like it's all slotted into place. For me, the sense of contentment I feel now came from leaving behind rocky relationships, and no longer polluting my body with alcohol and never giving myself a break – it came from making time for friends and family, and a loving, monogamous relationship. The Jamie of ten years ago, five years ago – would never have paused long enough to realise this. I could go back in time, and tell him, and once he'd asked me what the hell had happened to my hair and congratulated me on my guns (come on, allow it), he'd completely ignore all my advice. That's just who I was then. I remember reading about this Harvard study that went on for years, regularly analysing the brains of their graduates and seeing how their lives turned out, and apparently, the main factor in happiness was connections with friends and family.

I think it's also about facing my past and coming to terms with it. I take inspiration from people who've had much longer careers than I have, and more turbulent lives. I remember watching an amazing interview with Sir Anthony Hopkins, in which he was asked if he had any regrets. He was pretty honest; he said he didn't have time for regrets. He was a sinner, he said; he'd done some good things and some bad things. Realise what you've done and move on was his philosophy. I'm very much like that. I'm not in denial, by the way: I've done some things in my past that I'm not proud of. I've also done some things I'm really proud of. But there's no point in sitting with regrets and letting them get me down. I can't change any of them, all I can do is make my peace with them and make sure I don't repeat these mistakes. I actually think that mistakes are important – the more you make, the more you learn – but it's also about hurting as few people as you can along the way. I made every mistake under the sun possible. I drank too much, tried to do too much, ran away from commitment and broke people's trust in me. I've made a lot of people upset. It's very easy to say sorry, and I have done that a lot over the years, and I've meant every apology, but my apologies probably didn't help anyone else very much. But I did learn from each of these mistakes.

It took me a long time to admit that I had anxiety – admit it to myself, to others, and even to you, in this book. The hardest thing about having anxiety is being able to accept it – at first it feels like you're giving into it, in a way. Like I said, way back at the start of the book, I was the fun one, not the anxious one, and I was fighting against that side of me slipping away. But part of recovery and rebuilding is acknowledging anxiety, that it isn't just going to go away by itself. Anxiety is part of you, but doesn't have to define you. I'll admit to you right here, right now: I still feel vulnerable when talking about my anxiety, but accepting the problem and getting the help I needed – thanks again, Mal! – means I can live alongside it now and manage it, and I suppose in a way I respect it. It was important for me to be open with you about it, to show you, I suppose, that it can happen to anyone, and that the worst can be overcome. If it's happening to you, you're not alone. I'm still the fun one – that never changed. Even with anxiety, you're still you. Remember that.

Being obsessed with success was another one for me, wasn't it? Another thing getting in my way. It's weird how searching for happiness, or battling to do the things you think will make you happy, end up making things worse sometimes. Again, it's about balance. Maybe it's easy for me to say but money doesn't really make a difference as long as you can cover your bills, but I strived for success all the time and it's never as fulfilling as you think it's going to be, because then you're thinking: 'Well, okay, that's ticked off, what's next?' But having someone there who loves you is very fulfilling and the reason it's different with Sophie is because I'm in a place where I'm able to accept life as it is and am not constantly wanting more. I'm still ambitious, of course, but I'm more realistic now. A bit kinder to myself too, maybe. Taking time to celebrate the hits and learn from the misses.

The most amazing thing is that I have actually achieved one of my dreams. I've become a presenter! I have my own show, *I Like the Way U Move*, alongside the incredible Kaelynn 'KK' Harris – or just KK as I like to call her, saves time – on the BBC. I still pinch myself about this. This is seriously what I have always wanted – when I was a kid, I used to line up my teddy bears and pretend I was presenting to them, like my own little chat show. This show combines what I would politely call two areas of expertise – dating, which I've done a lot of, and dancing, which got me to a *Strictly* final. Like most things with me, it came along when I was least expecting it. I remember saying to my friend Toby a while ago that I still really hoped to get a proper presenting gig one day and he said, 'One day there'll be a moment where someone drops out or something happens, and they need you to fill in – that will be your moment to shine.' And, he was right! I got a call from Kelly, a producer I'd known for many years. She said she was shooting a pilot in South Africa and the host they'd lined up wasn't available, so could I just fill in this once to see how the format worked.

Look, I didn't need telling twice. It was only the pilot, no big deal, but maybe it would lead to other things. So off I went, under the shadow of a pandemic, to film this pilot with not many expectations other than it was going to be huge fun being back in front of the camera. Anyway, I went off, did my thing, had an absolute scream of a time doing it and . . . it went so well that they offered me the job. I couldn't believe it! Still can't! Pinch me, I might be dreaming. Oh. Well, okay, pinch the page of the book. OW. Yes, felt that. It's real. Thank goodness.

This really couldn't have come at a better time for me. Any younger and I think I'd be all over the place. I used to think that on TV you had to bring the energy, be turned up way past 100 per cent, but now I understand how to control my own personal levels more. I totally get it now and am much calmer and more comfortable in my own skin. I still get nervous, and I still panic I'm going to get something wrong, like a contestant's name, but I don't let the worries take over me – they help to push me a little instead. It's gone so great.

I don't know how you feel about me now you've (nearly) read the book. I've always been worried that people were going to judge me, but isn't it strange how I always put myself in situations where that's exactly what's going to happen? In the limelight, on TV, in competitive events or shows – there's always someone going to be judging you. There were things about me I didn't want people to know, because imagining them thinking badly of me was so terrifying. So I used to try to hide things, but hiding things can actually make you ill. I've been pretty selfish for lots of my life, and I've had to relearn and undo a lot of my past behaviour. Sounds cheesy, maybe, but I like the idea of giving something back. Like with my podcasting, I feel we genuinely help people by talking about mental health so openly and we also donate money every single month to people who deserve more. Helping others is a pretty important thing to do, and talking about stuff and being open and honest about things that are going on with you is really important. And you can't get much more open and honest than putting it all down in a book.

There's probably going to be a moment, when I first see the book in a shop, or online, where I think, 'Shit, this is actually happening, no going back now,' and I might feel a flutter of nerves in my chest. Maybe it's not the done thing to admit, but I am scared of what people might think and say after reading the book. I mean, I have literally – like, just a few paragraphs ago! – told you that I now feel calm and balanced and am focusing on what's important, yet . . . am still worried about what you think. It's a contradiction, I know. But life is like that. How you feel about me once the book is over is your decision; I can't influence that, I know. You may like me, you may hate me, you may adore me, or you may think I'm a complete twat. What's the right answer? Only you know. But what this is all about, is me being okay with whatever you decide. You can't please everyone, and you can't be loved by everyone, and that's okay. It's fine to be that way. I'm learning, all the time. A work in progress.

So now we've got the past out of the way, and we're dealing with the present, I suppose we should take a peek at the future, right? Well, okay, don't laugh, but I went to see a psychic. Why not? I'm not good with surprises, I like a bit of warning. We watch the weather channel to find out if it's going to rain, why not get a helping hand navigating the mists of times to come? They said that I was going to have a child one day, and that this child would be the making of me. This child will be everything to me and will open my eyes to the world. You may not believe in all that stuff, but it gave me a really warm feeling. I felt happy knowing that it might happen one day. You see, I get this now. My whole life, I've loved being part of a team, the big ensemble. I've been looking for this perfect team all these years, which is why I wanted the gang to carry on in *Made in Chelsea* long after everyone else had moved on. I have always been looking for somewhere to belong, to be able to join in. But what if, rather than search for this team, to be part of this big moment, I start it off myself? I've always wanted to put myself front and centre of everything for so long. Sometimes I've chased the approval of people who don't even know me, trying to please literal strangers.

We all want to make people happy, but actually making the people closest to you happy is more fulfilling. What better way to be front and centre than as a dad, in a family? And that's what I want, to share that spotlight with someone so we can all feel it. I want to be someone's hero, but not just for myself. That's what love actually means. It's putting others above yourself without even thinking about it. They're an extension of you, and you put a force field around them, and you. I suppose I see being a dad as being the ultimate hero.

I might knock it out the park, or I might fall flat on my face. Either way, I'm willing to give it a go. And that's all that matters.

Acknowledgements

Thank you to Vicky and everyone at Orion for giving me the opportunity to write my first book. I hope I don't let you down!

To Justin for helping me express what I wanted to say so beautifully on the page.

To all the many friends, acquaintances, fellow cast and crew members and colleagues who have been mentioned in the book. You have all guided, helped and shaped me in some way throughout my life, so thank you.

To my second family, everyone who works at Monkey Kingdom – I love you all!

To the teams at the BBC: thank you for all the fantastic opportunities you've given me.

To all my close friends who haven't been mentioned in the book! You know who you are, and I love you all. There aren't enough pages to express my gratitude to you, but also afraid your stories just weren't funny enough to make the edit. Sorry! Ha ha...

To Laura, Louise, Flora and Paul, my agents at the Independent Talent Group. God knows how you put up with me but thank you!

To my brilliant publicists Robbie and Tim at the Epilogue Agency, who continually make sure I don't say something stupid.

To my amazing business partner Ed, and the great team at Candy Kittens. I'm so proud of what we have all built together!

To my family, who have always been there and taught me what unconditional love is.

And finally, to my girlfriend Sophie, who loves me for who I am. For that I will always be grateful!

About the Author

Jamie Laing is one of the most recognisable faces on British TV, as the star of the BAFTA-winning series *Made in Chelsea*, first appearing in 2011 during its second series.

Jamie's career in entertainment has gone from strength to strength, seeing him star on *Celebrity Hunted*, *The Great Celebrity Bake Off for SU2C* and *Famous and Fighting Crime*, as well as hosting the *Private Parts* podcast with *MIC* co-star Francis Boulle and *6 Degrees from Jamie and Spencer* with Spencer Matthews. In 2020, Jamie went mainstream making it to the final of *Strictly Come Dancing*.

When he's not on our screens, Jamie's busy in the confectionery business as the founder of leading British sweet brand Candy Kittens.

CREDITS

Seven Dials would like to thank everyone at Orion who worked on the publication of *I Can Explain* in the UK.

Editor
Vicky Eribo

Copy-editor
Verity Shaw

Proofreader
Chris Stone

Editorial Management
Shyam Kumar
Jane Hughes
Bartley Shaw
Claire Boyle

Audio
Paul Stark
Jake Alderson

Contracts
Anne Goddard
Jakir Hussen

Production
Nicole Abel
Claire Keep
Fiona McIntosh

Design
Clare Sivell
Joanna Ridley
Helen Ewing

Finance
Nick Gibson
Jasdip Nandra
Sue Baker

Marketing
Folayemi Adebayo

Publicity
Francesca Pearce

Sales

Jen Wilson
Victoria Laws
Esther Waters
Frances Doyle
Georgina Cutler
Jack Hallam
Barbara Ronan
Dominic Smith
Deborah Deyong
Lauren Buck
Maggy Park

Operations

Jo Jacobs
Sharon Willis

Rights

Susan Howe
Krystyna Kujawinska
Jessica Purdue
Louise Henderson

Help us make the next generation of readers

We – both author and publisher – hope you enjoyed this book. We believe that you can become a reader at any time in your life, but we'd love your help to give the next generation a head start.

Did you know that 9% of children don't have a book of their own in their home, rising to 13% in disadvantaged families*? We'd like to try to change that by asking you to consider the role you could play in helping to build readers of the future.

We'd love you to think of sharing, borrowing, reading, buying or talking about a book with a child in your life and spreading the love of reading. We want to make sure the next generation continue to have access to books, wherever they come from.

And if you would like to consider donating to charities that help fund literacy projects, find out more at www.literacytrust.org.uk and www.booktrust.org.uk.

Thank you.

*As reported by the National Literacy Trust